Assessing EFL

Abdelhamid Ahmed
Hassan Abouabdelkader
Editors

Assessing EFL Writing in the 21st Century Arab World

Revealing the Unknown

Editors
Abdelhamid Ahmed
Faculty of Education
Helwan University
Cairo, Egypt

Core Curriculum Program
Qatar University
Doha, Qatar

Hassan Abouabdelkader
Ecole Nationales Supérieure
des Arts et Métiers
Moulay Ismail University
Meknes, Morocco

ISBN 978-3-319-87724-2   ISBN 978-3-319-64104-1 (eBook)
https://doi.org/10.1007/978-3-319-64104-1

© The Editor(s) (if applicable) and The Author(s) 2018
Softcover re-print of the Hardcover 1st edition 2018
This work is subject to copyright. All rights are solely and exclusively licensed by the Publisher, whether the whole or part of the material is concerned, specifically the rights of translation, reprinting, reuse of illustrations, recitation, broadcasting, reproduction on microfilms or in any other physical way, and transmission or information storage and retrieval, electronic adaptation, computer software, or by similar or dissimilar methodology now known or hereafter developed.
The use of general descriptive names, registered names, trademarks, service marks, etc. in this publication does not imply, even in the absence of a specific statement, that such names are exempt from the relevant protective laws and regulations and therefore free for general use.
The publisher, the authors and the editors are safe to assume that the advice and information in this book are believed to be true and accurate at the date of publication. Neither the publisher nor the authors or the editors give a warranty, express or implied, with respect to the material contained herein or for any errors or omissions that may have been made. The publisher remains neutral with regard to jurisdictional claims in published maps and institutional affiliations.

Printed on acid-free paper

This Palgrave Macmillan imprint is published by Springer Nature
The registered company is Springer International Publishing AG
The registered company address is: Gewerbestrasse 11, 6330 Cham, Switzerland

Dr. Abdelhamid Ahmed dedicates this volume to his late mother, and father, who was his first teacher of English, and spared no efforts in making his PhD journey a success. He also dedicates this volume to his wife, Dr. Lameya Rezk, who was always there for him academically, psychologically, and socially; and his kids Alaa and Esraa.

Dr. Hassan Abouabdelkader dedicates this volume to his children Soufiane, Otmane, Hamza, and Isabel. He would like to dedicate it to all academics who strive for global solutions to particular problems and help the whole world enjoy high levels of literacy and fight extremist thinking.

Foreword

Assessing EFL Writing in the Arab World Universities in 21st Century Arab World: Revealing the Unknown is the first volume to address assessment of writing in English as a Foreign Language (EFL) as it is an under-researched area in the Arab world. This edited collection comprises eleven research-based chapters, written by thirteen experienced EFL writing researchers and academicians whose academic ranks range from professors of education in Applied Linguistics/TESOL to doctoral candidates. These academics work at different higher education institutions in six different Arab countries; namely, Egypt, Morocco, Qatar, Tunisia, UAE, and Yemen. The represented Arab countries share many cultural, social, linguistic, and religious specifics.

It has been challenging for the book editors to find researchers interested and experienced in assessing EFL writing in the Arab world. First, authors received few responses from interested chapter contributors. The editors invested much time in finding different channels to call for book chapters. Second, the editors received a good number of research studies, but they were challenged by the unbalanced country distribution. Some countries were overrepresented, such as Egypt and Morocco, while other countries were underrepresented, such as Qatar, Tunisia, and Yemen, or not represented at all, such as Algeria, Oman, Palestine, Sudan, and Saudi Arabia. The editors did their best to balance the chapters and the countries. The third challenge was the reviewing process by Palgrave Macmillan,

UK, as the reviewers requested to remove some chapters that they believed were not up to the standards and add one more chapter to pave the way by addressing the challenges and issues of assessment of EFL writing in the Arab world university context. Finally, some chapter contributors apologised for not being able to write their chapters and meet the deadline, and they had to withdraw accordingly, leaving the editors in a state of helplessness.

The eleven chapters provide a critical examination of how EFL writing is assessed in different Arab world university contexts. These chapters address different aspects of EFL writing assessment as perceived by stakeholders, teachers, and students at the university level. The uniqueness of this edited collection lies in the diversity of perspectives presented in the different chapters. Each chapter draws on empirical research that portrays an important dimension of assessing EFL writing in one of the concerned Arab countries. All chapters of this book are original and unique as they address different aspects of assessments such as technology-enabled self-assessment and peer-assessment, assessment of EFL writing coherence, assessment procedures and outcomes, innovative assessment strategies, assessment literacy, assessment of writers' identities, E-rubrics, and assessment of academic writing. It is hoped that this book will enlighten assessment academicians, researchers, and practitioners about the different EFL writing assessment practices used in different Arab university contexts and the factors lying behind these current assessment practices. This edited volume is expected to appeal to the international readership as expected by the publisher and its audience. The chapters presented in this volume are not limited to the local and regional, but reach the international level. Each chapter focuses on one aspect of the assessment of EFL writing in an Arab university context. Altogether, the eleven chapters portray a comprehensive picture of EFL writing assessment in the Arab world region as represented by the six countries. The book's contribution to the Arab world region is knowledge on assessment of English writing as a foreign/second language worldwide in Asia, Africa, and Europe. The combination of six countries in the same Arab world region adds to the multiculturalism and diversity worldwide. Editors and chapter authors have collectively worked to produce this invaluable volume, with an international audience in mind. We drew upon our collective experience of assessment in different educational systems worldwide as reviewed in the literature. We consulted the literature available in books, local, regional, and international journals and on EFL writing assessment. We have largely succeeded in creating a multinational resource book that applies to the Arab world and many other parts of the EFL/ESL world, which gives it an international perspective.

We cannot claim to have a perfect volume about assessing EFL writing in the Arab world university context. We apologise in advance to our colleagues and readers for any academic myopia that might have happened unintentionally. If any aspects related to the assessment of EFL writing are not addressed in this volume, it would be due to some restrictions such as lack of researchers interested in contributing to this volume in the different Arab countries. The lack of researchers resulted in having fewer Arab countries represented in this volume. However, the available chapters address a wide range of issues and challenges of assessing EFL writing in six Arab countries. These chapters are varied and rich in their methodological design and perspectives; some chapters were quantitative, while others were qualitative and some used mixed methods research designs.

This edited collection is organised alphabetically by the represented countries. In other words, it starts with Egypt and ends by Yemen. It is divided into ten chapters along with the foreword and the conclusion. Despite representing six Arab countries, all chapters provide a critical examination of the context in which EFL writing is assessed and justify the different factors that have either contributed to or hindered the development and progression of these assessment practices.

The first chapter sheds light on some issues and challenges of assessing EFL writing in some Arab world university contexts. This chapter sheds light on how assessment of EFL writing takes place in nine Arab world university contexts including Algeria, Egypt, Morocco, Oman, Palestine, Saudi Arabia, Sudan, Tunisia, UAE, and Yemen. It has been reported in the literature that assessment of EFL writing in the Arab world does not seem to cope with the current trends in assessment worldwide for different reasons. First, Initial Teacher Education (ITE) programmes do not appear to create assessment-literate pre-service teachers, and professional development programmes at schools do not seem to focus on developing in-service teachers' assessment literacy. Second, teacher educators are not fully aware of the latest developments in assessment due to some institutional, cultural, financial, and administrative constraints. Third, teachers' beliefs about the assessment of EFL writing are incongruent with their practices. In addition, top-down management, lack of accountability, bureaucratic systems, teachers' workload, large classes, and lack of teachers' professional development opportunities for the assessment of EFL writing could account for the current embryonic assessment status in the Arab world.

The second chapter, contextualised in an Egyptian university context, examined the effect of self-assessment as a revision technique in English as a Foreign Language (EFL) writing to raise students' awareness of their common mistakes. More specifically, using a quasi-experimental design, the study examined the effect of self-assessment on the EFL students' overall expository writing as defined in terms of content, organisation, language, and overall writing ability. In addition, using a questionnaire, participants' attitudes towards self-assessment of their EFL expository writing were explored. Forty first-year engineering students at an Egyptian University were pre- and post-tested to examine the impact of the self-assessment rubric developed specifically for the study on students' writing proficiency. The results of the study indicated that self-assessment led to a highly significant improvement in students' expository writing (i.e. content, organisation, and language aspects, and overall writing ability). In relation to participants' attitudes, the findings showed that students favoured self-assessment as a technique that led to raising their awareness of their common mistakes and improving their essay writing proficiency.

The third chapter, also contextualised within an Egyptian university context, discusses the use of Topical Structure Analysis (TSA) to assess the internal coherence of EFL students' writing. It specifically examines the TSA and its three basic elements: parallel, sequential, and extended parallel progressions. Twenty-five argumentative essays written by first-year university students in the Arab Academy for Science and Technology and Maritime Transport (AASTMT) in Egypt voluntarily participated in the current study. Using Lautamatti's (1987) framework for the TSA, findings revealed that most students employed parallel progression in developing their topics (37.26%), followed by sequential progression

(35.62%), while extended parallel progression was the least employed (27.12%). These findings suggest that EFL students find difficulty in achieving coherence because of their poor lexical resources as EFL students. It is recommended that instructors use the TSA as a strategy to assess and teach both intermediate and advanced academic writing courses to enhance coherence in their EFL writing.

The fourth chapter reports the results of an empirical study within the Moroccan university context that focused on the procedures used to assess students' EFL writing composition skills. The study used a mixed-methods research design where quantitative and qualitative data collection and analysis are employed. The purpose of the current study is to investigate the relationship between the claims of the composition course and its outcomes. The current research argues that ineffective assessment strategies of composition will most likely lead to ineffective composing skills among students. The rationale underneath this claim is that lack of training in the constituents of the composing skills and attribution of the course to non-specialists are common practices in most Moroccan universities and that such outcomes are a sine qua non implication. Implications for the English departments in Moroccan universities are provided.

Within the Moroccan university context, the fifth chapter reports on an empirical study that investigated the effects of technology-mediated self- and peer assessment on L2 students' writing development in tertiary education. Informed by the socio-cultural and activity theories, the study rests on the understanding that effective learning results from collaboration, experiential learning and meaningful hands-on activities. Using a quasi-experimental pre/post-test between-group research design, a group of 48 semester-two students were exposed to a blended writing course over twelve weeks. Besides the process-based writing activities carried out in class, the students were divided into groups of four and were required to download multiple supplementary materials from Moodle and post their essays in an online workshop for discussion and exchange of feedback. Pre- and post-test score comparisons revealed that although both groups made progress in certain aspects of complexity and accuracy, the experimental group significantly scored higher on accuracy metrics. Qualitative analysis of students' comments showed that their noticing ability improved as demonstrated by a decrease in unhelpful comments and an increase in meaning-level comments. The implications of the results obtained for an effective blended writing course are discussed.

The sixth chapter analyses successful English writing assessment in Arabic-speaking medical student populations at Weill Cornell Medicine—Qatar (WCM-Q) from 2006-2016. Assessing L2 writers of English presents several unique challenges not only within the context of Science, Technology, Engineering, and Mathematics (STEM) academic writing but also within the American-style educational paradigm of Education City, Doha, Qatar. At WCM-Q, L1 Arabic students writing in English have specifically struggled with: the autonomous learning paradigm of American universities, English language deficits (limited vocabulary, difficulties with nuance and connotation), contextualised reading, audience, developing an authorial voice, and ethical sourcing of secondary materials (proper citation). The Premedical Program at WCM-Q evolved from no writing instruction in 2002 to a full Writing Program Curriculum and a Writing Centre, distributed Peer Tutor Network, and the development of literacy culture initiatives ten years later. Writing gained increasing prominence within the institution and eventually led to discussions about creating a longitudinal writing component in a newly revised curriculum. The WCM-Q Writing Program developed a variety of innovative assessment strategies including rubric development workshops, site visits by the John S. Knight Institute for Writing in the Disciplines, and an in-house written diagnostic essay test. A Foundation Program was added in 2007 to specifically address English language deficits.

Contextualised within the Tunisian higher education context, the seventh chapter explores Tunisian university EFL writing teachers' assessment literacy by investigating the way they perform their regular writing testing tasks. Data were collected using an open-ended questionnaire administered to a group of EFL writing teachers from different higher education institutions in Tunisia. Results showed that teachers did not receive any training in language testing as part of their university courses or during their professional development programmes. Results also showed that despite their ability to perform certain assessment tasks, the teachers seemed to have limited knowledge especially about aspects related to test construction.

The eighth chapter reports on a qualitative study that situates the discussion of EFL writing assessment by describing the assessment practices of writing teachers as perceived by first-year university students in the United Arab Emirates (UAE). The aim of the study was to explore how EFL university students construct and interpret their writer identities based on the assessments of past writing teachers, which, in turn, positions their current perceptions of writer identity once they enter university. Three themes emerged from the data in which the participants felt a lack of Perceived Academic Control (PAC) based on their secondary school teachers' writing assessments: feeling at fault for not understanding how to write academically, feeling forced to write academically, and feeling like the 'weakest' writer in the class. The study ends by suggesting that university-level educators in the Gulf region should engage in specific pedagogical and assessment practices to assist EFL students as they transition into using academic discourse at the university.

The ninth chapter, within another Emirati university context, explored professors' perspectives about the use of e-rubrics while assessing academic writing. Informed by an interpretive research framework, this exploratory case study investigates the perspectives of twenty-one English Language Teaching (ELT) professors about the use of e-rubrics in their assessment of academic essays. Undergraduates produced these essays in a series of required academic writing courses at an American University in the United Arab Emirates. Professors' perspectives on the usefulness of electronic rubrics in assessment and feedback were investigated through a survey and semi-structured interviews. Results revealed that while most participants agreed that e-rubrics helped them provide effective feedback to students' writing and saved the raters' time and energy, mixed feelings were reported about the effects of these e-rubrics in enhancing students' writing skills. The emphasis was rather on the role of the instructors in the classroom in developing the writing skills of their students.

Rubrics are also the focus of investigation within the Yemeni university context in the tenth chapter. This chapter investigates the reliability and validity of two scoring rubrics in the EFL writing assessment in Yemen: holistic and analytic. Using different psychometric statistics, the study compared Yemeni students' scores on a writing task using both holistic and analytic scoring rubrics. The participants in the study are 30 senior students of English at Taiz University, Yemen, and the raters of the writing samples are three experienced EFL instructors. The results of correlating the participants' performance on the writing tasks with the raters' holistic and analytic scores, and of examining the variations among the correlations, provide evidence for the reliability and validity of both rubrics. Analytic scoring rubrics, however, placed the participants along a more clearly defined scale of writing ability and are, therefore, more reliable and valid instruments for evaluating EFL writing for achievement purposes.

Finally, the conclusion chapter expresses a wave of challenges similar to the social unrest portrayed in the Arab social media and echoed globally. All these challenges express certain dissatisfactions with what occurs in their respective social contexts in an attempt to draw the attention of educational policy makers to take action and remediate the problems occurring in education. This edited collection is considered a 'red flag' raised in other western contexts and reveals the critical state of EFL writing assessment all over the world. The work combines different types of views and perspectives and provides useful insights into the assessment challenges and issues at stake. It is hoped that researchers, academics, and practitioners will benefit from the findings of the studies included in this volume and strive towards bridging the gap between the researchers' claims and the reality of EFL writing assessment in the modern classroom.

In closing this foreword, we cannot forget to thank some colleagues and participants, without whom this volume would not have come into being. First, we would like to thank the thirteen chapter authors who were devoted and committed to making this volume a success. We would also like to thank the reviewers who provided us with invaluable feedback that helped enrich the quality of this volume since its inception as a book proposal until it was completed as a full volume. In particular, we would like to thank Professor Icy Lee, Professor and Chairperson of the Curriculum & Instruction Department, Faculty of Education, the Chinese University of Hong Kong, for her valuable feedback and support. In addition, special thanks should go to Dr. Atta Gebril, Associate Professor of TESOL/Applied Linguistics, the American University in Cairo, for his valuable feedback and support. Moreover, we would like to thank the editorial team at Palgrave Macmillan, UK, particularly Judith Allan and Rebecca Wyde, for their continuous support since the beginning of the book proposal process till the completion of the journey of the book production. I am thankful for their great help.

Faculty of Education Abdelhamid Ahmed
Helwan University,
Cairo, Egypt

Contents

1. Assessment of EFL Writing in Some Arab World
   University Contexts: Issues and Challenges   1
   Abdelhamid Ahmed

2. The Effect of Self-Assessment as a Revision Technique
   on Egyptian EFL Students' Expository Essay Writing   21
   Nehal Sadek

3. Topical Structure Analysis: Assessing First-Year
   Egyptian University Students' Internal Coherence of
   Their EFL Writing   53
   Noha Omaya Shabana

4. Moroccan EFL University Students' Composing Skills
   in the Balance: Assessment Procedures and Outcomes   79
   Soufiane Abouabdelkader

5. The Impact of Self and Peer Assessment on L2 Writing:
   The Case of Moodle Workshops   111
   Abdelmajid Bouziane and Hicham Zyad

6 English Writing Assessment and the Arabic Speaker: A Qualitative Longitudinal Retrospective on Arabic-Speaking Medical Students in Qatar   137
   Alan S. Weber

7 Investigating Assessment Literacy in Tunisia: The Case of EFL University Writing Teachers   163
   Moez Athimni

8 EFL Assessment and the Construction of Positioned Writer Identities in Gulf University Students   191
   Lelania Sperrazza

9 ELT Professors' Perspectives on the Use of E-rubrics in an Academic Writing Class in a University in the UAE   221
   Rana Raddawi and Neslihan Bilikozen

10 EFL Writing Assessment and Evaluation Rubrics in Yemen   261
   Thikra K. Ghalib

11 Conclusion and Discussion   285
   Hassan Abouabdelkader

Index   297

List of Figures

Fig. 2.1	Rationale for the study	23
Fig. 2.2	The content mean scores of the experimental and control groups' pre- and post-tests	28
Fig. 2.3	Organisation means of the pre- and post-tests	29
Fig. 2.4	The language means of pre- and post-tests	30
Fig. 2.5	The total means of the pre- and post-tests	32
Fig. 3.1	Topical structure analysis of essay no. 1	64
Fig. 3.2	Topical structure analysis of essay no. 22	66
Fig. 3.3	Topical structure analysis of essay no. 5	68
Fig. 3.4	Topical structure analysis of essay no. 2	69
Fig. 3.5	Topical structural analysis of essay No. 6	69
Fig. 3.6	Topical structure analysis of essay no. 14—*Example of topical development of an essay using mostly parallel progression*	70
Fig. 3.7	Topical structure analysis of essay no. 15	71
Fig. 3.8	Percentages of the three types of progressions	72
Fig. 4.1	Students' composition grade dispersion	86
Fig. 5.1	An ELT writing peer and self-assessment activity system (adapted from Engestrom, 1999, p. 31)	115
Image 1	Screenshot of a student essay being graded and commented on using the department's common e-rubric	248
Image 2	The department's common e-rubric	248
Image 3	The screenshots of the e-rubric with comments typed under each category	249

Chart 1	Years of experience in teaching academic writing	252
Chart 2	Preferred method of giving feedback	252
Chart 3	Preferred medium of giving feedback and grading	253
Chart 4	Years of experience in using e-rubrics for writing assessment	253

List of Tables

Table 2.1	Descriptive statistics of the content variable in the pre- and post-tests	28
Table 2.2	Paired t-test results of the content variable of the experimental group	28
Table 2.3	Paired t-test results of the content variable of the control group	29
Table 2.4	Independent t-test results of the content variable of the post-test	30
Table 2.5	Descriptive statistics of the organisation variable in the pre- and post-tests	31
Table 2.6	Paired t-test results of the organisation variable of the experimental group	32
Table 2.7	Paired t-test results of the organisation variable of the control group	33
Table 2.8	Independent t-test results of the organisation variable of the post-test	33
Table 2.9	Descriptive statistics of the language variable in the pre- and post-tests	34
Table 2.10	Paired t-test results of the language variable of the experimental group	35
Table 2.11	Paired t-test results of the language variable of the control group	35
Table 2.12	Independent t-test results of the language variable of the post-test	36
Table 2.13	Descriptive statistics of the total of the pre- and post- tests	37

List of Tables

Table 2.14	Paired *t*-test results of the total variables of the experimental group	38
Table 2.15	Paired *t*-test results of the total variables of the control group	39
Table 2.16	Independent *t*-test results of the total variables of the post-test	39
Table 2.17	Results of item one of the post-treatment questionnaire	40
Table 2.18	Results of item two of the post-treatment questionnaire	41
Table 2.19	Results of item three of the post-treatment questionnaire	41
Table 2.20	Results of item four of the post-treatment questionnaire	42
Table 2.21	Results of item five of the post-treatment questionnaire	42
Table 2.22	Results of item six of the post-treatment questionnaire	43
Table 2.23	Results of item seven of the post-treatment questionnaire	43
Table 3.1	Lautamatti's (1987) Topical Structure Analysis—(TSA)	62
Table 3.2	The number of occurrence of each progression in essay no. 1	64
Table 3.3	Summary of topical development in the students' essays	65
Table 4.1	Students' grades distribution	87
Table 4.2	The mean of students' composing performance	89
Table 5.1	Participants' demographics	120
Table 5.2	Pre-test-post-test descriptive statistics for the experimental and control groups	125
Table 5.3	Within-group mean differences from the pre-test to the post-test	126
Table 5.4	Effect size of the progress made by the two groups as measured by Cohen's *d*	126
Table 5.5	Between-group mean differences from the pre-test to the post-test	126
Table 5.6	Descriptive statistics of the students' comments	127
Table 5.7	Developments in the nature of the students' feedback across three time intervals	128
Table 6.1	Expected first-year writing seminar goals	152
Table 6.2	Sample general rubric from the author	154
Table 7.1	Classification of the questionnaire items according to the assessment standards	170
Table 7.2	General profile of the participants	173
Table 8.1	Process coding: how lack of PAC (perceived academic control) positions writer identities	205
Table 9.1	Summary of interviewed faculty information	232
Table 9.2	Surveyed faculty demographics	234
Table 9.3	Challenges	255

Table 9.4	Benefits	255
Table 9.5	Perceived impact of e-rubrics on students	255
Table 10.1	Descriptive statistics for each of the scoring rubrics ($N = 90$)	272
Table 10.2	Descriptive statistics for each of the three raters within each of the two rubrics ($N = 30$)	273
Table 10.3	Descriptive statistics for each pair of the three raters and the overall across the two scoring rubrics ($N = 30$)	273

1

Assessment of EFL Writing in Some Arab World University Contexts: Issues and Challenges

Abdelhamid Ahmed

Introduction

Research has highlighted the need to assess students' skills in English as a Foreign Language (EFL) writing in more informative, accurate, and effective ways (Weigle, 2012). Gebril and Hozayin (2011) highlighted that assessment of EFL in general and English writing skills, in particular, are carried out in MENA nations for educational and professional purposes. In educational programmes, assessment of EFL helps make some decisions pertaining to screening, admissions, placement, programme exit, and scholarship selection. However, in professional contexts, it helps assess candidates' promotion, professional development, hiring, and proficiency in the English language for immigrants (ibid).

Research has shown that assessment training is needed. For example, Taylor (2009) noted that more people are involved in assessment despite

---

A. Ahmed (✉)
Faculty of Education, Helwan University, Cairo, Egypt

Core Curriculum Program, Qatar University, Doha, Qatar

not being well trained for this role. Similarly, Gebril and Hozayin (2011) pinpointed that the majority of educators in MENA countries, who are involved in creating and implementing policies of educational assessment, are not well prepared technically. This lack of training indicates an essential need to train educators in all areas of educational assessment including the diagnostic, placement, formative, summative, and technical aspects of testing such as validity and reliability (ibid).

The current chapter sheds light on some of the challenges and issues pertaining to the assessment of EFL writing in the following ten Arab world university contexts: Algeria, Egypt, Morocco, Oman, Palestine, Saudi Arabia, Sudan, Tunisia, United Arab Emirates, and Yemen. These countries are presented in alphabetical order.

Assessment of EFL Writing in Algeria

The EFL writing proficiency level of most Algerian first-year university students proved to be low intermediate. Researchers who assessed Algerian students' EFL writing distinguished two proficiency levels: low intermediate, nearly 80% of the new students; high intermediate, around 20% of the new students (Ourghi, 2002). Research findings revealed that low-intermediate students lack mastery of basic syntactic structures, knowledge of writing mechanics, vocabulary and useful composing strategies. In addition, findings of another study indicated that students' underuse or ineffective use of EFL writing strategies influenced the quality of their writing and low grades on their essays (Hamzaoui-Elachachi, 2006). Other writing deficiencies reported by first-year students include students' incapability of writing error-free sentences, unawareness of writing basics [i.e. mechanics of writing (e.g. capitalisation, punctuation, indentation], grammar (e.g. subject-verb agreement, use of pronouns) and vocabulary (e.g. frequently using anglicised borrowings from French). Furthermore, students' pieces of writing are just a list of ideas that lacks cohesion and coherence (Hamzaoui-Elachachi, 2010). Moreover, teaching EFL writing in Algeria has focused more on the product than the process of writing (Chelli, 2013). Consequently, students' written productions are assessed based on their test scores in EFL writing examinations instead of focusing on students' development in EFL writing (ibid). As an attempt to develop students' EFL writing accuracy, grammatical complexity and organisation, Chelli (2013) used self-assessment through portfolios. Findings revealed that students' writing abilities, attitudes towards writing and meta-cognitive skills have significantly improved.

Other researchers identified some reasons for students' EFL writing difficulties. These difficulties include students' negative affect towards writing, with particular reference to students' high writing apprehension and low writing self-efficacy, and the lack of regular assessment (Moussaoui, 2012) and of adequate responsive educational or pedagogical programmes (Bouhadiba (2000, p. 104). The lack of regular assessment takes place due to large class sizes and using traditional methods of teaching and assessing EFL writing, resulting in students lacking writing autonomy and critical thinking skills (ibid). Having measured the effect of peer evaluation on developing students' writing autonomy and positive affect, results showed that peer evaluation of students' writing enhanced their positive attitudes towards peer feedback, decreased their writing apprehension, increased their writing self-efficacy and led to the development of more autonomous student writers (Moussaoui, 2012).

Assessment of EFL Writing in Egypt

Research on assessment revealed that there is a shift in the purpose of assessment in Egypt (Ahmed, 2010; Gebril & Brown, 2014; Hargreaves, 2001). Hargreaves (2001) highlighted in her review of assessment in Egypt that the government aimed to improve assessment in an attempt to improve the educational system and individual learning. However, the use of formal written examinations based on memorisation and rote learning drifted away from any individual learning. In addition, Gebril and Brown (2014) investigated Egyptian teachers' beliefs about the assessment purposes. Results identified three assessment purposes: improvement, school accountability, and irrelevance. Moreover, another study investigated Egyptian students' problems with cohesion and coherence in EFL writing at a university in Egypt (Ahmed, 2010). Findings revealed that feedback and assessment practices are rare and traditional.

Other research about EFL writing assessment in Egypt showed that assessment is still a problematic area. For example, (Ahmed, 2011, 2016) examined EFL writing instruction in an Egyptian university. Based on data analysis, three important findings were reported: First, diagnostic assessment of students' EFL writing was rare as voiced by students and observed by the researcher. Second, attendance, classroom participation, and in-class assessments were the reported and observed formative assessment practices in the writing course. Third, the final examination was the only reported and observed summative assessment practice. Furthermore, Ahmed and Myhill (2016) explored the impact of the socio-cultural context of the L2 English writing on Egyptian university students. Some of the findings showed that the examination culture is viewed as an unchangeable challenge. Features of the examination culture include repetition of the writing topics in the final English writing examination and students' reliance on some memorised formulaic expressions.

Assessment of EFL Writing in Morocco

In the Moroccan context, assessment of EFL writing still suffers from challenges impeding its improvement and alignment with international standards. It can be argued that the Moroccan educational system lacks an efficient culture of evaluation that is fair and acceptable to educators and students. These problems have been isolated by local researchers. For example, Melouk (2001) highlighted that evaluation is in its initial stages in Morocco because of five factors. First, teachers and supervisors lack training in the technical aspects of evaluation. Second, evaluation field research is scarce in Morocco. Third, an independent body responsible for examination evaluation and production does not exist in Morocco. Fourth, the teaching and learning milieu in which national examinations are run makes teachers' incorporation of continuous assessment in their daily practices a difficult matter. Fifth, teachers share a common belief that they are not concerned with evaluation and testing issues. Consistent with these factors, other researchers conducted a study to evaluate Moroccan students' critical thinking skills (Amrous & Nejmaoui, 2017). Research findings revealed that Moroccan university students performed poorly in critical thinking tests. In addition, Moroccan EFL students still have some problems with their EFL writing skills. For example, Ouaouicha (1980) revealed that poor student writers underuse and misuse cohesive devices in their EFL writing. Furthermore, Bouziane (2017) surveyed the assessment of EFL reading and writing in Morocco and concluded that little attention has been devoted to the establishment of a systematic frame of EFL writing assessment. Findings revealed that assessment research of EFL reading and writing in Morocco is scarce and that writing assessment has been generally unfair and harmful to students during and after schools (ibid). In addition, the findings of the available research on language assessment, in general, show that scoring essays varied inconsistently among teachers in Morocco (Abouabdelkader & Abouabdelkader, 2017).

Assessment of EFL Writing in Oman

Some challenges and issues mark the assessment of EFL writing in the Omani context. For example, Al-Issaei (2012) explored the writing assessment challenges and issues in teaching English for Academic Purposes (EAP) in a higher education college in Oman. Analysis of the interviews showed that the writing assessment schemes in the Omani college needed some improvement. It has also been reported that the context of writing assessment is afflicted by four challenges (ibid). First, plagiarism prevails in students' written assignments. Second, the writing course materials and research skills needed to complete the writing projects are deteriorating. In addition, explicit constructive handouts that guide teachers and students in the research process are missing. Finally, the technical nature of the writing project challenged teachers and affected the quality of their evaluation process. In line with that, Al-Hajri (2014) evaluated the assessment practices used in the Foundation Programme at the Colleges of Applied Sciences in Oman. Findings revealed that the teaching and assessment are compatible, the assessment criteria are inconsistent, and general assessment standards are replicated. Moreover, Al-Azani (2015) explored ESL/EFL instructors' perceptions and practices of teaching and assessing writing in three tertiary educational institutions in Oman. Using questionnaires, interviews, and classroom observations as data collection tools, findings of Al-Azani's study revealed that ESL/EFL instructors rely on portfolios and written essays when they assess students' EFL writing. However, beliefs and practices were reported to be inconsistent on issues such as students' individual or group writing, using analytic or holistic rubrics, and assessing content or grammar first.

Other researchers investigated the assessment system in Oman and students' poor English writing (Al-Issa, 2005a; Al-Issa & Al-Bulushi, 2012; Al-Seyabi & Tuzlukova, 2014; Al-Toubi, 1998). For example, Al-Issa (2005b) criticises the assessment system in ELT in the Sultanate of Oman for training students to heavily focus on mastering content and achieving high grades through copying and memorisation, which negatively influence teachers and students' motivation and performance. In the same vein, Al-Toubi (1998) reported that Omani students' poor level of English is attributed to the examination-based system that is negatively influencing students' language development. Investigating Omani students' EFL writing underdevelopment, Al-Issa and Al-Bulushi (2012) found that the English language proficiency of Omani students joining higher education institutions is inadequate, which has negatively affected Oman's national development. Moreover, Al-Seyabi and Tuzlukova (2014) reported that high school and university students acknowledged that their English writing is problematic and students mostly struggle with lexical and content aspects of EFL writing.

Assessment of EFL Writing in Palestine

Assessment of EFL writing in Palestine is engulfed by challenges. Some studies in the Palestinian context shed light on some of the challenges facing assessment of EFL writing in Palestine (Sharawneh, 2012; Sobeh, 2007). For example, Sobeh (2007) conducted a descriptive analytic study that evaluated English writing in the 10th grade at Governmental Gaza schools. The questionnaire results indicated that most teachers still rely on the traditional methods of assessing their students' writing. These traditional methods of assessment, testing, and observation got the highest score in a percentage of 63.8% and 62.8% respectively. On the other hand, portfolios, self-assessment, peer-assessment, journals, interviews and conferences, rubrics, anecdotal records, and checklists received low percentages, ranging from 28.7% to 22.4%. Similarly, Sharawneh (2012) did empirical research to determine how English language teachers evaluate the writing section in the 11th and 12th grade examinations. Using a questionnaire, interviews with high school English teachers and supervisors, scoring compositions, and checking supervisors' reports, Sharawneh's findings showed that teachers' perceptions and practices towards the assessment of writing and the use of feedback are of medium level. Despite the Ministry's emphasis on the importance of writing assessment, this was incongruent with teachers' practices.

Other Palestinian researchers conducted research that spotlighted the different writing problems and challenges as reported by students and teachers (Abu-Shawish, 2009; Hammad, 2014). For example, Abu-Shawish (2009) analysed the written product of Palestinian English majors in three different national universities in Gaza Strip. Using a writing test, 120 mixed-gender undergraduate students were asked to write three paragraphs on a familiar topic. Test results indicated that students' performance in English writing proved to be below the pass level (i.e. 60%); their overall percentage was 52.43%. Students' most frequent errors were in coherence and grammar, whereas, the least frequent ones were in spelling and punctuation. Similarly, Hammad (2014) examined Palestinian EFL university students' essay writing problems as perceived by the students and their instructors. The researcher used an EFL writing test, an open-ended questionnaire with sixty students, and semi-structured interviews with three English instructors. Findings revealed that students' writing was marked by a lack of grammatical and lexical knowledge, word-for-word translation, cohesion errors, lack of academic writing style, lack of content, and lack of proofreading.

Assessment of EFL Writing in Saudi Arabia

In the Saudi context, a number of research studies have assessed students' English writing and identified some writing problems and challenges such as memorisation of written topics, poor English writing, and problems with punctuation, grammar, spelling, and capitalisation. For example, Al-Seghayer (2015) referred to Saudi students' memorisation of some written topics along with their list of words that have been discussed in class, as they know that they will be required to write an essay on one of these topics in the final examination. In addition, Saudi EFL students are commonly characterised as poor writers of English, as confirmed by the results of Shukri (2014), in which she explored EFL writing difficulties and challenges among Saudi university students. Moreover, Mohammad and Hazarika (2016) reported that Saudi Intermediate School students encountered problems in capitalisation, punctuation, language use, and spelling in their EFL writing. In the same vein, El-Tantawi, Al-Ansari, Sadaf, and AlHumaid (2016) assessed the scientific English writing of preparatory year dental students in Saudi Arabia. Analysis of 89 students' written assignments revealed that students had punctuation and grammar mistakes along with problems using references and documentation of resources, despite the many written words in their assignments. The study recommended having more than one scientific writing course in the preparatory year to strengthen students' scientific writing skills in English.

Assessment of EFL Writing in Sudan

In the Sudanese context, assessing students' EFL writing proved that students found EFL writing challenging (Alfaki, 2015; Zakaria & Mugaddam, 2013). For example, Zakaria and Mugaddam (2013) conducted a study in which 65 Sudanese EFL teachers and 240 senior English majors at five Sudanese universities participated. Based on their study findings, Sudanese students' written performance revealed that they have language problems, lack organisational skills, and are unable to meet the audience expectations. Additional writing problems that students encountered include the inability to use pre-activities and organisation as writing strategies, the lack of using teachers and peers' feedback while writing and a total lack of awareness of cohesive devices, which resulted in incohesive and disconnected writing. In support of the same argument, Alfaki (2015) identified Sudanese university students' writing problems in English and recommended some solutions. Twenty students were taught to write an essay that was assessed twice by ten English instructors. Results showed that Sudanese university students have morphological and syntactic problems in their English writing such as usage errors, spelling, punctuation, capitalisation, lack of writing development skills, cognitive problems, and graphomotor problems.

Assessment of EFL Writing in Tunisia

The Tunisian context is marked by some challenges and issues pertinent to English writing assessment that are similar to many other Arab university contexts (Athimni, 2017; Barakaoui, 2007; Daoud, 1999; Ghrib, 2001; Mahfoudhi, 1998). For example, Daoud (1999) claims that one of the underdeveloped aspects of English language teaching in Tunisia is language assessment. He attributed this for the paucity of research and expertise in assessment and the lack of preparation of testing in the Tunisian English departments. Highlighting the deficiencies in the Tunisian students' English writing, Mahfoudhi (1998) examined students' argumentative writing skills. He further reported that students have surface level deficiencies in EFL writing such as the inadequate use of mechanics, grammar, and vocabulary. At the global text level, he added that students lacked clear thesis statement and support for claims. In the same vein, Ghrib (2001) examined Tunisian EFL students' written essays. She found that Tunisian students' EFL writing difficulties were mainly in grammar and organisational skills. In addition, she reported that there were some discrepancies between students' self-assessments of their writing skills and difficulties and those reported by their teachers and their final exam results.

Furthermore, Barakaoui (2007) referred to the issue of impressionistic evaluation of EFL writing in Tunisia. In an attempt to improve the assessment practices of EFL writing in Tunisia, Barakaoui (2007) explored raters' scoring of Tunisian students' EFL writing. Findings revealed that evaluation of EFL writing at university is carried out impressionistically, with no written scoring criteria or instructions, but combining norm- and criterion-referenced approaches. However, Athimni (2017) described the assessment practices in Tunisia as not aligned with the international standards or best practices. He further attributed this status-quo to the lack of testing courses for English student teachers at university and the paucity of language assessment training for university teachers.

Assessment of EFL Writing in the United Arab Emirates (UAE)

Research showed that Emirati students' EFL writing needs more planning, reinforcement, and development (Hourani, 2008; Sperrazza & Raddawi, 2016; Raddawi, 2011; Al Naqbi, 2011). For example, Hourani (2008) explored the most commonly committed grammatical errors among 105 Emirati secondary students in their essay writing test. Findings revealed that students had the following grammatical problems in their English writing: passivisation, verb tense and form, subject-verb agreement, word order, prepositions, articles, plurality, and auxiliaries. The researchers attributed these grammatical mistakes to intralingual transfer. In addition, Sperrazza and Raddawi (2016) assessed Emirati students' academic writing and reported that students find critical thinking skills new and challenging because of the pre-university schooling system that relies heavily on rote learning and memorisation. These challenges are also similar to other Arab contexts such as the Omani context where Ministry of Education examinations relied on memorisation and rote learning rather than thinking (Al-Issa, 2002). Sperrazza and Raddawi (2016) added that most Arab EFL students are not used to selecting writing topics that are culturally challenging. In another study, 70% of 690 Emirati students took cultural restrictions into consideration before choosing a research topic (Raddawi, 2011). Similarly, Al Naqbi (2011) observed that Emirati students' written essays lacked planning, as there were too many specifics and not enough generalisations. Moreover, students' pieces of evidence were not well developed. Furthermore, students left out the best examples to support their argument.

Research identified some factors that contributed to the status of EFL writing assessment in the UAE. For example, Troudi, Coombe, and Al-Hamly (2009) explored EFL teachers' assessment roles and philosophies in two Arab countries, namely, UAE and Kuwait. Based on a qualitative study that used an open-ended questionnaire, findings revealed that teachers' different views on assessment were guided by their knowledge of EFL language learning and teaching as well as the contextual milieu and socio-political factors that governed their employment conditions. Additionally, findings also showed that the teachers did not play a major role in assessment because of two main issues: the top-down management approaches to education and the concern about the quality assurance in the educational programmes.

Assessment of EFL Writing in Yemen

According to the existing literature on the Yemeni context, little research addresses the different challenges that impede the learning and development of English writing skills. For example, Al-Shurmani and Al-Suhbani (2012) analysed 30 essays written by junior Yemeni students. Findings indicated that students encountered some problems in their English writing: semantic errors related to inappropriate use of lexicons, collocations, and structural norms. In addition, Yehia (2015) evaluated the quality of English writing of Yemeni undergraduate students to identify the most frequently used discourse markers used by Yemeni EFL students and the relationship between students' use of discourse markers and the writing quality. The study findings indicated that the most commonly used discourse markers in sequence are collateral, inferential, discourse activity, contrastive, discourse structure, causative, and topic change markers. In addition, students' writing quality correlated positively with participants' gender. EFL literacy studies in Yemen indicated that university students faced numerous problems in acquiring the EFL literacy skills necessary to meet the academic demands at university and that there was a lack of proficiency among students in higher education (Al-Hammadi & Sidek, 2014). Another problematic issue related to teaching writing in the current Yemeni situation is the absence of authenticity (Nasser, 2016).

Some reasons lie behind students' problematic writing. For example, Al-Shurmani and Al-Suhbani (2012) attributed this situation to the lack of a clear education policy for the higher educational programmes in general and EFL programmes in Yemen in particular. Other researchers attributed these problems to the gap between the current state of the preparation phase at secondary schools and the expected level required at university (Al-Hammadi & Sidek, 2014). Moreover, Nasser (2016) highlighted that students write pieces to pass the examination and to get marks, a factor that makes EFL writing meaningless and unauthentic. Finally, Muthanna (2016) highlighted that the EFL programme in Yemeni universities lacked an admission policy, material development and evaluation, instructors and classrooms, and a safe educational environment. Such challenges negatively affected students' acquisition of writing skills and made them hopeless candidates for pursuing postgraduate degrees that require more advanced writing competencies.

In reference to the assessment of EFL writing, researchers used scoring rubrics (Ghalib & Al-Hattami, 2015) and others used portfolios (Assaggaf & Bamahra, 2016). For example, Assaggaf and Bamahra (2016) compared EFL students' scores on a writing task using holistic and analytic scoring rubrics. Thirty English majors in a Yemeni university participated in this study. Analytic scoring rubrics helped diagnose students' writing ability against a clearly-defined scoring scale and are therefore more reliable than holistic scoring rubrics for evaluating EFL writing. In addition, two researchers used group discussions, written reflections, and a short questionnaire with Yemeni computer science students at university to explore students' views about portfolios in teaching English writing (Assaggaf & Bamahra, 2016). The study findings reported participants' positive views towards the use of portfolios in teaching writing in general and report writing in particular. Portfolios improved learning about report writing, made writing more fun, and monitored students' writing.

Conclusion

The reviewed literature has provided a bird's eye view of the assessment of EFL writing in the following ten Arab world university contexts: Algeria, Egypt, Morocco, Oman, Palestine, Saudi Arabia, Sudan, Tunisia, UAE, and Yemen. It has shed light on the different challenges and issues related to assessing EFL writing in these ten countries that share some characteristics: Arabic as the mother tongue, English as a foreign language, Islam as the most dominant religion, and similar cultural and religious customs and traditions. The following section will highlight EFL writing assessment challenges and issues among the concerned countries and the factors lying behind these challenges of assessment.

A number of assessment-related challenges have been revealed by scrutinising the pertinent literature and studies. First, it has been reported that the EFL writing proficiency level at most Arab world university contexts probably ranges from low to intermediate. Second, university students encountered problems in many EFL writing skills (i.e. syntactic features, semantic errors, lack of cohesion, coherence and organisation, ineffective composing strategies, lack of lexical repertoire and collocations, grammatical accuracy, and morphological and mechanical problems). Furthermore, students' EFL writing in some Arab university contexts are afflicted with plagiarism. In the same vein, other Arab contexts reported students' lack of in-text citations and references list in their written assignments. These EFL writing problems could be attributed to lack of regular assessment, large class sizes, students' L1 interference with L2 writing, traditional methods of assessment and teaching, lack of pedagogical programmes, and students' negative affect towards EFL writing in general and high writing apprehension and low writing self-efficiency in particular.

Regarding the assessment practices in most reviewed countries, the (meta-analysis) reviewed literature relates to some cultural specifics. For example, the cultures of memorisation, rote learning and stereotyped examination culture are quite common. Features of this examination culture include repetitive writing topics in final examinations and students' reliance on memorisation of formulaic expressions. These culture specifics negatively affected students' EFL writing development and progression. In addition, writing to pass the examinations and get grades was the most commonly reported purposes of EFL writing among Arab university students. Writing to pass examinations has negatively affected the need for authentic writing for real purposes and audiences. Moreover, lack of critical thinking skills and writer's autonomy are two other features of Arab students' EFL writing. Furthermore, some Arab university contexts have shown that impressionistic evaluation of students' EFL writing is highly common.

In relation to the noted assessment issues, the reviewed Arab countries showed the following issues. First, the assessment criteria are inconsistent, and general assessment standards are replicated. Second, the assessment practices of most reviewed countries have been proved not to be aligned with the international standards of writing assessment. Third, it was also noted that the culture of evaluation and assessment is in its embryonic stages, which signifies its underdevelopment. Additionally, diagnostic assessments are rarely used and traditional formative and summative assessment practices are reported. Moreover, the use of rubrics to assess students' EFL writing is rare and does not follow standardisation in terms of unified analytical or holistic rubrics. This results in inconsistent scoring schemes in the reviewed countries.

Some factors contributed to our understanding of the challenges and issues of EFL writing assessment in the Arab world university contexts. First, assessment-literate instructors and specialists seem to be rare to find. Second, many reviewed Arab university contexts reported the lack of assessment training/courses and evaluation in their institutions. In addition, superficial testing and assessment bodies contributed to the inadequate assessment status in many Arab university contexts. Furthermore, little research has been conducted on the assessment of EFL writing in many of the reviewed Arab world university contexts.

Finally, it is worth noting that the assessment of EFL writing in some Arab university contexts is affected by other factors. These include issues of accountability, funding, educational and admission policies, incongruent preparation at both the pre-university and university levels, independent assessment bodies, and discrepancies between teachers' beliefs and practices of assessment. Furthermore, some socio-political factors that governed teachers' employment conditions have affected the assessment-related decisions. Moreover, the top-down management approaches to education and the concern about the quality assurance in the educational programmes are believed to have affected the assessment of EFL writing in some Arab countries.

References

Abouabdelkader, H., & Abouabdelkader, S. (2017). Moroccan university students' EFL writing composition skills in the balance: Assessment procedures and outcomes. In A. Ahmed & H. Abouabdelkader (Eds.), *Assessing EFL writing in the Arab world universities in 21st century Arab world: Revealing the unknown* (1st ed.). London: Palgrave Macmillan.

Abu-Shawish, J. (2009). *Analysis and assessment of Palestinian EFL majors' written English*. Unpublished Ph.D. thesis, College of Graduate Studies, Sudan University of Science & Technology, Sudan.

Ahmed, A. (2010). Students' problems with cohesion and coherence in EFL essay writing in Egypt: Different perspectives. *Literacy Information and Computer Education Journal (LICEJ), 1*(4), 211–221.

Ahmed, A. (2011). *The EFL essay writing difficulties of Egyptian student teachers of English: implications for essay writing curriculum and instruction*. Unpublished Ph.D. thesis, Graduate School of Education, University of Exeter, UK.

Ahmed, A. (2016). EFL writing instruction in an Egyptian university classroom: An emic view. In A. Ahmed & H. Abouabdelkader (Eds.), *Teaching EFL writing in the 21st century Arab world: Realities and challenges* (1st ed.). London: Palgrave Macmillan.

Ahmed, A., & Myhill, D. (2016). The impact of the socio-cultural context on L2 English writing of Egyptian university students. *Learning, Culture and Social Interaction, 11*, 117–129.

Al Naqbi, S. (2011). The use of mind mapping to develop writing skills in UAE schools. *Education, Business and Society: Contemporary Middle Eastern Issues, 4*(2), 120–133.

Al-Azani, N. (2015). *Exploring English instructors' perceptions and actual practices regarding the strategies used in teaching and assessing writing in three tertiary education institutions in the sultanate of Oman*. Unpublished MA thesis, College of Education, United Arab Emirates University, UAE.

Alfaki, I. (2015). University students' English writing problems: Diagnosis and remedy. *International Journal of English Language Teaching, 3*(3), 40–52.

Al-Hajri, F. (2014). English language assessment in the colleges of applied sciences in Oman: Thematic document analysis. *English Language Teaching, 7*(3), 19–37.

Al-Hammadi, F., & Sidek, H. (2014). Academic writing in the Yemeni EFL context: History, challenges, and future research. Paper ID: ICLLCE 22014-82, pp. 167–174.

Al-Issa, A. (2002). *An ideological and discursive analysis of English language teaching in the sultanate of Oman*. Unpublished doctoral dissertation, University of Queensland, Australia.

Al-Issa, A. (2005a). An ideological discussion of the impact of the NNESTs' English language knowledge on Omani ESLpolicy implementation. *Asian EFL Journal, 7*(3), Article 9.

Al-Issa, A. (2005b, May). *An ideological discussion of the place & role of exams in the Omani ELT system*. Paper presented at Redesigning Pedagogy: Research,

Policy, and Practice Conference, Centre for Research in Pedagogy & Practice, National Institute of Education, Nanyang Technological University, Singapore.

Al-Issa, A., & Al-Bulushi, A. (2012). English language teaching reform in sultanate of Oman: The case of theory and practice disparity. *Educational Research Policymaking and Practice, 11*, 141–176.

Al-Issaei, N. (2012). A speculation on writing assessment issues in colleges of applied sciences in Oman. *Procedia: Social and Behavioral Sciences, 69*, 739–744.

Al-Seghayer, K. (2015). Salient key features of actual English instructional practices in Saudi Arabia. *English Language Teaching, 8*(6). https://doi.org/10.5539/elt.v8n6p89.

Al-Seyabi, F., & Tuzlukova, V. (2014). Writing problems and strategies: An investigative study in the Omani school and university context. *Asian Journal of Social Sciences & Humanities, 3*(4), 37–48.

Al-Shurmani, M., & Al-Suhbani, Y. (2012). Semantic errors committed by Yemeni university learners: Classifications and source. *International Journal of English Linguistics, 2*(6), 120–139.

Al-Toubi, S. (1998). *A perspective on change in the Omani ELT curriculum: Structural to communicative.* Unpublished MA dissertation, University of Bristol, UK.

Amrous, N., & Nejmaoui, N. (2017). *A developmental approach to the use of critical thinking skills in writing: The case of Moroccan EFL university students.* ASELS Annual Conference Proceedings, Mohammed V University of Rabat, Morocco.

Assaggaf, H., & Bamahra, Y. (2016). The effects of portfolio use in teaching report writing: EFL students' perspective. *International Journal of Applied Linguistics & English Literature, 5*(3), 26–34.

Athimni, M. (2017). Investigating assessment literacy in Tunisia: The case of EFL university writing teachers. In A. Ahmed & H. Abouabdelkader (Eds.), *Assessing EFL writing in the Arab world universities in 21st century Arab world: Revealing the unknown* (1st ed.). London: Palgrave Macmillan.

Barakaoui, K. (2007). Rating scale impact on EFL essay marking: A mixed-method study. *Assessing Writing, 12*, 86–107.

Bouhadiba, F. (2000). ELT and cross cultural communication. *Imago, 3*, 95–110.

Bouziane, A. (2017). Why should the assessment of literacy in Morocco be revisited? In S. Hidri & C. Coombe (Eds.), *Evaluation in foreign language education in the Middle East and North Africa* (pp. 305–314). New York: Springer International Publishing.

Chelli, S. (2013). Developing students' writing abilities by the use of self-assessment through portfolios. *Arab World English Journal, 4*(2), 220–234.

Daoud, M. (1999). The management of innovation in ELT in Tunisia. In M. Jabeur, A. Manai, & M. Bahloul (Eds.), *English in North Africa* (pp. 121–137). Tunis: TSAS.

El-Tantawi, M., Al-Ansari, A., Sadaf, S., & AlHumaid, J. (2016, April 28). Evaluating the English language scientific writing skills of Saudi dental students at entry level. *East Mediterranean Health Journal, 22*(2), 148–153.

Fraser, B. (1999). What are discourse markers? *Journal of Pragmatics, 31*, 931–952.

Gebril, A., & Brown, G. T. (2014). The effect of high-stakes examination systems on teacher beliefs: Egyptian teachers' conceptions of assessment. *Assessment in Education: Principles, Policy and Practice, 21*(1), 16–33.

Gebril, A., & Hozayin, R. (2011). Assessing English in the Middle East and North Africa. In A. Kunnan (Ed.), *The companion to language assessment* (1st ed.). Malden, MA: John Wiley & Sons, Inc.

Ghalib, T., & Al-Hattami, A. (2015). Holistic versus analytic evaluation of EFL writing: A case study. *English Language Teaching, 8*(7). https://doi.org/10.5539/elt.v8n7p225.

Ghrib, A. (2001). Thinking and writing in EFL: Cutting the Medusa's head. *Review of Applied Linguistics, 133/134*, 243–269.

Hammad, E. (2014). Palestinian university students' problems with EFL Essay writing in an instructional setting. *Journal of Second and Multiple Language Acquisition, 2*(1), 1–21.

Hamzaoui-Elachachi, H. (2006). *An exploration into the strategies used for essay writing across three languages: The case of EFL university students*. Unpublished doctoral thesis, University of Tlemcen, Algeria.

Hamzaoui-Elachachi, H. (2010). Development of a writing curriculum for academic purposes at tertiary level: The case of Algerian EFL university students. *ESP World, 1*(27), 1–9.

Hargreaves, E. (2001). Assessment in Egypt. *Assessment in Education: Principles, Policy & Practice, 8*(2), 247–260.

Hourani, T. (2008). *An analysis of the common grammatical errors in the English essay writing made by 3rd secondary male students in the Eastern Coast of the UAE*. Unpublished MA thesis, Institute of Education British University in Dubai, UAE.

Mahfoudhi, A. (1998). *Writing processes of Tunisian EFL students in argumentative essays*. Unpublished DEA dissertation, Faculté des lettres de la Manouba, University of Tunis.

Melouk, M. (2001). The state of EFL evaluation in Morocco: The testers and teachers' opinions. The Teaching and Assessment of English for Global Purposes. Paper presented at *MATE proceedings*, Essaouira, pp. 41–51.

Mohammad, T., & Hazarika, Z. (2016). Difficulties of learning EFL in KSA: Writing skills in context. *International Journal of English Linguistics, 6*(3). https://doi.org/10.5539/ijel.v6n3p105.

Moussaoui, S. (2012). An investigation of the effects of peer evaluation in enhancing Algerian students' writing autonomy and positive affect. *Procedia—Social and Behavioral Sciences, 69*, 1775–1784.

Muthanna, A. (2016). Teaching and learning EFL writing at Yemeni universities: A review of current practices. In A. Ahmed & H. Abouabdelkader (Eds.), *Teaching EFL writing in the 21st century Arab world: Realities and challenges*. Basingstoke: Palgrave Macmillan.

Nasser, A. (2016). Teaching the writing skill to Yemeni EFL learners: The importance and challenge. *South Asian Journal of Multidisciplinary Studies (SAJMS), 3*(6), 191–203.

Ouaouicha, D. (1980). *An analysis of learners' written discourse (with) special reference to the composition of Moroccan students*. Unpublished MA thesis, The University College of North Wales, Bangor.

Ourghi, R. (2002). *The implications of critical reflection and discourse awareness for educational change: The case of the writing curriculum, learner, and teacher development at the university level*. Unpublished doctoral thesis, University of Tlemcen, Algeria.

Raddawi, R. (2011). Teaching critical thinking skills to Arab university students. In C. Gitskaki (Ed.), *Teaching and learning in the Arab world*. New York: Peter Lang Publishing.

Sharawneh, I. (2012). *Evaluation of assessment practices in English writing for high school Palestinian students: A critical study*. Unpublished MA thesis, Faculty of Graduate Studies, Hebron University, Palestine.

Shukri, N. (2014). Second language writing and culture: Issues and challenges from the Saudi learners' perspective. *Arab World English Journal, 5*(3), 190–207.

Sobeh, H. (2007). *Evaluating English writing assessment in the 10th grade at Gaza schools with regards to the contemporary trends*. Unpublished MA thesis at Faculty of Education, The Islamic University of Gaza, Palestine.

Sperrazza, L., & Raddawi, R. (2016). Academic writing in the UAE: Transforming critical thought in the EFL classroom. In A. Ahmed & H. Abouabdelkader (Eds.), *Teaching EFL writing in the 21st century Arab world: Realities and challenges* (1st ed.). London: Palgrave Macmillan.

Taylor, L. (2009). Developing assessment literacy. *Annual Review of Applied Linguistics, 29*, 21–36.

Troudi, S., Coombe, C., & Al-Hamly, M. (2009). EFL teachers' views of English language assessment in higher education in the United Arab Emirates and Kuwait. *TESOL Quarterly, 43*(3), 546–555.

Weigle, S. (2012). *Assessment of writing. The encyclopaedia of applied linguistics.* Malden, MA: Wiley.

Yehia, T. (2015). Use of discourse markers: A case study of English writing by Yemeni students. *Language in India, 15*(6), 217–235.

Zakaria, A., & Mugaddam, A. (2013). An assessment of the written performance of the sudanese EFL university learners: A communicative approach to writing. *World Journal of English Language, 3*(4). https://doi.org/10.5430/wjel.v3n4p1.

Abdelhamid Ahmed is Assistant Professor of Education (TESOL/Applied Linguistics), Curriculum and Instruction Department, Faculty of Education, Helwan University, Egypt. He is experienced in teaching and researching EFL Writing as shown in his MEd and PhD theses as well as other research publications. He obtained his PhD in Education (TESOL/Applied Linguistics), Graduate School of Education, University of Exeter, UK. His areas of expertise include EFL writing problems, socio-cultural issues of EFL writing, assessing writing, written feedback, reflective journals, teachertraining, and teaching practicum. He is the co-editor of and a chapter author in *Teaching EFL Writing in the 21st Century Arab World: Realities & Challenges*. He also has a number of research publications in international peer-reviewed journals.

2

The Effect of Self-Assessment as a Revision Technique on Egyptian EFL Students' Expository Essay Writing

Nehal Sadek

Introduction

Teaching writing in the EFL classroom has undergone dramatic changes over the past decades. Traditionally, writing instruction focused on the final written product. With the advent of the Process Approach to Writing in the 1970s, however, EFL teachers started to respond to writing as work in progress rather than a final product (Zamel, 1985). In other words, writing is no longer viewed as a one-time activity starting with the assignment of a certain topic and ending with the submission of the final product (Hafez, 1996). A major paradigm shift has taken place in the writing pedagogy from a focus on product to process under the influence of exponents (e.g. Elbow, 1973; Emig, 1971; Murray, 1978; Zamel, 1982).

The process of writing, as defined by Murray (1985), consists of three main stages: prewriting, writing, and rewriting. *The pre-writing stage* includes everything that takes place before writing starts, including brainstorming and research for generating ideas. *Writing* is the act of producing

---

N. Sadek (✉)
Educational Testing Service (ETS), Princeton, NJ, USA

the first draft where learners focus on ideas and the organisation of these ideas. The final stage in the process of writing is *rewriting*, which is concerned with the revision of content, organisation, and language.

One of the advantages of adopting the Process Approach lies in developing the cyclical and recursive nature of writing, supposedly employed by native writers, where 'ordinarily pre-writing, writing and re-writing frequently seem to happen simultaneously' (Smith, 1982, p. 104). Moreover, the Process Approach empowers its students, thereby enabling them to make clearer decisions about the direction of their writing 'using discussion, drafting, feedback and informed choices encouraging students to be responsible for making improvements themselves' (Jordan, 1997, p. 168).

Being a problematic area for many EFL learners, the revision stage of the process of writing has received particular attention in EFL writing pedagogy over the last three decades. The reason for this increasing interest is that many learners complain about not knowing what to consider while revising their essays. A possible reason for this complaint is that they lack the criteria employed by teachers in evaluating their writing performance in assignments or achievement tests. The present study introduces a technique that can guide EFL learners while revising their drafts, namely, self-assessment. This could be done through the learners' use of a set of criteria covering the different aspects of writing, including content, organisation, and language.

Defining Self-Assessment

In an age where the Arab world is changing, and at a significant time described by many as the 'Arab Spring', the ability to question everything around oneself, including one's self, becomes crucial. Self-assessment is defined by Claxton (1995) as 'the ability to recognise good work as such and to correct one's performance so that better work is produced' (p. 339). In the revision stage of the writing process, self-assessment can provide learners with the basis of teachers' evaluation of writing by giving them a list of the criteria used by teachers to evaluate their writing.

Rationale for the Study

Self-assessment was employed as a revision technique in the process of writing to raise the learners' awareness of their common mistakes by providing them with a chance to locate these mistakes by themselves. The study examined the effect of self-assessment on the EFL learners' overall expository writing as defined in terms of content, organisation, language, and overall. The rationale for the study is summarised in Fig. 2.1 (see Figs. 2.2, 2.3, 2.4, and 2.5).

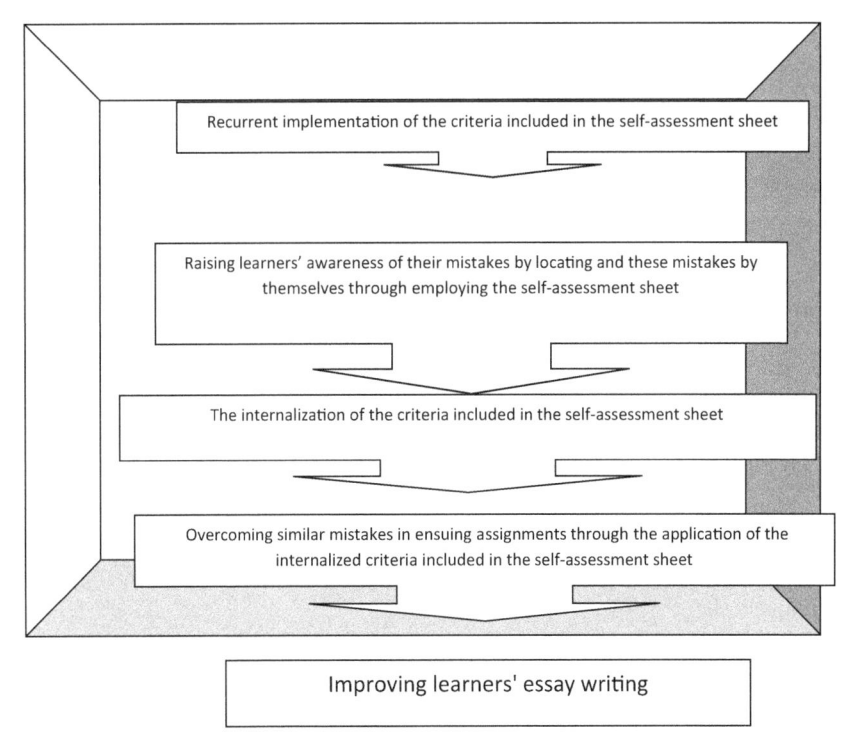

Fig. 2.1 Rationale for the study

Research Questions The study attempted to investigate the two following questions:

1. What is the effect of self-assessment on EFL Egyptian engineering students' writing performance?
   To answer the above question, the following sub-questions were raised:

   a. What is the effect of self-assessment on the content of EFL Egyptian engineering students' expository essay writing?
   b. What is the effect of self-assessment on the organisation of EFL Egyptian engineering students' expository essay writing?
   c. What is the effect of self-assessment on the language of EFL Egyptian engineering students' expository essay writing?
   d. What is the effect of self-assessment on the three writing aspects (i.e. content, organisation, and language)?

2. What are EFL Egyptian engineering students' attitudes towards self-assessment of their expository essays?

This study aims at providing EFL teachers and curriculum designers with a technique that could be exploited in the field of writing pedagogy. The importance of the study lies in the use of self-assessment as an effective revision technique. Self-assessment is employed in the process of composition in an attempt to raise EFL Egyptian engineering students' awareness of their recurrent mistakes so that they can overcome them in ensuing assignments and consequently improve their essay writing.

Furthermore, the study attempts to exploit self-assessment as a technique that could relieve teachers of correcting every single mistake found in learners' essays as well as help learners know the basis of their evaluation in writing. In addition, self-assessment can help learners see their writing mistakes for themselves to avoid them in ensuing writing assignments as opposed to the teachers' marking, which can sometimes be vague and discouraging.

Literature Review Findings

Previous research in the field of process writing focused on its different stages. The nature of the revision stage of the writing process was the major interest of many of those studies. Nevertheless, research in the field of revision focused on whether learners revised their writing or not and disregarded the nature of the revision stage itself (e.g. Emig, 1971; Honsa, 2011; Perl, 1979; Pianko, 1979; Stallard, 1974).

Oskarrson (1980) believes that self-assessment should be encouraged in EFL classrooms because of the following advantages. First, it promotes learning by training learners in evaluation, which results in benefits to the learning process. Second, it raises both learners and teachers' level of awareness of the different levels of abilities. Oskarrson's claim about the advantages of self-assessment was later supported by many researchers including Dickinson (1987), cited in Harris, 1997, and Harris (1997). Oskarrson differentiates between two forms of self-assessment: (1) global self-assessment, which is the learner's ability to make an overall impressionistic evaluation of his/her performance, and (2) criteria-based self-assessment, where learners evaluate specific language components that accumulate to give an overall evaluation of a certain ability using writing rubrics.

Another distinction made by Oskarrson relates to the uses of self-assessment. Self-assessment can be used for evaluative purposes, sometimes termed summative purposes (Bloom, Hastings, & Madaus, 1971), and for learning purposes, also termed continuous or formative purposes (Platt, 1997, as cited in Mears & Harrison, 2000). The use of self-assessment for evaluative purposes entails producing quantitative data to generate scores measuring the learner's performance and ability. Teachers resist this type of assessment because of doubts about the reliability of having students assess their ability, although self-assessment has been widely applied for learning purposes, and its use for evaluative purposes (Todd, 2002). Therefore, most of the studies conducted on self-assessment examined its effectiveness as a learning tool rather than an evaluative one.

Despite the numerous advantages reported by research on the effectiveness of both types of self-assessment, global and criteria based, it has been criticised. Much of the self-assessment debate, for example, focuses on the issue of reliability and feasibility factors. That is, there have been doubts about the reliability of learners' assessment of their performance (Dickinson,

1987, as cited in Harris, 1997). Schrauger and Osberg (1981), however, claim that the relative accuracy of self-assessment is at least comparable to other assessment methods. Thus, the historical perspective of self-assessment reveals that there is no consensus on its effectiveness.

Participants of the Study

The sample used for the study was a convenient one. Participants constituted two intact classes. The participants were 40 engineering freshmen at an Egyptian private University studying English as a requirement course. Hence, the sample was not randomly chosen, and the study was a quasi-experimental one. Nevertheless, the researcher does not aim to generalise the results, but rather the study can be replicated to examine the effectiveness of the treatment in a sample of different nature. The English course covered was a writing course. The participants were grouped into two groups, one experimental and the other control.

The Instrument: The Self-assessment Rubric

The self-assessment rubric included three sections covering content, organisation, and language. The rubric was designed to match the objectives of the course covered by the participants in the study. The rubric was developed in a way that avoided subjective wording including *to some extent*, fairly, *occasionally*...and so on. (For a copy of the instrument, see Appendix 0). The self-assessment rubric was pretested to ensure the reliability and validity of the instrument and minor wording changes were made accordingly.

Methodology

The experimental group received the treatment of the experiment, which included the application of the criteria included in the self-assessment sheet during the revision stage of the process of writing for 15 weeks. The control group, however, did not apply the treatment but rather implemented the different stages involved in process writing, i.e. pre-writing, drafting, and rewriting without self-assessment. The tools used to compare the two groups included pre- and post-tests to examine the subjects' writing proficiency before and after the application of the experiment. Moreover, a post-treatment questionnaire was given to the experimental group to measure students' attitudes towards self-assessment.

Results and Findings

Results demonstrated that self-assessment led to significant improvement in the experimental group's content, organisation, and language aspects of writing. Additionally, self-assessment significantly improved students' overall performance in the three aspects in comparison to the control group with a significance level of 0.05 and thus a less than 5% probability of type I Error.

Research Question One

1. What is the effect of self-assessment on the EFL Egyptian engineering students' writing skill as defined in terms of content, organisation, language, and overall performance?

To answer this research question four sub-questions were raised.

The Content Variable

a. *What is the effect of self-assessment on the content of EFL Egyptian engineering students' expository essay writing?*

The descriptive tests carried out to examine the effectiveness of self-assessment on the subjects' content aspect of writing include the means and standard deviation of subjects of the experimental group before and after the application of the treatment. The reason for conducting this test was to examine the effect of self-assessment on the experimental group's content variable before and after the application of the treatment. To do so, Table 2.1 presents the content means and standard deviation of the pre- and post-tests of the experimental group. Table 2.2 also provides the descriptive statistics of the control group related to the content variable to compare their results to those of the experimental group.

The results of the descriptive statistics show that the content means of the experimental group increased from 4.35 in the pre-test to 7.00 in the post-test, whereas the control group's content mean increased from 4.2 in the pre-test to 4.85 in the post-test. Figure 2.2 provides the content mean score of the experimental and control groups' pre- and post-tests (Tables 2.2 and 2.3).

Table 2.1 Descriptive statistics of the content variable in the pre- and post-tests

Variable out of 10	Group	N	Mean	Std. deviation	Std. error mean
Content-pre	Experimental	20	4.35	1.3089	0.2927
	Control	20	4.20	1.1050	0.2471
Content-post	Experimental	20	7.0000	1.0131	0.2265
	Control	20	4.85	1.0273	0.2297

Table 2.2 Paired *t*-test results of the content variable of the experimental group

Variable	Mean difference	t	Sig. (2-tailed)	Interpretation
Content pre and post Experimental group	−2.6500	10.760	0.000	Highly significant

*Results were found significant if ≤0.05

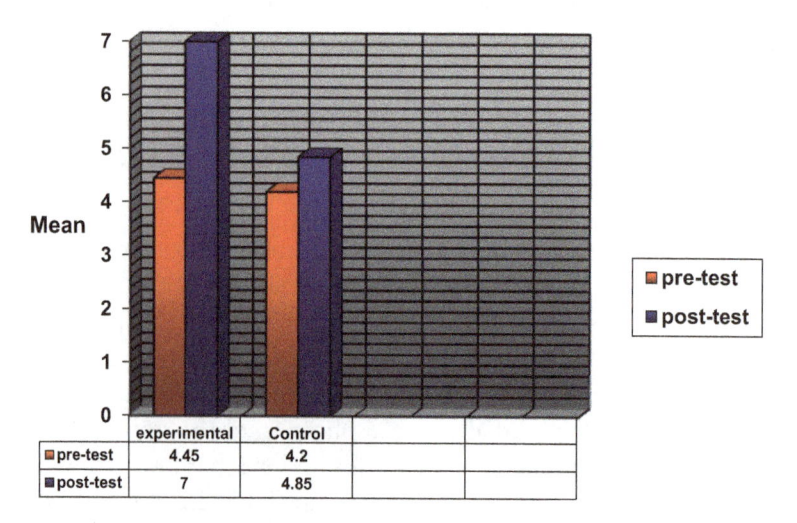

	experimental	Control
pre-test	4.45	4.2
post-test	7	4.85

Fig. 2.2 The content mean scores of the experimental and control groups' pre- and post-tests

Table 2.3 Paired t-test results of the content variable of the control group

Variable	Mean difference	t	Sig. (2-tailed)	Interpretation
Content pre and post Control group	−6.500	4.212	0.001	Highly significant

*Results are found significant if ≤ 0.05

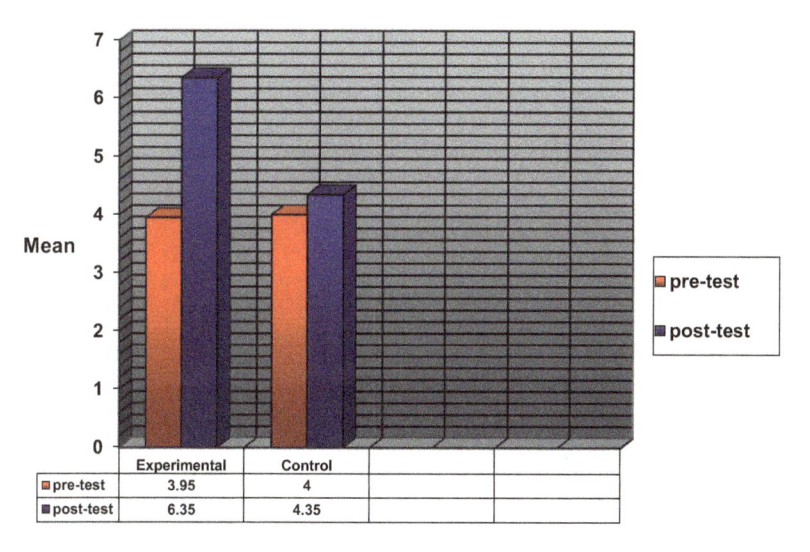

	Experimental	Control
pre-test	3.95	4
post-test	6.35	4.35

Fig. 2.3 Organisation means of the pre- and post-tests

The paired t-test was conducted to examine the significance of the increase found in the content variable of subjects of the experimental group. Table 2.4 provides the result of the paired t-test.

The results of the paired t-test demonstrate that subjects of the experimental group showed significantly improvement in relation to the content variable of their expository essay writing.

The paired t-test was also applied to the control group concerning the content variable to compare the significance of the improvement of this variable in this group before and after the experiment. The results of this test are presented in Table 2.3

The results of this test show that there was a highly significant improvement in the content aspect of the control group's expository essay writing. This implies that the English 101 writing course followed

Table 2.4 Independent *t*-test results of the content variable of the post-test

Variable	Group	Mean ± SE	t	Sig. (2-tailed)	Interpretation
Content	Control	4.8500 ± 0.2297	6.664	0.000	Highly significant
	Experimental	7.0000 ± 0.2265			

*Results are found significant if ≤0.05

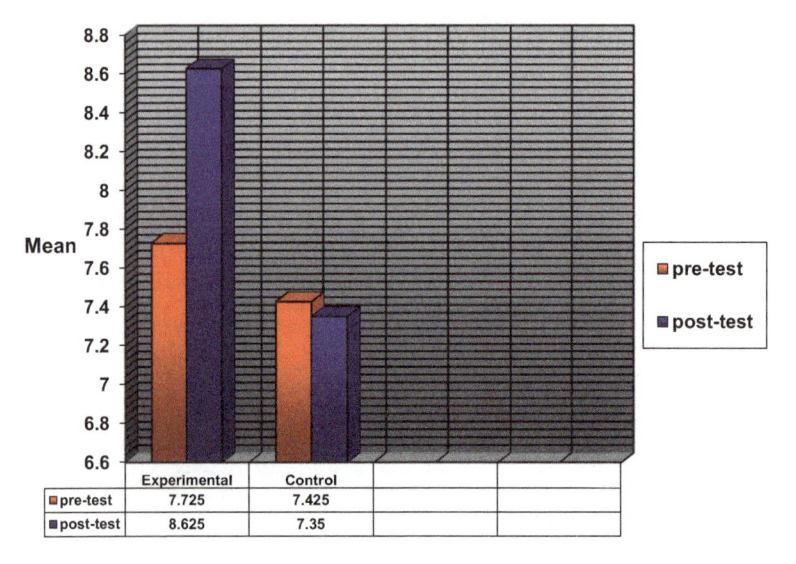

	Experimental	Control
pre-test	7.725	7.425
post-test	8.625	7.35

Fig. 2.4 The language means of pre- and post-tests

by MSA University led to highly significant improvement in the content of subjects' expository writing. However, comparing the paired *t*-tests of both the control and experimental groups showed that the significance of the content variable of the experimental group ($P = 0.000$) is slightly higher than that of the control group ($P = 0.001$). Nevertheless, to compare the significance between the control and experimental groups concerning the content variable, the independent *t*-test was conducted.

The independent *t*-test is usually conducted to compare two different groups. Therefore, this test was carried out to compare the control and experimental groups in relation to the content variable of the post-tests to trace the significance of the treatment.

The results of the independent *t*-test are highly significant in relation to the content variable. Therefore, this implies that self-assessment led to highly significant improvement in the experimental groups' content aspect of writing in comparison to the control group.

In short, the statistical tests conducted show that the application of self-assessment by EFL learners led to a highly significant improvement in the content of their expository essay writing, a finding that was not reported in the literature reviewed in the present study. Hence, the first hypothesis made by the study is accepted.

The Organisation Variable

b. *What is the effect of self-assessment on the organisation of EFL Egyptian engineering students' expository essay writing?*

This sub-question addressed the effect of self-assessment on the organisation of the EFL learners' expository essay writing. To address this question, descriptive and inferential tests were conducted. The descriptive tests compared the means and standard deviation of the experimental and control group's pre- and post-tests in relation to the organisation variable. The results of this test are presented in Table 2.5.

The results of the descriptive statistics demonstrate that the organisation mean of the experimental group increased from 3.95 in the pre-test to 6.35 in the post-test while the control group organisation means increased from 4.00 to 4.35. For further illustration, the following chart presents the mean scores of the organisation variable in both groups' pre- and post-tests.

Table 2.5 Descriptive statistics of the organisation variable in the pre- and post-tests

Variable	Group	N	Mean out of 8	Std. deviation	Std. error mean
Organisation pre	Experimental	20	3.95	1.2968	0.2900
	Control	20	4.00	1.4868	0.3325
Organisation post	Experimental	20	6.35	0.9747	0.2179
	Control	20	4.35	1.3582	0.3037

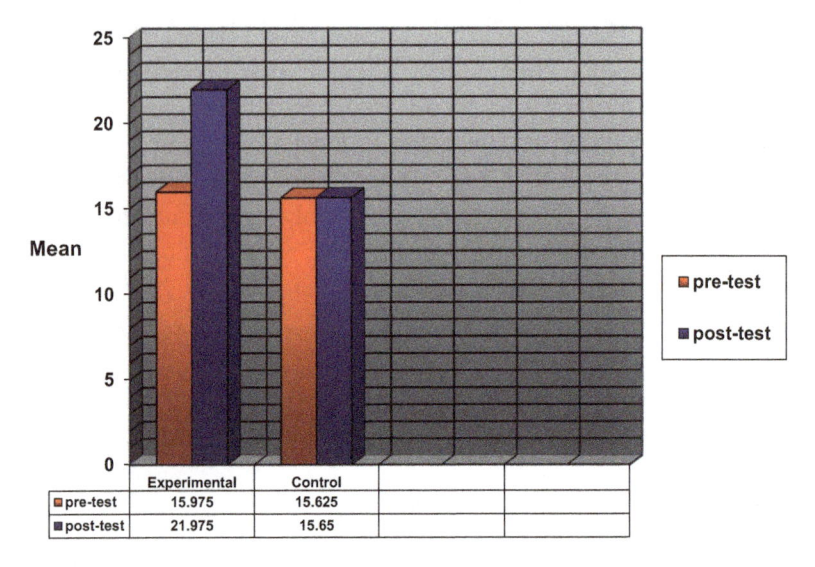

	Experimental	Control
pre-test	15.975	15.625
post-test	21.975	15.65

Fig. 2.5 The total means of the pre- and post-tests

Table 2.6 Paired t-test results of the organisation variable of the experimental group

Variable	Mean difference	t	Sig. (2- tailed)	Interpretation
Organisation pre and post Experimental group	−2.400	7.560	0.000	Highly significant

*Results are found significant if ≤0.05

To examine the significance of this increase, inferential tests were conducted, i.e. the paired and independent t-tests. The paired t-test was conducted to examine the significance of the increase found in the organisation variable of subjects of the experimental group in their pre- and post-tests. Table 2.6 provides the result of this test.

The results show that there was a highly significant improvement in the content variable of the organisation variable of the experimental group's expository essay writing. Therefore, this finding implies that subjects in the experimental group have significantly improved in relation to the organisation variable of their expository essay writing. As stated above, the paired t-test also was applied to examine the control's group expository writing as defined by content, organisation, language, and total. Therefore, the results of the paired *t*-test concerning the organisation variable of the control group are presented in Table 2.7.

The results of this test manifest that there was a very significant improvement in the organisation of the control group's expository essay writing. This means that the English 101 course led to very significant improvement in the organisation of subjects' expository writing. However, comparing the paired *t*-tests of both control and experimental groups showed that the significance of the organisation variable of the experimental group was highly significant ($P = 0.000$), whereas the significance of the same variable in the control group was very significant ($P = 0.027$). That is, the organisation variable improved more than that of the control group. To compare the significance of the organisation variable in both the control and experimental groups, the independent *t*-test was conducted.

The independent *t*-test was conducted to compare the organisation variable of both the control and experimental groups' post-tests. The test examines the effect of self-assessment on the organisation of the experimental groups' expository writing by comparing the change in this variable between both groups. The result of this test is reported in Table 2.8.

The results of the independent *t*-test for the organisation variable are highly significant. This means that self-assessment led to highly significant improvement in the experimental groups' organisation of writing in comparison to the control group.

Table 2.7 Paired *t*-test results of the organisation variable of the control group

Variable	Mean difference	t	Sig. (2-tailed)	Interpretation
Organisation-pre and post Control group	−3.500	2.405	0.027	Very significant

*Results are found significant if ≤0.05

Table 2.8 Independent *t*-test results of the organisation variable of the post-test

Variable	Group	Mean ± SE	t	Sig. (2-tailed)	Interpretation
Organisation	Control	4.3500 ± 0.3037	5.350	0.000	Highly significant
	Experimental	6.3500 ± 0.2179			

*Results are found significant if ≤0.05

In conclusion, the statistical tests used to examine the effect of self-assessment on the EFL learners' organisation of writing reveal that self-assessment results in highly significant improvement in the organisation of the EFL learners' expository essay writing. It is noteworthy that among the studies reported in the literature review, none reported the effect of self-assessment on the organisation of EFL essay writing.

The Language Variable

c. *What is the effect of self-assessment on the language of EFL Egyptian engineering students' expository essay writing?*

The third sub-question addressed the effect of self-assessment on the language of the EFL learners' expository essay writing. To address this question, descriptive and inferential tests were conducted. The descriptive tests, including the mean scores and standard deviation of the language variable of the experimental and control groups in both pre- and post-tests are presented in Table 2.9.

The descriptive test results show that the language mean score changed from 7.725 in the pre-test to 8.625 in the post-test of the experimental group. Chart 4 presents the above stated mean scores.

The descriptive tests conducted on the language variable of both groups revealed a rather surprising finding in relation to the control group. On examining the language variable in the pre- and post-tests, it can be seen that the language variable of the control group decreased from 7.425 in the pre-test to 7.35 in the post-test. This implies that the English course did not improve the language variable control group's essay writing. In other words, despite the fact that the course led to significant improve-

Table 2.9 Descriptive statistics of the language variable in the pre- and post-tests

Language variable	Group	N	Mean out of 12	Std. deviation	Std. error mean
Language pre-test	Experimental	20	7.725	1.4462	0.3234
	Control	20	7.425	1.0295	0.2302
Language post-test	Experimental	20	8.6250	1.4407	0.3222
	Control	20	7.35	1.132	0.2668

ment in the content and organisation of the control group's essay writing, it did not lead to a positive change in the language variable of the group's essay writing. The experimental group, on the other hand, showed improvement in the language variable as shown by the mean score of this variable, which increased from 7.725 in the pre-test to 8.625 in the post-test. To examine the significance of this change, in both the experimental and control groups, inferential tests were conducted.

The paired t-test was conducted on the pre- and post-tests of the experimental group as well as the control group to compare the language variable of their expository essays before and after the treatment. The results of the paired t-test conducted on the language variable of the experimental group are presented in Table 2.10.

Results of this test showed that the change in the language variable of the experimental group was highly significant. This means that self-assessment had a highly significant effect on the language of the subjects' expository essay writing. As mentioned above, this test was also used with the language variable of the control groups' pre- and post-tests to examine the significance of the decrease in the language mean. Table 2.11 provides the results of this test.

The results of this test are insignificant. That is, the decrease of the control group's language mean score from 7.425 to 7.35 is insignificant, which means that the course did not lead to any significant change,

Table 2.10 Paired t-test results of the language variable of the experimental group

Variable	Mean difference	t	Sig. (2-tailed)	Interpretation
Language pre and post Experimental	−0.9000	40.046	0.001	Highly significant

*Results are found significant if ≤ 0.05

Table 2.11 Paired t-test results of the language variable of the control group

Variable	Mean difference	t	Sig. (2-tailed)	Interpretation
Language pre and post Control	7.500E-02	.301	0.767	Not significant

*Results are found significant if ≤0.05

whether positive or negative, in the language of the subjects' expository essay writing. Considering that the language variable partially refers to grammar that is taught explicitly in the course, this finding supports earlier research conducted on the effect of formal or explicit teaching of grammar on learners writing in general including Braddock, Lloyd-Jones, and Schoer (1963), White (1965), and Whitehead (1966).

A possible interpretation of the insignificant results of the control group concerning the language variable relates to the course's achievement tests, including mid-term and final tests. That is, the achievement test in the course includes different language components where learners are asked to edit three passages including grammatical mistakes covered throughout the course. These mistakes include run-on sentences, fragments and so on. In other words, the mistakes covered in the tests are related to grammar and mechanics, including capitalisation and comma usage, which constitute a major part of what the language aspect implies. As for vocabulary, it is not assessed separately; rather it is considered in the essay-writing component of the test. However, grammar and mechanics constitute the larger part of the language aspects evaluated in course. Therefore, a possible reason behind the insignificant results of the language variable may be that learners were aware that grammar and mechanics would be evaluated separately in different components of the achievement tests; therefore, they might not have focused on these language aspects including grammar and mechanics while writing their essays.

To compare the control and experimental groups in relation to the language variable, the independent t-test was conducted on the language variable of subjects' post-tests. The results of this test are presented in Table 2.12.

The results of the independent t-test conducted on the language variable of subjects' post-tests reveal that self-assessment led to very significant ($P = 0.004$) improvement in the language variable of the experimental

Table 2.12 Independent t-test results of the language variable of the post-test

Variable	Group	Mean ± SE	t	Sig. (2-tailed)	Interpretation
Language	Control	7.3500 ± 0.2668	3.048	.004	Very significant
	Experimental	8.6250 ± 0.3222			

*Results are found significant if ≤0.05

group. Hence, the third hypothesis made by the study is also accepted. Moreover, the results of this test support the findings of Von Elek and Oskarsson (1973) who reported similar findings related to the positive effect of criteria-based self-assessment on the grammar of learners' writing as opposed to explicit instruction of grammar.

Thus, results of the different statistical tests reveal that both the control and experimental groups showed significant improvement about the content and organisation variables of their expository essay writing. The language variable, on the other hand, led to insignificant results in the control group. Unlike the control group, the experimental group showed highly significant improvement for the language variable. This implies that self-assessment has a positive effect on learners' language aspect of their essay writing.

The Overall Variable

d. *What is the effect of self-assessment on the overall of the three writing aspects measured, i.e. content, organisation, and language?*

This question examined the overall of the three variables mentioned above, i.e. content, organisation, and language. The reason behind examining the subjects' total is to determine the effect of self-assessment on the subjects' overall writing performance. That is, self-assessment can lead to different significances in the three variables of content, organisation, and language, which would consequently affect the total of the three variables and the subjects' overall essay-writing performance.

To examine this question descriptive and inferential tests were conducted. The descriptive tests, including means and standard deviation, conducted on the total of the experimental and control groups' pre- and post-tests are presented in Table 2.13.

Table 2.13 Descriptive statistics of the total of the pre- and post- tests

Variable	Group	N	Mean	Std. deviation	Std. error mean
Total pre	Experimental	20	15.9750	3.2015	0.7159
	Control	20	15.625	2.8831	0.6447
Total post	Experimental	20	21.9750	2.6778	0.5988
	Control	20	15.6500	3.0266	0.6768

The total mean of the experimental group showed improvement in the sense that it increased from 15.975 in the pre-test to 21.975 in the post-test whereas the control group total means increased from 15.625 in the pre-test to 15.65 in the post-test. The total mean scores are presented in the following chart.

Having found that self-assessment leads to significant improvement in the three variables that make up the overall total of subjects' essays, i.e. content, organisation, and language, it is logical that it would lead to significant improvement in the overall performance of subjects' essays. Nevertheless, to examine the degree of significance of this improvement inferential tests were conducted.

The inferential tests used included the paired *t*-test for both the experimental and control groups to examine the change within each group, whereas the independent *t*-test was conducted to compare between the control and experimental groups' post-tests.

The first paired *t*-test was used to test the degree of significance of the treatment on the experimental group's overall total. This is done by comparing the total of both the pre- and post-tests to determine the difference between the variables under consideration before and after the application of the treatment. Table 2.14 presents the results of this test.

Results of the paired *t*-test show that subjects of the experimental group showed highly significant improvement in the total variable. The interpretation of this is that the applied treatment, i.e. self-assessment, led to highly significant improvement in the subjects' overall expository essay writing performance as defined by content, organisation, and language.

As with the previous research questions, the paired *t*-test was also conducted on the pre-and post-test results of the control group to determine the effect of their writing course on the total variables to compare it with the results of the applied treatment. Table 2.15 presents the results of this test.

Table 2.14 Paired *t*-test results of the total variables of the experimental group

Variable	Mean difference	t	Sig. (2-tailed)	Interpretation
Total pre and post Experimental group	−6.000	12.295	00.000	Highly significant

*Results are found significant if ≤0.05

Table 2.15 Paired t-test results of the total variables of the control group

Variable	Mean difference	t	Sig. (2-tailed)	Interpretation
Total pre- and post Control group	−2.50E-02	0.031	00.976	Not significant

*Results are found significant if ≤0.05

Table 2.16 Independent t-test results of the total variables of the post-test

Variable out of 30	Group	Mean ± SE	t	Sig. (2-tailed)	Interpretation
Total	Control	15.6500 ± 0.6768	7.000	0.000	Highly significant
	Experimental	21.9750 ± 0.5988			

*Results are found significant if ≤0.05

Results of the test conducted on the total variables of the control group's post-test reveal that there was no significant improvement in the subjects' total variable. This finding implies that the course did not lead to any significant improvement in the subjects' overall expository essay writing as defined by content, organisation, and language. This finding needs to be addressed by the university's curriculum designers.

To compare the experimental and control groups concerning the total of their post-tests, the independent t-test was conducted. Table 2.16 presents the results of the independent t-test conducted on the total variables of the control and experimental groups' post-test.

The results of this test were highly significant ($P = 0.000$). The interpretation of the results of this test is that self-assessment led to highly significant improvement in the total variables of the experimental group in comparison to the control group who did not implement the treatment of the study. Therefore, the fourth hypothesis made by the study is also accepted.

Thus, results of the statistical tests conducted to examine the previous four sub-questions provided an answer to the first research question, which referred to the effect of the treatment, i.e. self-assessment, on the subjects' writing proficiency in general. The statistical tests reveal that self-assessment led to highly significant improvement in the experimental groups' content and organisation of writing, while it led to very significant improvement in their language aspect of writing. Moreover, it was found that self-assessment led to highly significant improvement in the subjects' overall expository essay-writing performance.

To address the second research question, which traces the subjects' attitudes towards the applied treatment, i.e. self-assessment, a post-treatment questionnaire was given to the experimental group. Items 1–4 of the questionnaire address the subjects' attitudes towards self-assessment in general. Items 5–7, however, probe into the three different sections included in the self-assessment sheet applied in the experiment, i.e. content, organisation, and language (see Appendix 0).

The results of the seven questionnaire items are presented below:

1. *I feel that applying self-assessment to my essays has improved my writing proficiency in general.*

Item one of the post-treatment questionnaire traces the subjects' attitudes in general towards the treatment of the study, i.e. self-assessment. The subjects' responses are presented in Table 2.17.

Item one shows that all the subjects (100%) consider self-assessment a technique that led to the improvement of their writing skill in general. This positive attitude towards self-assessment is also reflected in the subjects' results in the post-treatment test, where it was found that their expository essay-writing proficiency has significantly improved as indicated by the t-tests.

2. *I would like to apply self-assessment to my other courses.*

Item two of the post-treatment questionnaire investigates whether subjects would like to apply self-assessment in their other courses. The results of this item are presented in Table 2.18.

Table 2.17 Results of item one of the post-treatment questionnaire

Response	Strongly agree	Agree	Disagree	Strongly disagree
%	45	55	0	0
No.	9	11	0	0

Table 2.18 Results of item two of the post-treatment questionnaire

Response	Strongly agree	Agree	Disagree	Strongly disagree
%	30	45	15	10
No.	6	9	3	2

Table 2.19 Results of item three of the post-treatment questionnaire

Response	Strongly agree	Agree	Disagree	Strongly disagree
%	0	25	65	10
No.	0	5	13	2

Although all the subjects noted that self-assessment had enhanced their writing skills, 25% of them mentioned that they would prefer not to carry out this procedure in their other courses. A possible reason for this might be that they found self-assessment a difficult or time-consuming procedure to carry out; this is manifested by the results of the following item. Nevertheless, the majority of the subjects (75%) expressed their willingness to implement self-assessment in their other courses (Table 2.19).

3. I think that self-assessment is a very difficult technique to carry out.

Item three examines whether self-assessment is a difficult technique to carry out from the subjects' points of view. The subjects' responses to this item were as follows.

The difficulty of applying self-assessment was the core of this item. Seventy-five per cent of the subjects believe that self-assessment is not a difficult procedure to carry out. The remaining 25% of the subjects, however, consider it a difficult technique but did not state the reasons. A probable interpretation of the results of this item is that the subjects who consider self-assessment a difficult technique to carry out (25%) are the same as those who do want to implement self-assessment in other courses (25%). However, this finding was not investigated on an individual basis simply because subjects answered the post-treatment questionnaire anonymously.

4. *I like applying self-assessment in general because it allows me to see for myself the mistakes I make.*

This item intended to highlight the subjects' positive attitude towards the applied treatment (Table 2.20).

All the subjects (100%) favoured self-assessment as a technique that helped them to see their mistakes in an attempt to overcome them in ensuing assignments. The item also intended to determine whether the subjects consider self-assessment a technique that raises their awareness of their mistakes. All the students indicated the effectiveness of self-assessment in allowing them to see their mistakes for themselves.

5. *I like the content section of the self-assessment sheet more than the other two sections (language, organisation).*

Item five tackles the subjects' attitude toward the content section of the sheet and the self-assessment sheet in comparison to the two other sections of the self-assessment sheet, i.e. organisation and language. The results of this item are presented in Table 2.21.

The majority of the subjects (60%) indicated that this section was not their favourite one. However, a considerable percentage (40%) noted that the content section was their favourite section of the self-assessment sheet. The reasons given by subjects for their preference of this section included that it helped them evaluate their ideas employing well-defined concrete criteria, and therefore could be easily applied, which was some-

Table 2.20 Results of item four of the post-treatment questionnaire

Response	Strongly agree	Agree	Disagree	Strongly disagree
%	45	55	0	0
No.	9	11	0	0

Table 2.21 Results of item five of the post-treatment questionnaire

Response	Strongly agree	Agree	Disagree	Strongly disagree
%	20	20	40	20
No.	4	4	8	4

thing they had lacked before. It is worth mentioning that although the majority of the subjects indicated that this section was not their favourite, the *t*-tests indicated highly significant improvement concerning the content variable of the subjects' expository essays.

6. *I like the organisation section of the self-assessment sheet more than the other two sections (language, content).*

This item examines the subjects' attitudes towards the organisation section of the self-assessment sheet. The results of this item are presented in Table 2.22.

Half the subjects (50%) expressed that they favoured this section because, according to them, it helped them organise their ideas as well as being easy to apply. The remaining 50%, however, did not consider it their favourite section. Similar to the findings of the previous item, although 50% of the subjects noted that the organisation section of the self-assessment sheet is not their favourite, the *t*-tests indicated highly significant improvement in the organisation aspect of the subjects' expository essay writing.

7. *I like the language section of the self-assessment sheet more than the other two sections (organisation, content).*

Item seven deals with the final section of the self-assessment sheet, i.e. the language section. Table 2.23 and the chart provide the subjects' responses to this item.

Table 2.22 Results of item six of the post-treatment questionnaire

Response	Strongly agree	Agree	Disagree	Strongly disagree
%	30	20	45	5
No.	6	4	9	1

Table 2.23 Results of item seven of the post-treatment questionnaire

Response	Strongly agree	Agree	Disagree	Strongly disagree
%	15	30	40	15
No.	3	6	8	3

The results of this item show that the majority of the subjects (55%) did not consider the language section their favourite. Yet, the remaining 45%, which is still a considerable percentage, noted that they favoured this section more than the other two. The reasons given by subjects who favoured this section included that this section helped them improve their language by locating their mistakes as well as being easy to implement because all they did was count their mistakes.

Apparently, some subjects chose more than one section as their favourite, which explains why items five, six, and seven do not add up to 100%. A possible explanation for this is that subjects preferred more than one section in the self-assessment rubric.

Thus, the post-treatment questionnaire, in general, shows that subjects of the experimental group have favourable attitudes towards the application of self-assessment to the subjects' writing. This is a similar finding reported by previous research conducted on the learners' attitudes towards criteria-based self-assessment including Von Elek and Oskarsson (1973); Donetta (2003).

However, there was some disagreement about what writing aspects subjects favoured or found most useful, content, language, or organisation. The questionnaire, however, did not further probe into the reasons why subjects disfavoured certain sections of the self-assessment sheet, a procedure that could have led to a further insight into the subjects' attitude towards the applied treatment, i.e. self-assessment.

The findings of the study in general shed light on the possible positive effects of self-assessment in improving the EFL learners' expository essay writing. Further research, however, is still needed on the effect of this technique on other genres including narrative, argumentative, and descriptive writing.

Discussion

The results of this study can provide insights for writing teachers in relation the effectiveness of criteria-based self-assessment as a revision technique, EFL learners' attitudes towards self-assessment, and explicit grammar instruction.

The key finding that emerged from the current study is that the use of criteria-based self-assessment is a highly effective revision technique, which leads to significant improvement in the EFL learners' expository essay writing. This finding supports Oskarrson (1980) and Flower and Hayes (1981), who previously stressed the importance of providing EFL learners with a set of criteria to revise their essays. Moreover, the study supports earlier findings of Von Elek and Oskarsson (1973) in relation to the effectiveness of self-assessment on the EFL learners' language aspect of writing mainly grammar. The present study goes further to add another finding, which is the highly significant effect of self-assessment on the content and organisation aspects of EFL essay writing. This finding was substantiated by the results of the pre- and post-tests of the experimental group, where a highly significant improvement in the subjects' content and organisation of writing in addition to their language was found.

Another major finding of the study is related to the EFL learners' attitude towards self-assessment. In support of Von Elek and Oskarsson (1973) and Donetta (2003), it was found that EFL learners who implement self-assessment in their writing have a positive attitude towards it.

A final finding worth mentioning is related to the effect of explicit grammar instruction on EFL learners' writing. Studies in the 1960s conducted on explicit or formal grammar teaching concluded that it does not lead to significant improvement in the EFL learners' writing performance (e.g. Braddock et al., 1963; White, 1965, as cited in Williams, 2003; Whitehead 1966, as cited in Williams, 2003). Similar to the findings of previous studies, the present study found that explicit teaching of grammar did not lead to significant improvement in the EFL learners' essay writing, but that the implementation of a set of criteria to revise writing led to improving the language aspect of their writing, in addition to the two other writing aspects, i.e. organisation and content.

Limitations of the Study

The limitations of the study are related to the duration of the treatment, the layout of the self-assessment sheet, the sample, and the post-treatment questionnaire.

The treatment was applied for 15 weeks where subjects wrote five essays and applied self-assessment five times only because the treatment covered 33% of the class time. It is recommended that subjects have a chance to apply self-assessment on more essays, which can lead to more insightful findings.

The layout of the self-assessment sheet is one of the limitations of the study. The language section, for example, included a 'correction' category where subjects were required to correct the mistakes they located in their essays. It was found that the space allocated for this category was not enough for participants' corrections. Another limitation related to the self-assessment sheet includes the 'Additional mistakes not mentioned' section. This section was intended to address the mistakes participants identified in their essays but they were not included in the self-assessment sheet. However, this section was not allocated a score; therefore, students completely disregarded this section of the self-assessment sheet.

Another drawback of the study is related to the degree of correspondence between the learners' and teacher's scores employing self-assessment. That is, the study did not investigate the percentage of correspondence between the subjects' and teacher's scores. Moreover, the study did not examine whether a relationship exists between the score the subjects assign themselves and other factors including writing proficiency. As for the sample, the fact that the sample was not randomly chosen as well as the limited number of participants can act as yet another limitation of the study.

This study was intended to contribute to the research conducted in the field of EFL writing by examining the effect of self-assessment on EFL learners' expository essay writing. Nevertheless, further research is needed on the effect of this technique on different writing genres other than exposition, i.e. description, argumentation, and narration.

Conclusion

Self-assessment can lead to significant improvement in other EFL learning environments; therefore, it should be employed in the EFL classroom to guide learners through the revision stage of process writing. In addition, self-assessment can provide learners with a chance to participate in their learning process by assessing their writing performance, which can consequently lead to learner autonomy, a valued concept in EFL pedagogy in general and much needed in the Arab world in particular. Most curricula in the Arab world rely on memorisation of key concepts rather than metacognitive strategies where students learn how to learn and where learning is focused on skills rather than rote learning. Employing self-assessment could help move teaching in Egypt and the Arab world from mere memorisation to creating critical thinkers, a much-needed skill in this ever advancing world.

Appendix 1: Self-assessment Sheet

Name:
Essay Topic:
Date:
Score: _____
           30

Directions:
I. Circle the answer that best corresponds to your writing then use the following key to score your essay.

II. Use the following code to score your essay:

    Give yourself two marks for each "yes" answer
    Give yourself one mark for each "To some extent" answer
    Give yourself zero for each "No" answer.

Content
Introduction:

1. The introduction of my essay includes a statement of the essay's central point.
    a. Yes.   b. To some extent .   c. No.

2. The introduction of my essay includes the ideas that are discussed in the body.
    a. Yes.   b. To some extent .   c. No.

Body: 3. Each idea is explained, clearly supported and illustrated in the body.
    a.Yes.   b. To some extent.   c. No.

Conclusion: 4. The conclusion clearly summerises the information discussed and/or gives an opinion.
    a. Yes.   b. To some extent.   c. No.

5. The conclusion refers to a central point and draws the essay to an end.
    a. Yes.   b. To some extent.   c. No.

Total:

Organization:

6. The opening of each paragraph has a clear focus or purpose.
    a. Yes.   b. To some extent.   c. No.

7. Information is written in logical sequence.
    a. Yes.   b. To some extent.   c. No.

8. Ideas are tied together using transition words.
    a. Yes.   b. To some extent.   c. No.

9. Each paragraph in the body has only one central idea.
    a. Yes.   b. To some extent.   c. No.

Total

Language use Section
Directions:
For each of the following language components choose the category that you find applicable to your essay. Then assign a score out of two in the column on the right. Finally add up your marks and write the total out of 12 in the space left at the end.

Language Component	No mistakes 2marks	From 1-3 mistakes 1.5 marks	From 4-6 mistakes 1 mark	More than 7 mistakes 0.5 mark	Corrections	Score
Mechanics (Spelling & Punctuation)						
Verb-Tense Choice, & formation						
Subject-Verb Agreement						
Fragments						
Vocabulary (Correct word choice)						
Word-Order (Sentence Structure)						
Total Score						

Additional mistakes not mentioned:

....

Appendix 2: Post-treatment Questionnaire

Directions: Dear student, after applying self-assessment to your essay writing, please answer the following questions.

1. I feel that applying self-assessment to my essays has improved my writing proficiency in general.
   a. Strongly Agree. b. Agree. c. Disagree. d. Strongly Disagree.
2. I would like to apply self-assessment to my other courses.
   a. Strongly Agree. b. Agree. c. Disagree. d. Strongly Disagree.

3. 3. I think that self-assessment is a very difficult technique to carry out.
   a. Strongly Agree. b. Agree. c. Disagree. d. Strongly Disagree.

If your answer is 'a' or 'b' please mention why?
....
....

4. I like applying self-assessment in general because it allows me to see for myself the mistakes I make.
   a. Strongly Agree. b. Agree. c. Disagree. d. Strongly Disagree.

5. I like the content section of the self-assessment sheet more than the other two sections (language-organization).
   a. Strongly Agree. b. Agree. c. Disagree. d. Strongly Disagree.

If your answer is 'a' or 'b' please mention why?
....

6. I like the organisation section of the self-assessment sheet more than the other two sections (language-content).

   a. Strongly Agree. b. Agree. c. Disagree. d. Strongly Disagree.

If your answer is 'a' or 'b' please mention why?
....

7. I like the language section of the self-assessment sheet more than the other two sections (organization-content).

   a. Strongly Agree. b. Agree. c. Disagree. d. Strongly Disagree.
   If your answer is 'a' or 'b' please mention why?

References

Bloom, B., Hastings, T., & Madaus, G. (1971). *Handbook on formative and summative evaluation of student learning*. New York: McGraw-Hill.

Braddock, R., Lloyd-Jones, R., & Schoer, L. (1963). *Research in written composition*. Champaign, IL: National Council of Teachers of English.

Claxton, G. (1995). What kind of learning does self-assessment drive? *Assessment in Education, 2*, 339–343.

Dickinson, L. (1987). *Self-instruction in language learning*. Cambridge: Cambridge University Press.

Donetta, J. (2003). *Students' use of and perspectives on rubrics*. A paper presented at International Education Research Conference by the Australian Association for Research in Education. Retrieved July12, 2005, from http//:www.aare.edu.au/members/mem-form.htm

Elbow, P. (1973). *Writing without teachers*. Oxford: Oxford University Press.

Emig, J. (1971). *The composing processes of twelfth graders*. Urbana, IL: National Council for Teaching English.

Flower, L., & Hayes, J. (1981). The pregnant pause: An inquiry into the nature of planning. *Research in the Teaching of English, 15*, 229–244.

Hafez, O. (1996). Peer and teacher response to student writing. In *Proceedings of the first EFL-skills conference: New directions in writing* (pp. 159–165). Cairo: American University in Cairo Press.

Harris, M. (1997). Self-assessment of language learning in formal settings. *English Language Teaching Journal, 51*(1), 12–20.

Honsa, S. (2011). *Self-assessment in writing: A study of intermediate EFL students at a Thai University*. Lancaster: Lancaster University Press.

Jordan, R. (1997). What's in a name? *English for Specific Purposes, 16*(1), 167–171.

Mears, R., & Harrison, E. (2000). *Assessment and standards in sociology: A resource handbook*. Retrieved November 17, 2001, from http://www.bathspa.ac.uk/socassess/sectiontwo.html

Murray, D. (1978). The internal revision: A process of discovery. In C. Cooper & L. Odell (Eds.), *Research on composing: A source book for teachers and writers* (pp. 53–59). Urbana, IL: National Council for Teaching English.

Murray, D. (1985). *A writer teaches writing*. Boston: Houghton Mifflin.

Oskarrson, M. (1980). *Approaches to self-assessment language learning*. Oxford: Pergamon.

Perl, S. (1979). The composing process of unskilled college writers. *Research in the Teaching of English, 17*, 535–552.

Pianko, S. H. (1979). A description of the composing process of college freshmen writers. *Research in the Teaching of English, 13*, 39–83.

Schrauger, J. S., & Osberg, T. M. (1981). The relative accuracy of self-predictions and judgments by others in psychological assessment. *Psychological Bulletin, 90*(2), 332–351.

Smith, F. (1982). *Writing and the writer*. London: Heinemann Educational Books.

Stallard, C. K. (1974). An analysis of the writing behavior of good student writers. *Research in the Teaching of English, 8*, 206–208.

Todd, R. (2002). Using self-assessment for evaluation. *English Teaching Forum, 40*(1), 16–19.

Von Elek, T., & Oskarsson, M. (1973). *Teaching foreign language grammar to adults: A comparative study*. Stockholm: Almqvist & Wiksell.

Williams, J. (2003). *Preparing to teach writing: Research, theory, and practice* (3rd ed.). New Jersey: Lawrence Erlbaum Associates, Inc.

Zamel, V. (1982). Writing: The process of discovering meaning. *TESOL Quarterly, 16*(2), 195–209.

Zamel, V. (1985). Responding to student writing. *TESOL Quarterly, 19*(1), 79–101.

Nihal Sadek earned her Ph.D. degree in Composition and TESOL from Indiana University of Pennsylvania, USA. She has an MA in Teaching English as a Foreign Language (TEFL) from The American University in Cairo and an MA in Applied Linguistics from Cairo University. She currently works at Educational Testing Service (ETS) where she develops items for the TOEFL iBT reading and writing sections. Her research interests include exploring second language writing assessment models that promote, and not just measure, learning. Dr. Sadek has also been an ESL instructor for over 17 years and has taught numerous ESL courses at some universities including the American University in Cairo, Egypt, NYU, and Columbia University, USA.

3

Topical Structure Analysis: Assessing First-Year Egyptian University Students' Internal Coherence of Their EFL Writing

Noha Omaya Shabana

Introduction

Writing is an important aspect of undergraduate education in both colleges and universities all over the world (Lee & Subtirelu, 2015; Schneer, 2014). A major difficulty that faces students is achieving coherence in their writings. It is considered difficult for both native and non-native English speakers (Almaden, 2006). They both have the same target, which is to help readers understand the logical connections between different parts of their texts through creating coherence (Almaden, 2006; Grape & Kaplan, 1996; Almaden, 2006). Nevertheless, 'the challenge of producing coherent texts is even more intense for these second language learners who come from a different cultural background' (Almaden, 2006, p. 129). It is reported in the literature that ESL students find difficulty in organising and joining all the semantic and rhetorical discourse elements in a written text, clearly and logically (Almaden, 2006;

N. O. Shabana (✉)
German University in Cairo (GUC), Cairo, Egypt

© The Author(s) 2018
A. Ahmed, H. Abouabdelkader (eds.), *Assessing EFL Writing in the 21st Century Arab World*, https://doi.org/10.1007/978-3-319-64104-1_3

Liangprayoon, Chaya, & Thep-ackraphong, 2013). One of the reasons behind this problem is that coherence is hard to grasp (Barabas & Jumao-as, 2009). This is why L2 learners experience the pressure of transferring their culture writing conventions into the second language writing discourse (Zainuddin & Moore, 2003). Furthermore, finding a relation between the writer and the reader and establishing a connection between clauses, sentences, and paragraphs are the keys to successfully written texts (Almaden, 2006; Liangprayoon et al., 2013).

A common problem that is widely noted by both teachers and researchers is the frequent use of transitional signals in some students' writings without achieving coherence in their texts (Almaden, 2006; Cheng & Steffensen, 1996). This is because students usually 'focus more on the lexical and sentence levels rather than on the discourse level' (Almaden, 2006, p. 128). To achieve coherence in a written discourse, writers should not only link sentences to each other but should also have logic and sense in their argument development (Almaden, 2006; Wingate, 2011).

All of the problems mentioned above necessitate adopting certain strategies to achieve coherence in a written text. Furthermore, it is necessary to teach ESL and EFL students the concept of textual coherence in writing to fully comprehend it and be able to produce well-written texts (Liangprayoon et al., 2013). Lautamatti's (1987) Topical Structure Analysis (TSA) is a strategy that is considered one of the most effective methods of teaching students how to detect coherence problems in their writings (Barabas & Jumao-as, 2009; Connor, 1990; Connor & Farmer, 1990; Liangprayoon et al., 2013).

Theoretical Background

Lautamatti's Framework

Lautamatti used TSA to determine the thematic development in paragraphs in written discourse. According to Lautamatti (1978), readers expect a certain meaningful structure of a written text. They expect a related, coherent piece of discourse. Furthermore, the written text consists of sentences that are composed of topics and subtopics ordered in a particular sequence of ideas. This relationship between sentences and discourse topics and subtopics is called the topical development of discourse (Lautamatti, 1978). Moreover, TSA was developed by Lautamatti to describe coherence in written texts 'focusing on semantic relationships that exist between sentence topics and the overall discourse topic' (Connor & Schneider, 1989, p. 413). The process of the topical progression is defined by Lautamatti (1978) where:

> Sentences in discourse can be thought of as contributing to the development of the discourse topic using sequences that first develop one subtopic, adding new information about it in the predicate of each sentence, and then proceed to develop another. (p. 72)

TSA is an analytical tool that measures the coherence of texts by tracking the progression of themes and rhemes and their development in each sentence throughout a written discourse. Connor (1990) describes TSA as a means to analyse the organisational patterns and coherence of a text. According to Almaden (2006) students achieve coherence when they focus more on 'thought progression' or on the relationship between ideas. Without this relation between concepts and ideas in a text, readers would rather find any written discourse would be rather 'plain' and hard to understand or process (Almaden, 2006). Thus by establishing a relationship between lexical and semantic items of a written text in addition to its concepts and ideas, a coherent piece of writing is achieved. TSA 'has enabled ESL researchers and teachers to describe student writing by going beyond the sentence to the discourse level' (Connor & Schneider, 1989, p. 423). It has been argued as well that TSA is a suitable framework to explain and assess differences between high and low-rated essays (Connor, 1990).

TSA has three basic elements, which are parallel progression, sequential progression, and extended parallel progression. In *parallel progression*, the sentence topics are semantically identical. In *sequential progression*, the sentence topics are always different, as the comment of the previous sentence becomes the topic of the next sentence and so on. In *extended parallel progression*, a parallel progression may be temporarily interrupted by a sequential progression (Lautamatti, 1987).

Several researchers adopted and added to Lautamatti's TSA in their attempts to analyse and assess the thematic and topical style of individual's writings (Almaden, 2006). Connor and Schneider (1988) investigated whether TSA would affect a reader's judgments of the quality of writing. In their study, they examined 15 high-rated compare-and-contrast essays and another 15 low-rated essays. Their results showed no significant differences between high- and low-rated essays regarding the proportion of parallel and extended parallel progressions. However, a significant difference was found between these two groups regarding the proportion of the sequential progression where high-rated essays used it more than low-rated essays. One interpretation of their results was the length of the essay in the sense that the longer the essay is, the more opportunities for the writer to use sequential progressions. A follow-up study was done by Connor and Schneider (1989) to check if these differences between high- and low-rated essays are independent of essay length. The results showed again that high-rated essays used more sequential topics and fewer parallel topics than low-rated essays. Connor and Schneider (1989) suggest that lacking criteria for identifying sentence topics was the reason behind differences across studies between what counts as parallel, sequential, or extended parallel progression.

Connor and Schneider's (1989) results were different from a study by Witte (1983) regarding the use of sequential progression in low-rated essays. They explained that difference by a reinterpretation of what sequential progression is. Witte (1983) related more use of sequential progression to low-rated essays, which indicate less coherence in a written text. The more new sentence topics are introduced, the fewer developed topics are in a written text, which complicates the discourse and makes it hard to follow (Connor & Schneider, 1989). On the contrary, Connor and Schneider's (1989) results suggest that sequential progression may help in elaborating on previous topics as long as they are related to that topic, despite the difference in form, and thus can contribute to the coherence of a written text. They also agree that sequential progression would characterise low-rated essays if they were indirectly related or totally unrelated to the topics of previous sentences, which would result in failure in achieving coherence.

Furthermore, in a comparative study of academic paragraphs in English and Spanish, Simpson (2000) used TSA in analysing 40 paragraphs written by experts in the field of humanities in both languages. The results of her study revealed that the Spanish rhetoric is different from the English rhetoric in being elaborate in style. Spanish writers use long sentences and many clauses, unlike the English writers who tend to have more repetition of keywords and phrases in their writings. Moreover, she added to Lautamatti's three types of sentence progression a fourth type of progression, which is extended sequential progression. It is when the rheme element of one sentence becomes the theme element of a non-consecutive sentence. According to Simpson's (2000) analysis, this fourth progression appeared in the Spanish texts, where they used it as a strategy to link ideas together within their paragraphs. Spanish writers are found to prefer describing the topic and providing examples for elaboration rather than repeating the topic immediately.

Another recent study using Lautamatti's TSA to investigate its relation to students' coherence in writing was done by Almaden (2006). It was conducted to determine the types of progressions used by Filipino first-year university students in their attempt to achieve coherence in their writing using the TSA proposed by Lautamatti. According to Almaden's (2006) results, parallel progression was the type of progression used the most by all students indicating weak thematic development mostly through repetition of key words and phrases in successive sentences. Students were not able to repeat these key words and phrases in non-consecutive sentences or across paragraphs, nor were they able to achieve more sequential progressions through taking the rheme of one sentence as the theme of the succeeding sentence. This finding agrees with Simpson's (2000) where both English and Spanish writers used more parallel progressions in their writings. Despite writing essays of one rhetorical pattern, students employed different styles in their writings, especially in connecting ideas between sentences and within paragraphs. Also, the frequency of the most predominant progressions used in their writings varied. This means that 'second language learners of one culture do not limit themselves to only one topical structure but employ different combinations of patterns of progression made available for them in their desire to impart meaning' (Almaden, 2006, p. 150).

The study by Barabas and Jumao-as (2009) aims at exploring the common and least type of progression used by Cebuano multilingual students in their writings. Twenty students of a Bachelor of Science in Accountancy are each to write a definition essay. Their results showed that Cebuano ESL students employed mostly the sequential progressions in the selected paragraphs for the analysis. Moreover, Barabas and Jumao-as's (2009) results attest that coherence is crucial for a written text to be successful and that Lautamatti's (1987) TSA framework is a valuable determiner of the students' coherence and thematic development in their writings.

Contrary to examining the thematic development in students' academic writings, a study by Carreon (2006) aimed at examining the topical development of students' journals. Carreon used TSA in investigating cohesion in 20 journals of two ESL composition classes. She involved Lautamatti's (1978), and Simpson's (2000) different types of progressions referred to earlier in this review. Her TSA results indicate no use of parallel progression, limited use of extended parallel progression, and more use of sequential progression. Carreon claims that the intermediate to advanced language level of her students helped them refrain from the constant repetition of the key topics in their journals. Moreover, the paucity of the extended parallel progression occurrence is attributed to the personal and informal nature of the journals, which does not oblige the students to write a well-structured pattern that offers closure to the readers by employing extended parallel progressions. Finally, Carreon argues that employing more sequential progressions indicates full awareness of the content, where the students freely elaborated and expressed their personal opinions on the subject matter.

In addition to investigating and analysing the students' coherence in writing using TSA, other recent studies have investigated the effectiveness of implementing TSA into writing instruction (Liangprayoon et al., 2013). In their study, Liangprayoon et al. investigated TSA instruction and its effect on enhancing the writing quality of university students. Moreover, they sought to trace the thematic development of skilled and unskilled writers, through exploring the proportions of the different types of progressions in the students' essays. Results indicate that coherence was higher in the experimental group that was taught TSA with the process approach in instruction, unlike the control group, which was taught through the process approach only. Moreover, sequential progression was the mostly employed progression by both skilled and non-skilled writers in both groups, whereas parallel progression was slightly higher in successful writers than less successful writers. Furthermore, extended parallel progression was mostly employed by high proficiency writers compared to low proficiency writers. The study concluded that students' coherence improved in their writings after learning TSA, which enhanced their writing quality.

It can be concluded from this review of the literature regarding using TSA, whether as a method of analysis or as a method of instruction, that it is a valid and reliable method for determining the thematic development and assessing the coherence of the students' written compositions. Consequently, it is of prominent importance that students and teachers acquire some knowledge about this method to be able to produce coherent developed texts.

Research Question The present study attempts to find an answer to the following research question:

What are the most prevailing types of progressions that characterise the Egyptian university students' argumentative essays in the AASTMT?

Significance of the Study

As highlighted by the reviewed literature, there is a pressing need for unravelling the thematic development that characterises the Egyptian university students' (EUS) argumentative essays. The focus of the present study is to detect coherence in the students' essays that appear to be problematic for EUS as non-native English speakers. The results of the present study are significant to many stakeholders including faculty members, students, English courses designers, and English language instructors in departments of English that offer English courses for specific purposes (ESP).

The current study is significant in two respects: teaching and learning purposes. Regarding teaching, highlighting the topical development that characterises the argumentative essays of EUS will help teachers revisit the coherence problems of students' essay writing and will give them instructional insights into developing English writing curricula in schools and universities. Compiled data of the current study shed light on the most and least prevailing types of progressions in the argumentative essays of EUS and consequently will benefit teachers in improving instruction on the areas of weaknesses. Regarding learning, orienting EUS to the TSA will enhance the internal coherence of their essays, which will consequently improve their writing quality.

In summary, the present study contributes to detecting coherence through the topical structure analysis of the argumentative essays of EUS. The current study is of considerable practical value for generating useful pedagogical recommendations and practical implications for improving coherence in the argumentative writing of EUS.

Methods

The present study adopts a cross-sectional, applied, and exploratory design. It attempts to explore the most prevailing types of progressions that characterise argumentative essays of EUS. The present study adopts a quantitative design that attempts to highlight patterns of occurrence of the examined variables using the instrument of analysis. Tables and pie charts are used to show the distribution and the occurrence rate of the variables across the sample.

Participants

The random sampling technique is used in drawing the sample from The Arab Academy for Science and Technology and Maritime Transport (AASTMT), where English is the Medium of Instruction (EMI). The initial size of the sample used in the study was 100 students in four different classes, with 25 students each. For the purpose of the study, the researcher reduced the sample size by randomly selecting 25 sample essays from the four classes. Consequently, the final sample in the study is 25 first-semester, upper-intermediate undergraduate students in the Faculty of Engineering of the academic year 2012–2013. Their level of proficiency is determined by a placement test given by the English Department in the AASTMT. The selected sample for the present study ranges in age from 16 to 18 years old. All students speak English as their foreign language. First-year students, in particular, were chosen as they only receive the argumentative essay instruction during this year before they move to more specified ESP courses.

Argumentative essay writing is taught in ESP II, and the course book is Oshima and Hogues's (2006). The students receive two 90-minute writing classes per week. They are taught different genres of academic essays such as compare and contrast, cause and effect, and argumentative essays. Special attention is given to the argumentative genre in particular with an average of two classes during the whole course. Teachers explain the organisation of the argumentative essay. Moreover, they explain the components of an argumentative essay as indicated in Oshima and Hogues (2006). Furthermore, students do not receive pre-readings regarding their topic of writing. They only discuss the topic of argumentation with their teachers before writing their essays.

Instruments

The coherence of the sample essays is analysed according to Lautamatti's (1987) Topical Structure Analysis (TSA) for detecting coherence and organisation of a written text. It inspects coherence through the relationships between sentence topics and overall discourse topics and investigates the use of the three different types of progressions in the sentences namely parallel, sequential, and extended parallel (Lautamatti, 1987). Table 3.1 describes the function of each of the three types of progressions. The table includes as well some examples of each progression, adopted from Connor and Schneider (1990) for illustration.

Lautamatti (1987) explains the three basic elements that are essential in identifying the thematic progression or sequence of sentences. The first one is the initial sentence element, which comes first in a sentence. It may come in whatever type or form; it could be the subject of the sentence or any introductory phrase. The second element is the mood subject, and it functions as the grammatical subject of the sentence. The topical subject is the third element, and it refers to the topic of the sentence or the idea discussed in a clause. It does not have to be the grammatical subject of the

Table 3.1 Lautamatti's (1987) Topical Structure Analysis—(TSA)

Type of progression	Function	Example (Connor & Schneider, 1990, p. 413)
Parallel progression	Topics of successive sentences are the same	1. Over 500 million *bags* are handled on airplane flights each year 2. Sometimes that *luggage* is lost, delayed or damaged
Sequential progression	Topics of successive sentences are always different, as the comment of one sentence becomes the topic of the next	3. *Airline employees* sometimes are to blame 4. In many cases, *passengers* themselves are to blame
Extended parallel progression	The first and the last topics of a piece of text are the same but are interrupted with some sequential progression	5. It is not surprising that *lost luggage* is the number one complaint in the airline industry

sentence. It could come in any other lexical form, yet still could be referred to as the topical subject since it is directly related to the discourse topic. For the purpose of this study, the researcher only identifies the topical subject in each independent clause.

Data Analysis and Procedures

Sampled essays were collected and read, and then the number of sentences was counted for each essay for the purpose of sentence identification. In the process of the analysis of the argumentative essays in regards to TSA, only the independent clauses were used to detect the topical development of the sample essays. Consequently, the researcher had to further code the independent clauses in each sentence to identify the topics of each independent clause, since the students included complex sentences in their essays. As a result, the (a, b, c) coding was added next to the initial number of each sentence to identify the independent clauses of each essay.

Finally, an inter-rater agreement was performed to limit subjectivity. Six essays were randomly chosen by the researcher for the inter-rater. The researcher and the inter-rater have the same background in teaching academic writing, and in particular the argumentative genre. They teach students at the university level and use Oshima and Hogue's (2006) book in teaching academic writing.

The sample students' essays were typed to facilitate the topical development analysis, and they were copied with the students spelling and grammatical mistakes. The numbers of independent clauses and sentences per essay were counted to establish differences on the face value of the data. A clause is defined as a unit of thought that consists of both a subject and a predicate, and it could be dependent or independent (Simpson, 2000). On the other hand, a sentence defines one unit of thought, and it can consist of either a single clause or series of clauses as per each case.

The first step in the analysis was to identify all the topical subjects of each independent clause in all the essays. The second step was to construct a diagram corresponding to the topical structure of the essays, where the topical subjects were plotted in this diagram to recognise the type of progression, topical depth, and topical development. The relations of the sentence structure and the discourse topics were charted using the three types of topical progression. Furthermore, the researcher applied the same diagram format in reporting the topical depth and development of each sentence, as provided in the literature (Liangprayoon et al., 2013; Barabas & Jumao-as, 2009; Connor & Schneider, 1989; Lautamatti, 1978). This diagram is constructed by placing the topical subject of each independent clause of parallel progression exactly below each other. Then, sequential topics are indented progressively. Finally, topics of extended parallel progression are placed under the parallel topics to which they refer. This progressive indentation on the charts represents the topical depth. The following figure illustrates the topical development of essay no. 1 concerning the three progressions.

Figure 3.1 shows that essay one contained 14 independent clauses, with only two topics. It can be noticed that the writer employed mostly the parallel progression (9), (3) extended parallel, and only (1) sequential progression as shown in Table 3.2. Consequently, these results mean that the initial topic was not developed since the writer resorted to the repetition of topics all through the essay.

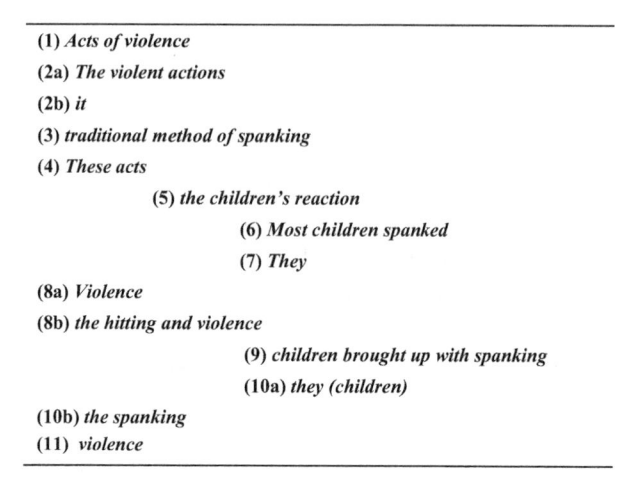

(1) *Acts of violence*
(2a) *The violent actions*
(2b) *it*
(3) *traditional method of spanking*
(4) *These acts*
    (5) *the children's reaction*
        (6) *Most children spanked*
        (7) *They*
(8a) *Violence*
(8b) *the hitting and violence*
        (9) *children brought up with spanking*
        (10a) *they (children)*
(10b) *the spanking*
(11) *violence*

Fig. 3.1 Topical structure analysis of essay no. 1

Table 3.2 The number of occurrence of each progression in essay no. 1

Item	Number of occurrences
Parallel progression	9
Sequential progression	1
Extended parallel progression	3

Inter-rater Agreement

The disagreement between the raters was mainly in identifying the topic of each independent clause, as each topic was not necessarily the topical subject of the sentence. Deciding the topic of each independent clause required a certain amount of intuition, and was not thought of as being the same by two different raters, because of their different perspectives (Dumanig et al., 2009; Simpson, 2000). Subsequently, for each of the six essays, a final agreement was reached about the focus of each independent clause. The two raters discussed the topic progression of each essay and agreed on one set of topics for each essay. The rest of the analysis of the three different types of progressions was based on this set of topics.

Findings and Discussion

The quantitative numerical data are analysed by calculating the frequencies and percentages of occurrence of the three types of progression according to Lautamatti's (1987) TSA. The data collected from the students' argumentative essays describe the physical and internal structure of the paragraphs. The total number of independent clauses and topics is identified as indicated in Table 3.3.

Table 3.3 indicates that there are 390 independent clauses in the students' argumentative essays. Moreover, 155 new topics are also being introduced in 390 clauses. The three types of progressions identified by Lautamatti's (1987) TSA are all manifested in the students' argumentative essays. However, Table 3.3 indicates that parallel progression was prevalent in the students' argumentative essays (37.26%), where the sentence topics are semantically identical. This finding confirms the results of the study conducted by Almaden (2006), which revealed that parallel progression was the most common type of progression used by all students. This topical structure analysis indicates a weak thematic development mostly through repetition of keywords and phrases in successive sentences. It is also observed that most essays that employed more parallel progression introduced the topical subject in the first independent clause in the initial position. This topical subject is repeated in the succeeding clauses. Students used nouns, pronouns, and noun phrases in referring to their topical subject introduced in the initial clause.

Table 3.3 further shows that the EUS employed 35.62% of sequential progressions in their essays, in which topics of successive sentences are always different, as the comment of one sentence becomes the topic of

Table 3.3 Summary of topical development in the students' essays

Aspects of comparison	Frequency	Percentage
Total no. of clauses	390	–
Total no. of topics	155	–
Parallel progression	136	37.26%
Sequential progression	130	35.62%
Extended parallel progression	99	27.12%
Total no. of progressions	365	100.00%

the next or is used to derive the topic of the next sentence. Among the 25 essays, only 8 employed more sequential progression than parallel progression or extended parallel. This result showed that EUSs are not able to show a logical succession of their ideas. The majority failed to increase the number of new topics in their essays.

Moreover, Table 3.3 indicates that a small difference occurs in the percentage of usage between parallel progression and sequential progression. This shows that some students also employed sequential progressions, which helped achieve coherence in their essays. Furthermore, the same table shows that students used extended parallel progression the least. It is noted that the majority of the appearance of this type of progression is in the concluding parts. This means that students were able to pull back to their main idea in the initial clause. That is, students introduced a topical subject in the initial clause and then sequentially introduced other ideas, but in the closing sentences, they were able to pull back to the initial clause or their main idea as shown in Fig. 3.2 below.

Figure 3.2 shows that the writer started the essay by using 'spanking children' as the main topic in clause (1a) and ended the essay using the same topical subject 'it' referring to spanking children, which was already introduced at the beginning of the essay.

(1a) *spanking their children*		
	(1b) *some others*	
(1c) *it*		
(2a) *spanking*		
(2b) *it*		
	(2c) *the kids*	
(2d) *spanking*		
	(3a) *some truth*	
(3b) *it*		
(3c) *it*		
(4) *it*		
(5a) *it*		
		(5b) *the goal*
(6a) *spanking children*		
(6b) *it*		

Fig. 3.2 Topical structure analysis of essay no. 22

On the other hand, it is noted that some essays are incoherent mainly because of either not employing the extended parallel progression or because of the paucity of extended parallel among the other progressions. This is noticed in the following example of essay no. 5, Fig. 3.3.

What is problematic in this essay is that the writer is not able to go back to 'spanking', which is the main topic in clause (1). The writer instead introduced another topic in (8b), which is the concluding clause of the essay namely 'a lot of ways'. Thus, there was no closure of this essay. It only had an incoherent succession of topics that were not able to go back to the topical subject in the initial clause.

Figure 3.3 shows that the writer is not focused and has introduced many new, unrelated topics. The writer starts by introducing the initial topic 'spanking' in clause (1), followed by another new topic in clause (2), 'parents', followed by parallel progressions in (3–4), (4–5a), and (5a–5b), and then a series of different topics in clauses (6a), (6b), (6c), (6e), (6f), (6g), (7a), (7b), (8a), and (8b), indicating incoherence in the essay. This finding is congruent with Connor and Schneider (1989), where they also agree that the sequential progression could characterise low-rated essays in some cases if they are indirectly related or unrelated to the topics of previous sentences, which would result in failure in achieving coherence. Moreover, it is congruent with the results of Witte's (1983) study, which characterised the low-rated essays by using more sequential progressions. Witte (1983) claims that the more new sentence topics are introduced, the fewer developed topics are in a written text. This indicates less coherence in a written text.

Essay no. (2) exemplifies the writer's overuse of sequential progression and shows no use of parallel progression. It is worth mentioning that the essay lacks topical depth and is incoherent through introducing new topics in each clause. The result is a total diversion from the main topic, 'spanking children', and an incoherent, incomprehensive piece of writing. Figure 3.4 shows the topical development of essay (2).

Furthermore, essay no. (6) exemplifies the least occurrence of extended parallel progression in students' essays as shown in Fig. 3.5. What is problematic in this essay is that almost no extended parallel progression is employed except for only two, which are (3b–5a) and (1a–4a). This can be attributed to the difficulty in L2 composing or the students' lack of

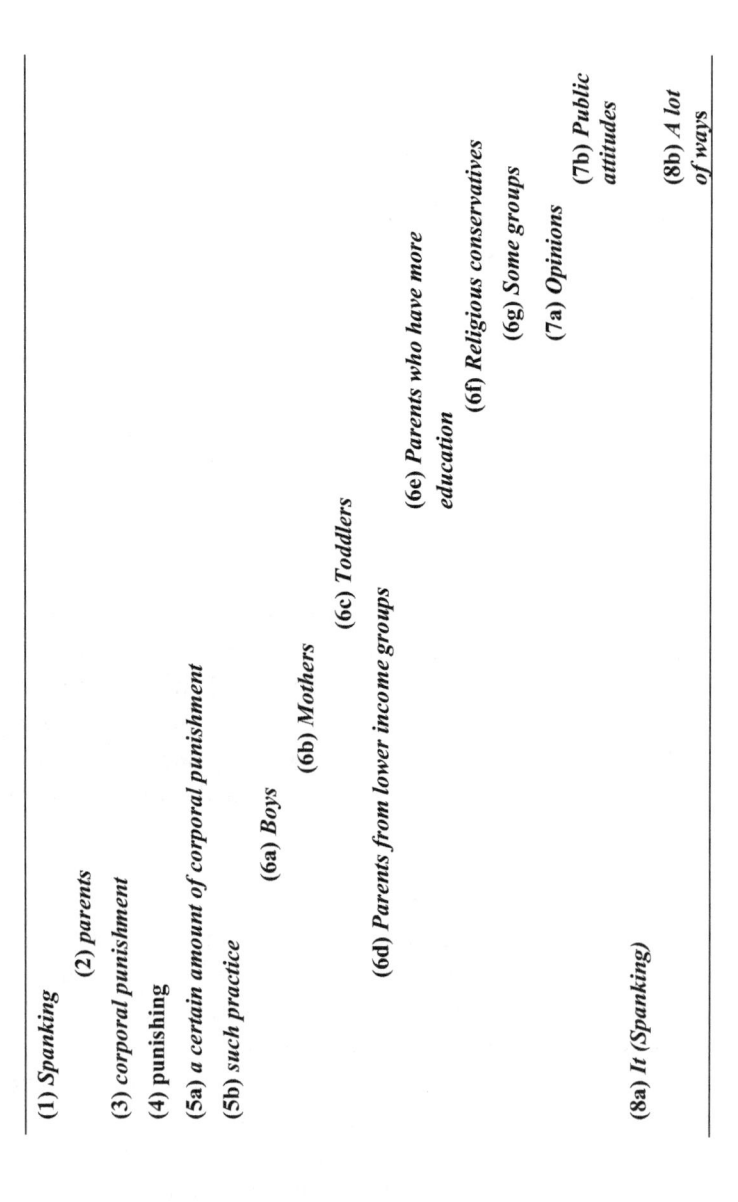

(1) Spanking
    (2) parents
(3) corporal punishment
(4) punishing
(5a) a certain amount of corporal punishment
(5b) such practice
        (6a) Boys
            (6b) Mothers
                (6c) Toddlers
                    (6d) Parents from lower income groups
                        (6e) Parents who have more education
                            (6f) Religious conservatives
                                (6g) Some groups
                                (7a) Opinions
                                    (7b) Public attitudes
(8a) It (Spanking)
                                        (8b) A lot of ways

Fig. 3.3 Topical structure analysis of essay no. 5

```
(1a) Spanking
    (1b) Parents child relationships
        (2) Children who are spanked
(3) Spanking children
        (4) Male
            (5a) Worry
        (5b) It (being spanked)
                    (6) It (when authority figure spank)
(7) The spanking
```

Fig. 3.4 Topical structure analysis of essay no. 2

```
(1a) Spanking children
(1b) it
(2) It
        (3a) Most of us
        (3b) we
    (4a) These actions
                (4b) they
        (5a) we
                    (5b) the way
                            (6) our children
                                    (7a) kids
                                    (7b) they
                                            (8a) you
                                                (8b) that
```

Fig. 3.5 Topical structural analysis of essay No. 6

lexical resources. It is noteworthy that the writer employed eight sequential progressions against only four parallel progressions. This indicates topical development where the rheme of one clause would be the theme of the following one.

It is worth mentioning that sometimes students employ more sequential progressions in their essays, but the topic is still not well developed. This complicates the discourse and makes it hard for the reader to follow. For example, in the TSA in essay (5) referred to in Fig 3.3, the writer employed nine sequential progressions against only four parallel progressions and three extended parallel progressions. The number of new topics introduced in this essay is 12, whereas the number of independent clauses is 17. Despite the number of new topics introduced in this essay, it was less coherent.

Figure 3.6 is an example of the topical development of an essay using mostly parallel progression.

In this essay, the writer started by introducing 'what would come to your mind' as the main topic in clause (1). In clause (2), 'this topic' served as the main topic, which is a sequential progression, taking the comment of the previous clause 'spanking children' as its topic. In clause (3), 'hitting or spanking children' served as the topical subject, which is parallel to the main topic in clause (2). In clause (4), 'this' served as the main topic, which is still in reference to the main topic in clause (3). The 'hitting them' in clause (5) also refers to the main topics of the preceding clauses (3) and (4). In clause (6a), 'hitting or spanking children' served as the main topic which is parallel to the main topics in clauses (2), (3), (4), and (5). In clause (6b), 'this', which serves as the main topic, still has parallelism to the main topics in clauses (2) to (6a). Again 'this' in clause (7) functions as the topical subject and refers to the main topics in clauses (2) to (6b). The 'beating children' in clause (8) functions as the topical subject and is still about the main topics in clauses (2) to (7). In clause (9), 'hitting children' is the topical subject and still refers to the previously mentioned main topics of the preceding clauses from (2) to (8). In clause (10a), the writer used 'hitting' as the topical subject, which still refers to the preceding clauses. Finally, the writer used a new topic 'we' in clause (10b) as the topical subject of the last sentence, which serves as a sequential progression. Thus, the convention of this essay mostly follows the parallel progression.

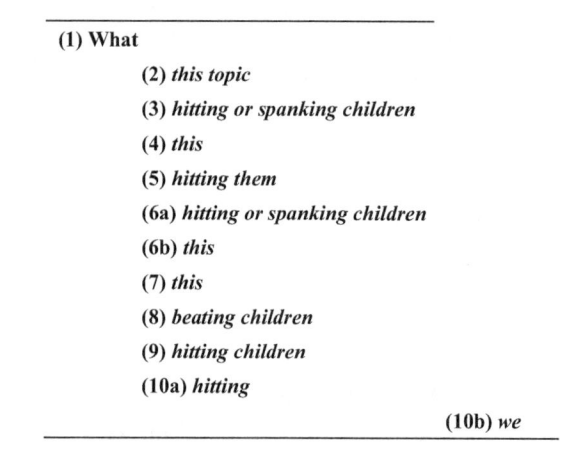

(1) What
    (2) *this topic*
    (3) *hitting or spanking children*
    (4) *this*
    (5) *hitting them*
    (6a) *hitting or spanking children*
    (6b) *this*
    (7) *this*
    (8) *beating children*
    (9) *hitting children*
    (10a) *hitting*
                                                      (10b) *we*

Fig. 3.6 Topical structure analysis of essay no. 14—*Example of topical development of an essay using mostly parallel progression*

Figure 3.6 reveals that the writer did not use any extended parallel progressions. This emphasises that some EUS were not able to pull back to the initial topic mentioned at the beginning of the essay and thus provided no proper closure, which yielded an incoherently written text.

It is noteworthy that sometimes using more parallel progression is advantageous and indicates more topical depth. Employing more parallel progressions in written texts indicates strong topical focus. This is shown for example in essay 15, Fig. 3.7, where there are seven parallel progressions against four sequential progressions. Despite using only five new topics in this essay amidst 16 clauses, it is still well developed without the heavy use of repetitive keywords. The writer started the essay by talking in general about the topic explaining that spanking children is an important issue to discuss and then moved to the second paragraph explaining the point of view of the proponents of spanking children. Afterwards, in the third paragraph, the writer explained the counterargument of the opponents of spanking children and then finally provided his/her opinion in the concluding paragraph.

The parts of the pie chart in Fig. 3.8 conclude the comparison and the percentages of the three types of progressions after analysing the EUS sample essays. As this figure indicates, students employed parallel and sequential progressions with a similar frequency, yet with parallel progression slightly higher (PP: 37.26%, SP: 35.62%). Extended parallel progression, however, was employed the least, in 27.12%.

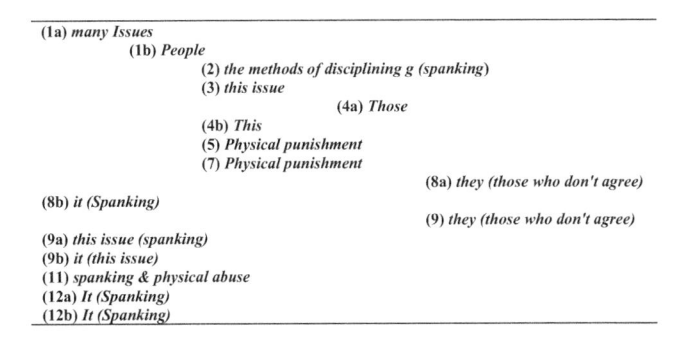

```
(1a) many Issues
    (1b) People
        (2) the methods of disciplining g (spanking)
        (3) this issue
                    (4a) Those
        (4b) This
        (5) Physical punishment
        (7) Physical punishment
                                (8a) they (those who don't agree)
(8b) it (Spanking)
                                (9) they (those who don't agree)
(9a) this issue (spanking)
(9b) it (this issue)
(11) spanking & physical abuse
(12a) It (Spanking)
(12b) It (Spanking)
```

Fig. 3.7 Topical structure analysis of essay no. 15

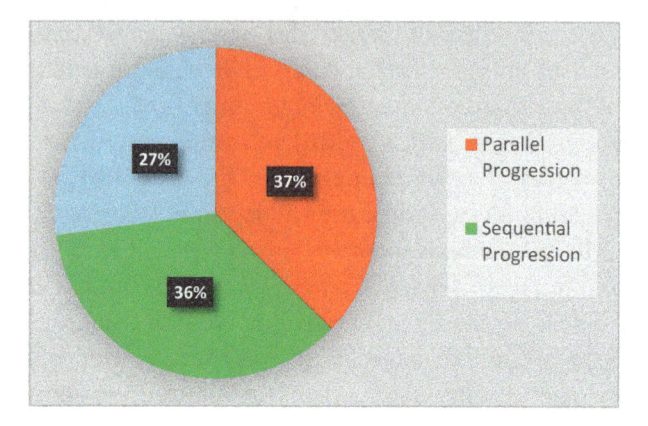

Fig. 3.8 Percentages of the three types of progressions

Relating the Results to the Research Question

To answer the research question concerning the most prevailing type of progressions utilised by the EUS, Lautamatti's (1987) TSA is used. Results indicate that parallel progression is the most employed progression by the sample students in their argumentative essays by repeating words, nouns, and pronouns. The second most employed progression by the sample students is sequential progression, where students increased the number of new topics introduced in the essay. It is also indicated that extended parallel progression is the least employed by the sample students in their essays, where they use it in their concluding sentences.

In describing how the progressions mentioned above are utilised in the sample students' argumentative essays, it is observed that the majority of students who employed mostly the parallel progression introduced their topical subject in the initial part of the sentence, making the word both the topical and grammatical subject of the sentence. The students frequently repeated this word or the reference of this word to the following sentence and shifted to the next sentence by introducing another topical subject. Students who employed mostly sequential progressions in their essays increased the number of new topics introduced in each sentence. Nevertheless, students who can employ a good number of extended parallel progressions in their essays repeated their initial topics by using parallel progression at the beginning of their essays. Then they increased the number of new topics by employing sequential progression, and, finally, they went back to their initial topical subject that had been mentioned and repeated earlier in the essay by referring to it again in the concluding sentences.

Employing more parallel or sequential progression in the students' sample essays is not a determinant of high-quality essays. This is because employing mostly parallel progressions means that students repeated the topical subject several times down to the concluding sentence. Moreover, employing more sequential progressions means that students increased the number of new topics introduced in each sentence, which made the essay less coherent. Moreover, because EUS are second language learners, it is difficult for them to find the right words that would help them organise their thoughts and ideas in their essays, which contributed to the difficulty in achieving coherence. For the essays to be coherent and of high quality, students should learn how to logically and clearly introduce their ideas and topical subjects. Ideas in their essays should be clear from the beginning of the essay to the concluding sentences. The shift from one topical subject to another should be performed in a smooth pattern from one sentence to the other.

The study results are in disagreement with the results of Barabas and Jumao-as (2009), Carreon (2006), and Connor and Schneider (1990), where their EFL students usually employed sequential progressions, unlike the EUS who employed mostly parallel progressions. Barabas and Jumao-as (2009), for example, attributed their results to the expository rhetorical mode and the text types written by students. Their EFL students were assigned classification and compare-and-contrast types of essays, which postulate that students would add details and give examples of the topic in their essays to develop their ideas. Consequently, the sequential progression is mostly employed since it helps in developing topics by adding details elaborating on an idea.

However, Connor and Schneider (1990) attributed their results to the length of essay factor, and its relation to the quality of the essays, where the longer the essay is, the higher quality it achieves. Moreover, they believed that the various interpretations of what stands as a sequential progression have contributed to their results, where some researchers such as Witte (1983) related the low-rated and less coherent essays to their excess use of sequential progressions. Furthermore, presenting many new discourse topics complicates the discourse topic of the essay and causes less topical development. On the other hand, Connor and Schneider (1990) claim that employing sequential progressions aids in elaborating on previous topics in the form of different yet related topics that follow logically from previous ones in the essay. In their opinion, coherence in written texts is achieved when sequential topics are related to preceding topics together with the discourse topic of the whole composition.

Furthermore, Carreon (2006) attributed her results of employing more sequential progressions to the journal type of writing where students are familiar and fully aware of their personal content they include in their writings, unlike the unfamiliar topics of academic writing. This enabled them to explore and elaborate on the subject well, which affirmed using different sequential topics.

Moreover, the results of the current study are not in line with those of Liangprayoon et al. (2013), where their students succeeded in maintaining a good balance between the use of parallel and extended parallel progressions. Consequently, their essays were perceived as high quality and more coherent. On the contrary, the EUS had a low percentage of the extended parallel progressions employed in their essays, which indicates a gap between the use of extended and parallel progressions.

Furthermore, the results of the current study are in disagreement with Carreon's (2006) results, where her students employed 'zero' parallel progressions in their journals. On the contrary, the EUS sample employed the parallel progression excessively in their argumentative essays. Carreon (2006) explains that her students belong to the intermediate to advanced language learners' category, which in her opinion was the reason for not employing a single parallel progression in their journals. Carreon (2006) argues that the students who constantly repeat the same topic of their initial sentence element mostly belong to the beginner language learner category. This again is in disagreement with the current research, where the EUS sample also belongs to the upper-intermediate language learner category, yet employed mostly the parallel progression.

Nevertheless, Barabas and Jumao-as' (2009) results indicate that their EFL students' use of extended parallel progression is small in percentage, which is congruent with the results of the current study, where EUS used extended parallel progression the least. Their results are also in agreement with the current study results in that there was a small difference in the percentage of usage between the sequential and the parallel progressions. This result shows that the EUS sample also used an appropriate number of sequential progressions in their essays.

Implications of the Study

The results of the study are significant to many stakeholders: faculty members, students, and English-Language instructors. Understanding the topical structure that characterises EUS' argumentative essays will enable teachers and academic writing course designers to assess the strengths and weaknesses of the internal coherence of the students' essays. Moreover, increasing teachers' awareness of monitoring the thematic development in the students' essays has positive effects on enhancing the students' coherence in their writings. Therefore, the practical implications of the results of the present study can be summarised as follows:

> Regarding analysing the TSA in the sample of EUS argumentative essays, the total number of topics is 155 whereas the total number of clauses is 390. This indicates less topical development and more repetition of the initial subject or the keywords and thus makes the EUS argumentative essays less coherent. The repetition of keywords shows a lack of lexical resources. Consequently, students should improve their vocabulary and lexical items to enable them as L2 learners to be more productive and fluent.

Moreover, it is highly recommended for teachers to introduce TSA as one of the strategies in teaching intermediate and advanced academic writing courses. Students should be familiar with the TSA framework to be able to increase coherence in their writings. In this light, teachers should encourage more use of the other types of progressions that are rarely used by students to increase the quality and coherence of their written texts. In addition, ESL teachers should strive to enrich the students' vocabulary bank instead of focusing on writing short sentences with good grammar. Enriching students' vocabulary will enable them to produce more words in sentences.

Fragments and dependent clauses were used frequently in the sample of the EUS essays. Thus, ESL instructors should teach students how to distinguish between types of sentences, such as simple, compound, and complex, to use them effectively in building a comprehensive argument. Furthermore, instructors should give the students enough time to revise their writings to avoid any grammatical or lexical mistakes that could eventually negatively affect the coherence and hence the development of the argument.

Conclusion

The current study reported the different types of progressions employed in the argumentative essays of EUS, indicating the most and the least prevailing ones. It can be concluded that it is difficult for the EUS to achieve coherence because of their inability as L2 learners to find the right words that would help them organise their ideas in their essays.

In the current study the researcher aimed at equipping EFL/ESL instructors and designers of academic writing courses with the necessary information about the thematic development that characterises the argumentative essays of EUS. Moreover, revealing the most and the least prevailing types of progressions in the argumentative essays evokes insights into developing the teaching material needed to assess coherence to enhance the quality of the EUS written product. The researcher used the TSA, which is a rhetorical measure that enables students to improve their writings by judging their own product. Finally, the ultimate goal of the researcher is not only to improve the academic writing of EUS in general, but also to equip them with the necessary coherence strategies that would help them express their ideas clearly and communicate their messages effectively.

References

Almaden, D. (2006). An analysis of the topical structure of paragraphs written by Filipino students. *The Asia-Pacific Education Research, 15*(1), 127–153.

Barabas, C. D., & Jumao-as, A. G. (2009). *Topical structure analysis: The case of the essays written by Cebuano multilingual students.* Paper presented at the 15 Annual Conference of the International Association of World Englishes, Cebu City, Philippines, pp. 1–21.

Carreon, M. (2006). Unguarded patterns of thinking: Physical and topical structure analysis of student journals. *The Asia-Pacific Education Research, 15*(1), 155–182.

Cheng, X., & Steffensen, M. S. (1996). Metadiscourse: A technique for improving student writing. *Research in the Teaching of English, 30*(2), 149–181.

Connor, U. (1990). Linguistic/rhetorical measures for international persuasive student writing. *Research in the Teaching of English, 24*(1), 67–87.

Connor, U., & Farmer, M. (1990). The teaching of topical structure analysis as a revision strategy for ESL writers. In B. Kroll (Ed.), *Second language writing. Research insights for the classroom* (pp. 126–139). Cambridge: Cambridge University Press.

Connor, U., & Schneider, M. (1988, March). *Topical structure and writing quality: Results of an ESL study.* Paper presented at the 22nd Annual TESOL Convention, Chicago.

Connor, U., & Schneider, M. (1989). Analyzing topical structure in ESL essays. *Studies in Second Language Acquisition, 12*, 411–427.

Connor, U., & Schneider, M. (1990). Analyzing topical structure in ESL essays. *Studies in Second Language Acquisition, 12*(04), 411–427.

Dumanig, F. P., Esteban, I. C., Lee, Y. P., & Gan, A. D. (2009). Topical structure analysis of American and Philippine editorials. *Journal for the Advancement of Science & Arts, 1*(1), 63–72.

Grabe, W., & Kaplan, R. B. (1996). *Theory and practice of writing.* New York: Addison Wesley Longman.

Lautamatti, L. (1978). Observations on the development of the topic in simplified discourse. In V. Kohonen & N. E. Enkvist (Eds.), *Text linguistics, cognitive learning and language teaching* (pp. 71–104). Turku, Finland: University of Turku. Retrieved from https://www.jyu.fi

Lautamatti, L. (1987). Observations on the development of the topic of simplified discourse. In U. Connor & R. B. Kaplan (Eds.), *Writing across languages: Analysis of L2 text* (pp. 87–114). Reading, MA: Addison-Wesley Publishing Company, Inc.

Lee, J. J., & Subtirelu, N. C. (2015). Metadiscourse in the classroom: A comparative anslysis of EAP lessons and university lectures. *English for Specific Purposes, 37*, 52–62. Retrieved from http://www.sciencedirect.com

Liangprayoon, S., Chaya, W., & Thep-ackraphong, T. (2013). The effect of topical structure analysis instruction on university students' writing quality. *English Language Teaching, 6*(7), 60–71.

Oshima, A., & Hogues, A. (2006). *Writing academic English.* White Plains, NY: Pearson Education.

Schneer, D. (2014). Rethinking the argumentative essay. *TESOL Journal, 5*(4), 619–653. Retrieved from http://onlinelibrary.wiley.com

Simpson, J. (2000). Topical structure analysis of academic paragraphs in English and Spanish. *Journal of Second Language Writing, 9*(3), 293–309.

Wingate, U. (2011). 'Argument!' helping students understand what essay writing is about. *Journal of English for Academic Purposes, 11*(2), 145–154.

Witte, S. P. (1983). Topical structure and writing quality-some possible text-based explanations of readers judgments of student writing. *Visible Language, 17*(2), 177–205.

Zainuddin, H., & Moore, R. A. (2003). Audience awareness in L1 and L2 composing of bilingual writers. *TESL-EJ, 7*(1), 1–18.

Noha O. Shabana is an English language instructor at the German University in Cairo (GUC). She holds an MA in Applied Linguistics from Ain Shams University and is currently a doctoral candidate at Helwan University. Ms. Shabana is passionate about teaching writing, as well as integratingcritical thinking into writing. Her academic and research interests in Applied Linguistics and Discourse Analysis resulted in conducting a comprehensive analysis of the rhetorical features in the Egyptian university students'argumentative essays as the focus of her Master's dissertation. Her researchresults generated valuable practical implications for EFL/ESLteachers and English language courses designers.

4

Moroccan EFL University Students' Composing Skills in the Balance: Assessment Procedures and Outcomes

Soufiane Abouabdelkader

Introduction

This chapter reports the results of an empirical study that focused on the procedures used to assess students' composing skills in some Moroccan state universities. It is an attempt to assess the progress achieved during the last two decades regarding the pragmatic realisations of both teachers and researchers in the field of EFL assessment. By the same token, it is an attempt to discover the dysfunctions existing in the composition assessment practices adopted for the purpose of college graduation.

Given the complexity of the problems related to composition assessment, this study seeks to depict the assessment principles and practices of Moroccan university teachers in assessing students' composing skills. It

---

S. Abouabdelkader (✉)
Ibn Tofail University, Kenitra, Morocco

incorporates the analysis of corpora collected from two different universities. These corpora include students' end-of-term composition examinations, on the one hand, and teachers' views and perceptions of assessment on the other. These two sets of data were collected and analysed quantitatively and qualitatively by observed features and concerning the claims made by four composition instructors involved in the study.

The analyses try to focus on the contextual factors that may provide insight as to where writing interventions might be most successful at the three levels under investigation: (1) students' performance in composition, (2) teacher-designed composition tests, and (3) teachers' conceptions of assessment and their actual assessment practices. The two levels of university instruction that have been examined are Semester 1, in which the focus is on the language mechanics, and Semester 3, in which students are trained to write full compositions (see course description in Appendices 1, 2, and 3). The focus was on Semester 3 data, as all the students were required to write a composition under examination conditions; all of them had similar levels of motivation to upgrade to the next level of education. The topics of the tests are reported and analysed in the study, and their effects on students' performance are reported. Guidance to perform these analyses is drawn from a set of rubrics that have been used in a study on the improvement of writing skills by Oppenheimer, Zarombb, Pomerantzc, Williams, and Park (2017). This study has made use of a set of well-designed rubrics that seem consistent with the objectives of the present research. These rubrics are made according to each of the genres tested and delineate the degree of performance of each composition.

It is assumed in this research study that ineffective composition assessment strategies naturally correlate with the ineffective learning of composing skills among the students. The rationale underneath this claim is that lack of training in the constituents of the composing skills as well as attribution of the course to non-specialists is a common practice in most universities and that such outcomes are a sine qua non implication of lack of clear criteria for learning and assessment. The questions raised in this regard address the validity and reliability of these tests and their effects on academic life.

1. What are the major features of composition assessment in higher education?
2. Do teachers test students' compositions in proportion to a set of criteria that match clear standards and specified objectives? Or
3. Do they test students' composing skills just for the purpose of coming to terms with the content of the modules we are assigned at a specific semester?

These questions seek to delineate the skills targeted in the composition tests as well as the testing procedures adopted by the composition instructors. The data collected for this purpose have been analysed and interpreted according to a mixed methods research paradigm, based on the context under investigation, as depicted in the review of the literature.

State of the Art of EFL Writing Assessment

Back in 1983, the Moroccan Association of Teachers of English (MATE) devoted its annual conference to 'Testing in EFL', featuring several dimensions of the problem by researchers and experts from Morocco, the United States, and Great Britain. The contributions provided for the purpose of the conference illustrate the limitations of the existing trends of EFL assessment in both secondary and tertiary education. By then, most of the tests aimed to test the students' knowledge of the foreign language structure and functions, a trend that was opposed by several advocates of the issue of culture as a crucial component of language that requires further consideration (Johnson and Riazi, 2016).

The recurrent shifts of focus in English language teaching, as revealed in the literature, have had some impact on composition teaching and assessment in Moroccan universities. The major milestones of innovation and progress in this area have been laid by scholars whose experience in assessment time has been the major incentive for the changes and improvements brought forth by the educational reform. These scholars' contributions laid the ground for the uprising of discontent about the way assessment is done in higher education. Ouakrime (1986), for example, says that the problem of assessing students' proficiency skills relate to the use of inadequate scoring rubrics that would maintain learners' confidence. He says that the examination system "increases the risk of examination results being perceived as subjective judgments made on students performance than a "fair" evaluation of the range of their knowledge and abilities" (Ouakrime, 1986, p. 238). In fact, the situation has not changed much since then. Bouziane (2016) maintains a status quo of the operation, confirming that the system has evolved since 2009, in spite of the efforts made by the first higher education reform. He says that 'There is still a large difference between at the conceptual level of teachers' attitudes and practices in the composition track'. As reported below, most of the problems related to EFL assessment in Morocco have been mentioned in the existing literature. Abouabdelkader and Bouziane (2016) report that the persistence of these problems is due to the limited use of the existing local research in the field.

What matters most in this chapter is that researchers within this area are becoming increasingly conscious that testing foreign language skills should be aligned with the course content and objectives. As evidenced in the literature, this view is not new; several researchers in the 1980s raised it. The contention between language and content was amply addressed, and several views were reported. Ezzroura (1993) reported for example that, because students still grapple with the language at the earlier stages, it is fair to give more importance to vocabulary and grammar. He says: 'we must account for this medium [i.e.; language] before establishing any view of the text' (p. 50). Later on, Ennaji (1987) expressed the concern of academia to make assessment reflect the teaching course objectives, with more focus on language at earlier stages and a shift towards meaning at advanced stages and advocated the use of scoring rubrics. In a doctoral dissertation, Abouabdelkader (1987) demonstrated that, in addition to language proficiency, student writers at the university level have problems that relate to how to guide them in the act of writing and usually lack knowledge of text structure. Nothing has been done to sort out this and many other composing ills, such as attention to the notions of cohesion and coherence, raised by previous researchers (Dahbi & Britten, 1989; Ouakrime, 1986) through clearly stated rubrics is still inexistent.

Now, the issue of assessing university students' composing ability is thornier than ever before. The huge number of students involved in the English studies department makes it difficult for teachers to score students' compositions in a short time. Given the absence of scoring rubrics for composition skills, both the learning and the teaching of the composition will remain unsystematic and unproductive. Awareness of these problems is growing among the teaching community, and it is not surprising that new directions and practices have now emerged. One of these practices is teachers' resorting to the plethora of tests available on the internet to use for examination purposes since they are designed by professionals in the field. The use of tests that have been designed by other test specialists poses a threat to the requirements and only sour grapes and simply further intensifies the problem. In fact, some researchers, such as Raddaoui et al. (this volume), contend that the use of e-rubrics might serve as a means to overcome the problems associated with EFL students' writing.

Among the most important points raised by these scholars is that university faculty need to be aware of the risks and dangers of unreliable and invalid testing procedures of students' compositions. In a recent groundbreaking chapter on the assessment of EFL writing in Morocco, Bouziane (2017) highlights the main issues related to assessing writing in Moroccan higher education institutions. He reports the cries of most researchers and tries to raise some questions that call for urgent treatment. Not only is this an impediment to social equity among students, but also a handicap for the promotion of the whole educational system. The argument is that the success of education highly depends on how assessment is accountable and how it impacts the students' motivation to learn. Internationally, this awkward state of a central issue is even felt dramatically. In a well-detailed report, the Commission on the Future of Higher Education (2006, cited in Oppenheimer et al., 2017) in the United States brought accountability to the forefront of policy discussions about higher education, noting that 'Student achievement…must be measured by institutions on a "value-added" basis that takes into account students' academic baseline' (Spellings Commission, 2006, p. 4, reported by Oppenheimer et al., 2017). It is assumed in this research that the achievement of this objective lies partly in the language assessment, which needs to be separated from language teaching without making it a profit for businesses.

In a substantive study, Oppenheimer et al. (2017) report that the demystification of learning outcomes cannot be achieved through tests that are not validated, as they are either based on insufficiently sensitive assessments that measure the wrong construct or other forms of measurement error. This rising of the 'red flag' over the state of research on learning outcomes and the mismatch between the existing assessment practices and the teaching is amply justified. One of the worries expressed in the report that seems to apply to the Moroccan context as well is that the type of 'outcome-only assessment' used in the assessment of students' composing skills is inadequate because it measures what students know rather than what they have learned (Astin & Antonio, 2012). This fact is easily discernible in the topics analysed in the present study.

As reported in the study on of EFL assessment in the UAE (Raddaoui, this volume), this state of affairs has urged some critics to suggest some extreme views, calling for stronger recommendations, such as applying uniform accreditation standards that provide a valid and reliable measurement of student learning (Staub, 2017). The main focus of this type of research is on the reliability of the assessment instruments (Huot, 2002) as a means of providing a reliable assessment of learner outcome. As demonstrated in the present study, resorting to such measurements is unlikely to yield positive results in higher education, and more reliable sources of assessment are in the hands of the faculty themselves.

Composition Assessment in Higher Education

The educational reforms introduced in 2000 brought many changes to higher education in Morocco and actively prompted several improvements, but also left a much freedom to the teachers regarding several pedagogical practices. Unfortunately, this freedom has often proved unproductive as it sometimes leads to the proliferation of varying trends. With regard to the issue of assessment, university students' composing skills have been the liability of the faculty, and students usually do not play any role in these practices. The real issue at stake with these tests is that they lack the validation norms that would strengthen the bond between assessment and instruction. Johnson and Riazi (2017, p. 18) say that 'the validation of an institution's locally created and rated writing test produced a number of insights that were beneficial for the host institution and its stakeholders and offers valuable information for the language and educational testing community as well'. The argument is that the quality of assessment the teachers are in charge of contributes to the reputation of the institution and its entire staff and that the achievement of this success is dependent upon the teachers' ability to design effective tools for this endeavour.

Results of the Study

Results of the three levels of investigation investigated in the study, namely: (1) students' performance in composition, (2) teacher-designed composition tests, and (3) teachers' conceptions of assessment and their actual assessment practices, are reported in this section. As gleaned from the analyses of the data, these three levels of enquiry have yielded features that are positive and others that have negatively impacted both the learning and teaching of composition in higher education. Interestingly, the problems associated with university teachers' assessment of students' composition are found to be inherent at several levels, including the conceptual and the practical aspects of composition assessment. These problems are reported below for each of the levels investigated.

Overall Students' Composing Abilities

The results obtained in the composition tests administered by the four instructors are indicative that the students' composing skills are below expectations. The distribution of students' grades in the composition in the end-of-term examinations shows two extreme picks, one at the top and the second at the bottom, and that the dispersion of students' grades displays a normal statistical distribution, with the base consisting of poor students whose grades do not exceed 5 out of 20. The causes of this low performance can be attributed to both instruction methodology and assessment practices. Though this bimodal distribution is symmetrical, these data do not represent a normal distribution, and the teaching and assessment of students' composing skills need to be reconsidered. As displayed in the histogram in Fig. 4.1, this low performance represents 48% of all the subjects involved in the study, with a pick of 20.7% at the bottom of the scale for students who obtained 2/20 in composition, indicating that composing is a problem for EFL students.

On the other hand, the distribution of the upper grades (from 10/20 to 16/20) displays a normal distribution. The figures displayed in Table 4.1 (below) show that the grades awarded to the students by both tutors range from 00/20 to 16/20. These results show that 40% of the students received less than 4/20, a grade far below average that calls for urgent treatment.

Overall, the performance of university students in the composition tests shows that students' composing skills are low and that the dispersion is greater in both groups. The variations between the members of the groups are big, varying from 00/20 to 14/20. Analysis of the samples indicates that the papers that received a 00/20 grade are not that bad and that the grading did not consider what the students could do as it tested what the instructors wanted them to do. Further exploration of these

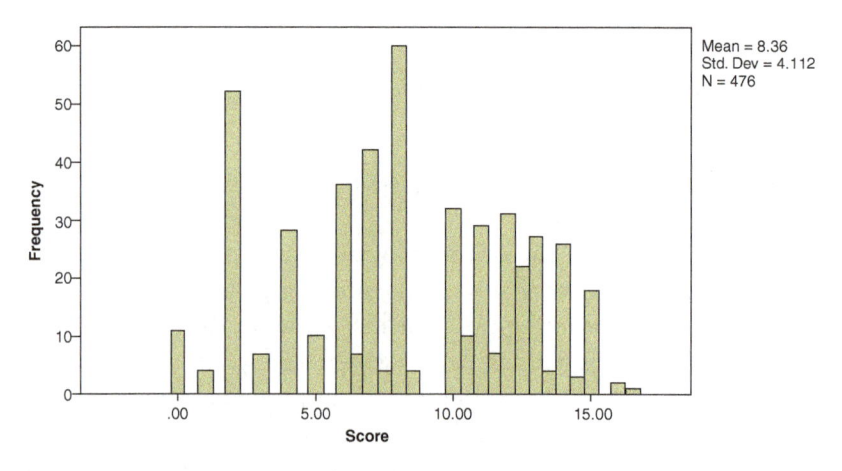

Fig. 4.1 Students' composition grade dispersion

Table 4.1 Students' grades distribution

Valid	Frequency	Per cent	Valid per cent	Cumulative per cent
0.00	10	4.1	4.1	4.1
1.00	4	1.6	1.6	5.7
2.00	51	20.7	20.7	26.4
3.00	7	2.8	2.8	29.3
4.00	27	11.0	11.0	40.2
5.00	10	4.1	4.1	44.3
6.00	16	6.5	6.5	50.8
7.00	9	3.7	3.7	54.5
8.00	10	4.1	4.1	58.5
10.00	18	7.3	7.3	65.9
11.00	17	6.9	6.9	72.8
12.00	18	7.3	7.3	80.1
13.00	14	5.7	5.7	85.8
14.00	20	8.1	8.1	93.9
15.00	13	5.3	5.3	99.2
16.00	2	0.8	0.8	100.0
Total	246	100.0	100.0	

grades shows that these students were penalised for reasons that relate to the instructors' conceptions of composition. It is worth noting, however, that distribution of the examination score data is very close to normal and that it is similar to the findings of other researchers. Peters and Van Houtven (2010, cited in Oppenheimer et al., 2017) report that the results of students' performance in L2 writing at university do not reach the threshold level. Unfortunately, most of the research attributes this failure to students (Deygers, Van den Branden, & Peters, 2017) rather than teachers and testing practices.

A comparison of the means of the grades obtained by the two sample groups of students indicates that the scoring procedures used by the two instructors vary and give different results (9.5 is the mean of group 1 while 7.3 is the mean of group 3).

The low performance of group 3 indicates that one teacher teaches better or gives higher grades than the other. These results may also suggest that the students of one group are more skilled than those of the other group or that the test assigned to group 1 is easier than that assigned to group 2. All these possibilities suggest that students' performance is a pedagogical matter and that its assessment needs to be more systematic. The question now is 'how accountable are these results?'

Composition Test Accountability

The findings of this study reveal that the composition tests included in the data collected for the purpose of the study do not explicitly examine writing proficiency differences related to the competencies and skills described in the guidelines provided by the department and reflected in the course description. This failure to discriminate between the compositions produced by the students objectively can be attributed to several factors. As described in the ensuing sections, the validity of the assigned the teacher-designed tests is disrupted by the fact that they do not indicate the features of writing tested and hardly tap the composing strategies used by students (e.g. Torrance, Thomas, & Robinson, 2000) in the construction of their compositions, the problem of moving from the abstract to the concrete, from what is general to what is specific

Test Design and Topic Formulation

'Topic formulation' refers to the multiple considerations taken by the test designer during the writing of a writing task. This process involves the measures that make the writing task understandable and doable for the student-writer, in as much as it is reliable and accountable for the instructor and the establishment. Analysis of the tests collected for the purpose investigation indicates that they are deficient regarding the measures required for the validity of a writing assignment as illustrated by the following three features: (1) the ease of the topic of the composition, (2) the genre addressed, and (3) the competencies required. 'Ease of the topic' means the facility, do-ability, and suitability of the task to the level of instruction and thinking ability of students. It is essential to give these landmarks their due, as they may impede the creativity and logical flow of thinking in the students' writing. The following samples of the composition test have been copied as used in the examination sheet. Does study contain the following topics as prompts for composition writing?

A first reading of the assignment shows that the two choices offered by the instructor are badly written, confusing, inconsistent, and full of mistakes. The first one is too vague and difficult to understand. What do the words 'grounds', 'entails', and 'repercussion' refer to? It also does not provide a proper instruction that indicates the nature of the task nor does it provide a question on what the students need to talk about. Worse than that, the statement also contains a grammar mistake ('entail' instead of 'entails'), and there is no full stop. The second topic is not any better; it is ungrammatical and cognitively demanding. Like the first one, this topic does not provide a clear instruction to the students.

The test provided by the second instructor is as follows:

> Choose ONE of the two topics below and write a 250-word essay about it. Please remember that it should be a five-paragraph essay.
>
> 1. In some countries, teenagers have jobs while they are still students. Do you think this is a good idea? Support your opinions by using specific reasons and details.
> 2. Many teachers assign a lot of homework to students every week. Do you think that weekly homework is necessary for students? Use specific reasons and details to support your answer.

At first glance, the topics of the two composition writing tests display several irregularities. First, it is easy to notice the big difference between the two tests in terms of ease and do-ability. As the results indicated in Table 4.2, this variance of difficulty seems to have affected the level of performance of the two groups, indicating that care has not been taken to ensure that students of all groups enjoy equal opportunities.

A second more important finding is that the topics of both tests are ambiguous and demand knowledge states that are not taught in the course. Bearing in mind the level of instruction of the students, it seems that the intellectual demands of the assigned tests seem to exceed those

Table 4.2 The mean of students' composing performance

Group	Mean	N	Std. deviation
Group_1	9.5000	230	2.79191
Group_3	7.3008	246	4.81059
Total	8.3634	476	4.11150

proclaimed in the course description. In other words, the tests examine students' ideas about knowledge of issues that do not relate to intellectual hierarchies deriving from cognitive levels that have not been closely considered. As reported in research studies, the topics of the composition tests need to avoid asking questions that require cognitive skills that are harder than the students' cognitive abilities (Mcewan, 2016).

A third and equally interesting finding is that, even in cases where the teachers use or get inspired by tests provided in standardised tests like the TOEFL, or propose topics from internet resources as well as other written sources, as might be the case in the choices proposed in Test 2, the composition topics used for the semester 3 examination poses a puzzling interrogation about teachers' knowledge of assessment theory and practice.

The analyses reported for these locally designed tests show that they lack high levels of reliability and validity. None of them provides features that are measurable. The teachers' interviews reveal that none of them used any criteria by which the theme will be evaluated. The interviews have revealed that one of the teachers is not aware of the features of valid and reliable tests and ignores the appropriate computational reliability formulas. To compensate for this gap, most of them report that they resort to composition assignments provided in some standardised tests, on the ground that these tests have already been tested, on the one hand, and seem to cater for the characteristics of university students' needs, on the other. The negative side of these topics is that they are designed for a different purpose and a different context and audience. It is, therefore, unlikely that they would yield discriminatory scores of students' written communicative skills.

What do the composing tests address? The content of the first composing assignment deals with an issue that might be alien to many students. The topic assigned to students addressing the importance of 'online' courses in education is not an easy task. The topic pertains to a field that is unfamiliar to most students. At the surface level, the terms 'online' and 'conventional' are very frequent, yet both of them are complex concepts.

With regard to topic 1, analysis of the compositions written by the students for the purpose of the examination shows that none of them has defined or given a clear idea of what an online course is. None of them has said anything about a conventional course. In fact, both concepts are part of pedagogy. At the level of background knowledge, the issue at stake is pedagogical and addresses the problem of learning, a subject that requires knowledge of several related fields. Besides, many of these students do not have any knowledge of what an online course is and none of them has ever had any such an experience. How can we, then, test them on what they have never seen or experienced?

A closely related issue is that the topic requires a jargon that is specific and different from what students at this level of instruction are being taught in the course. This makes the assignment an even bigger burden at the level of vocabulary knowledge. Such complexity refutes the validity ratio of the topic and puts a question mark on the test itself.

Regarding skill evaluation, the teachers' interviews reveal that the tests have not been devised on the basis of any rubrics, nor are provided with a scoring rubric, which is counter-productive. At university levels, these guidelines provided by the reform have encouraged and implicitly recommended the implementation of evaluation-type frameworks commonly involving the isolation learning outcomes (i.e., statements of the knowledge, skills, and dispositions targeted by the course). These requirements are part of the mandate stipulated for all accredited institutions in the United States (Mcewan, 2016). What is important for the present research is that, in the absence of these criteria, it is not possible for students to choose an appropriate line of thinking that matches the teachers' impressionistic scoring procedure. Research on the composing process reports that students' deficiencies in composing in English as a foreign language are multifaceted and that assessment of their compositions for graduation purposes needs to be theoretically grounded, valid, and reliable (Turner & Purpura, 2015). In the absence of these criteria, accountability of the learners' outcome assessment provided in some universities for graduation purposes is not guaranteed.

The Teaching-Testing Connection

It is assumed in this study that the accountability of the composition course depends on the extent to which it reflects the milestones of the educational system. The fact that the results highlight students' poor performance in the composition tests is an indicator that the composition course needs more care and that the tests need to be in tune with the foci of the course. In fact, the results obtained by the semester 1 students are more consistent than those of semester 3 students. In fact, the course description of semester 1 shows that it is based on a set of language features, such as sentence formation, punctuation, and other simple writing components. The advantage of these elements is that they can be converted into clear assessment items. Recent research on the validity of tests highlights these interesting poles for the promotion of literacy and the establishment of strong milestones. The importance of accountability is also proclaimed by the European Framework of Reference:

> The current demand for accountability in education is unlikely to wane, and neither is the expansive use of tests to inform high-stakes decisions about individuals, programs, and institutions. As a result, there has never been a greater need: to answer questions about when, how, and why tests are used; to ensure the use of a test has beneficial consequences for stakeholders, and to make sure the ethical obligations of test developers and users are met. (p. 181)

The questions raised in the above statement cannot be answered by one single teacher. While the assessment of students' composing skills is a burden for university teachers, it is also a nightmare for students and administration staff. The challenge of getting this practice in agreement with all the stakeholders' expectations is a matter of making all parties aware of the targeted outcomes of learning/teaching, as reported in the related research. As reported by Bouziane and Abouabdelkader (2016), the discrepancy between research and practice is huge not only at the level of assessment of composing skills but also in terms of the teaching and testing boundary. Much of the research done on teaching and testing has been done, and yet very little use has been made of it, so far. Reluctance to convert theory into practice is probably a risk not taken. The reason is that this transfer of knowledge into practice is itself a skill that needs training and practice. Besides, change is usually feared on the ground that it may arouse unrest among the students.

Lack of Collaboration

The absence of collaboration among the faculty, a factor that drastically affects the assessment process, is raised by all the participants in this research. As reported by Instructor 2: 'It's impossible to work together; we don't meet as often as possible because our work schedules do not coincide and most of us have other commitments'.

Not getting enough assistance in the construction of valid and reliable tests from their peers, most composition teachers struggle to design their own tests. Their main worry, as reported by Instructor 2, is to make the assessment of the composition module fit the guidelines provided by the English department: 'The important thing is that I do all my best to design good tests that correspond to the module description'. Theoretically, the claims made by the instructors are sound; what is worrying is that they are based on idiosyncratic beliefs and conceptions of what composing skills are made of. The pedagogical repercussions of this practice are drastic as the college graduation tests under investigation serve as end-of-term examinations and, therefore, impact the future of the students.

Teachers' Conceptions of Composition Writing

Theoretically, all the instructors have reported well-grounded views of composing. Their conceptions are broad, general and advance complex terminology. As reported by the three teachers interviewed for the purpose of this study, effective composing is defined in terms of broad categories that consider composing as the ability to produce a coherent discourse in response to a prompt/task provided by the composition instructor, bearing in mind the level of the students, the specifications included in the instructions proposed, and the writer's mode of communication, as represented by their reasoning skills and thinking patterns.

For instructor 1, 'assessing students' composing skills involves both the students' manipulation of the content knowledge and their communicative skills in the foreign language'. He says that 'This ability to carry out the exigencies of the writing test involves the use of effective language and thinking patterns that apply to the task [...]. This is part of the composition course and, therefore, needs to be an integral part of its assessment'. Assessing composition tests, in these terms, is more than analysing the students' mastery of the foreign language and their ability to use it as a tool to perform specific tasks; it is looked at as a process through which students display their level of creativity and command of the English language. In response to how these features of composing can be assessed, the instructor replies:

> With experience, we can easily detect these skills...We see them reflected in the quality of the language, first. We can then visualise it in the ideas.

The main point raised in the teachers' statements is that their conception of composing consists of broad terms and paradigms, the realisation of which in concrete and controllable terms is demanding. At the surface level, these concepts seem common, but their conversion into clear consensual rubrics requires a lot of effort and time. It is not surprising, then, that most of these teachers call for impressionistic value judgments to gauge students' composing skills.

Other teachers express their concern with language. Instructor 2 looks at composing as 'a communicative skill that demonstrates the students' ability to grapple with the language to convey their ideas'. To the question: how can you assess these skills? He replies, 'Good compositions are mistake free and full of good ideas. Moreover, good compositions contain logical markers and structures taught in the course [...] Assiduous students do that'. Such claims are not without critics.

Composition Tests Design

The findings of the study reveal that the deficiencies of the tests derive partly from the teachers' conceptions of what makes a test in concrete terms. These findings also suggest that there is a big gap between the claims of the course descriptions and their assessment.

The assessment of composition skills among undergraduate students at the end of each semester is a common practice in Moroccan universities. As can be seen in the appendices, the courses are well structured and focus on all the components of written composition; yet, the scores obtained in the course are indicative that their implementation has not been done properly. The first two courses in the first year of college focus on the elements of writing, such as the sentence, and give a lot of importance to the mechanics. In the second year, the students' focus is oriented towards the paragraphs and the ways they can be written. How can we justify the bad grades obtained in the composition test by these students?

These tests are always designed by the teachers in charge of the composition course to test students' degree of assimilation of certain skills or abilities prescribed in that course. They are made for the purpose of graduation rather than training, a very common practice through which students' performance is diagnosed in proportion to loosely defined norms and standards to discriminate between them in terms of ability and competence. Here are some of the composition test types usually assigned at the end-of-term examinations at the faculty of letters.

Many of the administered tests are short of supplementary instructions that clarify the purpose of the test, its context, and its targeted audience. The students are often left on their own to make their interpretation of the task. One of the instructors said that 'This is usually part of the testing process. Students must show their understanding and the topic itself'. This suggests that the composition test is also a test of comprehension. Scaled descriptors are not provided to assist the learner to be more succinct and the test to be more accountable. The tests do not indicate any of the scaled descriptors provided in the European framework of reference or any other empirical testing procedure. Very little is provided to indicate the type of information requested or creates a scenario that might trigger students' creativity and reasoning.

Another important feature of the composition tests administered by the four instructors is that they are not homogeneous. Though they are designed for the same level of instruction, each of the tests addresses the issues contained in the course description through a different format and content, favouring some students over others. The decision to provide different tests within the same level of instruction is motivated by the instructors' willingness to test students on what has been taught in class. 'I should not expose my students to what they have not learned. I am responsible for the module, and I should assess it'. Unfortunately, this claim is not put into practice.

Teachers' Composition Tests Scoring Procedures

The results of the interviews reveal that the composition assessment procedures adopted by teachers to score the end-of-term graduation tests are holistic. No rubrics have been used to gauge students' performance, and the teachers' scores attributed to the compositions are based on teachers' impressions rather than a specific scale. In the absence of scoring scales that would secure some degree of accountability, the English departments do not intervene in the grading procedures; they simply provide a set of recommendations to assess students' composing courses on the basis of the principles stipulated in the educational reform. According to the statements reported in the interviews, this unjustified practice is motivated by the time constraints and other unfavourable conditions. In reality, it is partly due to the deficiencies of the department guidelines, as well as the reform, that are short of clear details on the content of the test, the scoring procedures, or even the level of proficiency to be addressed.

While teachers are responsible for achieving certain standards at the end of every course, checking if these standards have been achieved is another responsibility that teachers undertake for the purpose of college credit. The relationship between these two tasks is complementary, as both instruction and module outcome assessment in a foreign language are two sides of the same coin, leaving a lot of freedom for teachers to design their course content and tests the way they feel more appropriate, and their decisions are incontrovertible. Unfortunately, this advantage becomes an impediment to educational excellence, on the one hand, and social equity, in some instances. As reported in this study, this freedom is not without risks, and its drawbacks outweigh its advantages. This means that testing students' composing ability should not be left ungrounded and that rigorous measures should be taken to strengthen its credibility and accountability, on the one hand, and the objectives of the curriculum, on the other.

The Value of the Current Research

By compiling and analysing the actual features of assessment as it happens in real-time, the study tries to uncover the different visions and conceptions of the faculty and the existing trends that need further treatment. This alignment is bound to consolidate the confidence of students and faculty, on the one hand, and the faculty and the social environment, on the other. It is, however, not the intention of the present study to evaluate the progress achieved in the teaching and assessment of composition in English; what is sure is that the findings of the study reveal that the progress achieved in the way composition is assessed in some Moroccan universities is still limited and that it needs improvement of all its features.

Generally speaking, all teachers involved in the study are concerned about the adverse effects that assessment can have on their students. They admit that this awkward situation urges them to think of alternatives that might help them overcome this challenge. One of them says: 'in order to provide reliable tests, I sometimes use model tests from renowned universities whose assessment systems are theory-grounded'. One point, though, is that while they devise their tests on the basis of these models, all the teachers say that they adopt their own scoring procedures. One of the teachers who enjoy a lot of experience as a teacher of English says: 'using the scoring scales of the model tests is not possible to and inappropriate for us; we have large groups and little time; we have to use a holistic approach in order to be in the deadlines'. What they refer to by 'holistic' is an impressionistic procedure that takes into consideration several categories without making use of a succinct and focused scoring scale.

The point is that such practice is that lack of specific rubrics that match the content of the syllabus is hazardous and counter-productive (Rakedzon & Baram-Tsabari, 2017). In addition to social equity, educational excellence, improvement of the assessment strategies and practices in English language teaching, and understanding assessment procedures and principles adopted by instructors of composition at the university are crucial steps to quality assurance in education.

Teachers' Knowledge and Training

At the level of knowledge and training, the findings of this study reveal that the teaching community feels concerned with the problems associated with assessment, yet, apart from the teachers who experienced secondary education, the others have scant information about testing, and all their knowledge of the issue comes from what they have experienced as students. The worry of this second category is less acute than those with experience in testing. The instructors with little experience in teaching uphold the use of tests proposed in the existing composition textbooks or directly drawn from the internet. They simply map existing tests onto the examination canvas to suit their intentions sometimes without making any transformation, contending that these tests are made by native speakers who have better knowledge of the English language. As reported in the interviews, those who are informed about testing, contrariwise, strive to design their own tests and include the grading scales and checklists used in other local and international universities. In other terms, the assessment practices adopted by teachers to test their students' composing skills vary from one teacher to another. In some cases, teachers leave the writing test unspecified to give room for different interpretations. In fact, the proliferation of new private and semi-private universities in Morocco has provided new instruction pedagogies and testing procedures within the field of English language composition.

These findings indicate that the problems of assessment in language education in many universities are due to a number of barriers that hamper the work of teacher and undermine the validity of the tests. These findings are also supportive of the view that the achievement of well-founded testing results in composition assessment is likely to uncover the hidden secrets of the teaching of written communication. In fact, the developments achieved in composition research indicate that assessment is an integral part of the whole educational system. Oppenheimer et al. (2017, p. 14) proclaim that 'insufficiently sensitive assessments, measuring the wrong construct, or other forms of measurement error can lead researchers to fail to observe legitimate academic growth'. In fact, the practices that have long been in use in higher education do not accommodate the requirements of the new millennium.

In concrete terms, the major implication of this research is that assessment is the reflection of the outcome of learning outcomes and that both the course designer and the course evaluator need to share the same vision of the outcome to be reached. In the absence of this common ground, teachers' assessment of students' products is likely to yield subjective judgments of students' composing skills and competence. The teaching-testing dichotomy is not easy to settle down unless the purpose of assessment is determined in terms of mutually agreed-upon rubrics between the learners and the assessors. Now is the time for setting clear rubrics; the metrics of this view underscore the constructivist approach to learning, which establishes a strong bond between teaching and learning (Richardson, 2003).

Proponents of this trend conceive of the assessor as cognizant of the course objectives and the principles underneath language assessment, which consolidates the view that assessing language skills needs to have stronger levels of validity and reliability. This trend views assessment as an independent profession (Weigle, 2002), i.e., an issue that should be provided by professionals in the field of assessment and guarantee a higher level of confidence (Rakedzon & Baram-Tsabari, 2017; Raddaoui, this volume). This view is not without critics, either. Some researchers suggest that even these standardised tests fail to provide correct judgments of communicative competence in English as a foreign language. Graddol, in a personal communication, confirms that some Japanese companies sent representatives to the United States for business negotiations and that, in spite of their high grades in the TOEFL, these representatives failed to carry out their mission with their counterpart American businessmen in English. Based on the way standardised tests are prepared for, it is argued in this chapter that this type of proficiency is not supported by the knowledge states that bear a close relation to real-life situations.

A closely related implication of the findings for the issue of writing ability is that a systematic approach that considers the bond between the objectives of the composition course and its assessment requires the pledge of the following four components of the course: (1) awareness of the targeted composing skills, (2) knowledge of the procedures through which the test content can be achieved, and (3) knowledge of the validation measures of the tests. To realise these objectives, composition test designers need to be cognizant of the principles of assessment, the objectives of the composition course, and the purposes of assessment. The first step to identifying these requirements is to set up criteria of learning that can be tested for each level of instruction through an effective assessment system.

These objectives cannot be achieved without the involvement of the English departments in the design and administration of the end-of-term composition tests and contributing to the training of its staff in pedagogical matters involving learner outcome assessment principles and procedures. By making the English departments responsible for designing, implementing, and scoring tests of students appropriately, learning outcomes will be clearly isolated, and the roles of the stakeholders will be well defined within a systematic framework that involves the following three features:

- The first level concerns the instructor as a producer whose role is to check that the extent the learning of the targeted competencies has been achieved by the learners and the extent to which the learners are aware of these objectives.
- The second level concerns the department and the institution and relates to the extent to which they can contribute to students' learning and their discrimination in terms of efficient assessment schemes.
- The third is the establishment of norms of accountability that address the different competencies sought by the composition course students' learning outcomes and purposes.

The above features of composition assessment are only part of the requirements of higher education in the twenty-first century. Fortunately, all the teachers involved in the study corroborate the value and worth of research in the field of composition assessment and support its promotion through the exploitation of already available information and research.

Conclusion

As a conclusion, the findings of the study support the claims of previous research on EFL writing that stress that composition assessment in some Moroccan universities could be characterised as unstructured and unsystematic and that its negative 'washback effect' on students (Bouziane, 2017) highly affect the accountability of assessment in general, and composition, in particular.

The features investigated relate to the EFL composition assessment principles and practices adopted in higher education in some Moroccan state universities. The major focus has been on the procedures adopted by the faculty to assess students' composition skills their repercussions on the quality of instruction in composition.

Altogether, the results of the study indicate that, in spite of the progress achieved in the organisation and teaching of composition, the grades obtained by semester 1 and 3 students in composition indicate that the state of composition teaching is alarming and that assessment of composition needs to be revisited to suit the claims of the reform it represents.

Analysis of the interviews collected for the purpose of the study has revealed that the deficiencies observed in some teachers' designed tests are indicative that teachers lack the appropriate knowledge of skills and expertise to design their own tests. Investigation of these teachers' claims also indicates that the design of the composition tests administered to these students was done without any collaboration between the teachers, which largely contributed to the difference in performance between the two groups. These disadvantages along with the lack of professional development programmes in the field of assessment are cited by the faculty as instigators of the problems associated with composition assessment and teaching.

On the other hand, examination of the students' papers shows that composing is a real problem for EFL students, that both semester 1 and 3 students seem to grapple with the linguistic, communicative, and cognitive aspects of composing in English as a foreign language, and that the first step to isolating these barriers to excellence in higher education is to set up clear criteria of learning that can be tested for each level of instruction through an effective assessment system.

To conclude, the advances made in the study confirm that the problems associated with EFL composition assessment in some Moroccan universities are closely related to teaching practices adopted in these institutions and that the improvement of any of them requires the improvement of the other. The study also stresses the importance of rubrics in writing assessment and assessment research and deplores the lack of teacher training and guidelines documenting rubric development or analysis of students' abilities in writing. The results of the study suggest that achievement of these objective needs, all the stakeholders need to cooperate to establish common frameworks for language assessment, in general, and that of composing skills, in particular.

Appendix 1: Course Description Guidelines (U1)

Course Description

Semester 2: Objective of the Course

The purpose of this course is to initiate students to writing skills by writing small paragraphs. The focus is on basic components of writing, such as the word, the sentence, the punctuation, the capitalisation, and the paragraph as a constitutive part of the essay.

Learning Outcomes

Upon successful completion of the course, students should be able to:

- Write clear topic sentences and concluding sentences.
- Write paragraphs considered appropriate for the college level in a variety of rhetorical modes.
- Exhibit effective unity, support, coherence, and mechanics in paragraphs.
- Use punctuation and capitalisation effectively.
- Understand the patterns of organisation, the structures, and the discourse markers involved in descriptive writing and process writing.
- Evaluate their own and others' writing.

Teaching Method

The course will be based on the three-stage writing strategy (whole class practice, group practice, and individual practice).

Course Requirements

- Regular attendance is advised
- Active participation is advised
- Regular practice of writing

Course Content

Sessions	Content
Session 1	Paragraph structure 1: the main idea
Session 2	Paragraph structure 2: the topic sentence
Session 3	Paragraph structure 3: body paragraph1: outlining paragraphs
Session 4	Paragraph structure 4: body paragraph 2: supporting ideas
Session 5	Paragraph structure 5: the concluding sentence
Session 6	Coherence 1 + punctuation 1
Session 7	Coherence 2 + combining sentences

Sessions	Content
Session 8	Unity + capitalisation 1
Session 9	Descriptive writing 1: describing places + punctuation 2 and capitalisation 2
Session 10	Descriptive writing 2: describing people + punctuation 3 and capitalisation 3
Session 11	Descriptive writing 3: describing events + run on sentences 1
Session 12	Process writing 1 + run on sentences 2
Session 13	Process writing 2
Session 14	Process writing 3
Session 15	Review + mock examination

References

Imhoof, M., & Hudson, H. (1979). *From paragraph to essay.* Harlow: Longman.

Jupp, T. C., & Milne, J. (1972). Guided paragraph writing: A first course in English composition with structural practice. Reprinted in 1979. Heinemann Educational Books.

Appendix 2: Course Description Guidelines (Univ. 2)

Composition 1 (Semester)

This course emphasises the expository, analytical, and argumentative writing that forms the basis of academic and professional communication, as well as the personal and reflective writing that fosters the development of writing facility in any context. In addition, it teaches students that the expository, analytical, and argumentative writing they must do is based on reading as well as on personal experience and observation.

 1.4. DESCRIPTION DU CONTENU DU MODULE ♣ Fournir une description détaillée des enseignements et/ou activités pour le module (Cours, TD, TP, Activités Pratiques, ….). ♣ Pour le cas des Licences d'Etudes Fondamentales, se conformer au contenu du tronc commun national. Composition 1 Semester 2 Course Description

Week 1. S 2 course will cover the following: Review of paragraph structure—Paragraph structure—Formatting a paragraph—The topic sentence—Paragraph unity—Coherence in a paragraph

Week 2. From paragraph to short essay: The paragraph and the short essay: Different structures—Short essay organisation—Types of essays

Week 3. Exploring the Writing Process: The Writing Process—Subject, Audience, and Purpose Week

Week 4. The Process of Writing an Essay (part 1): (3 paragraphs)—Prewriting to Generate Ideas—Generating Ideas for the Body—Outlining

Week 5. The Process of Writing an Essay (part 2): (3 paragraphs)—Writing introductions: Hook—Background information—Thesis statement, Cycle licence 42/145 2014

Week 6. The Process of Writing an Essay (part 3): (3 paragraphs)—Thesis statement vs. topic sentence—The title—The Conclusion: Different types

Week 7. Ordering and Linking Paragraphs in the Essay: Writing and Revising Essays Cohesion: Practice Coherence: Practice—Revising Essays: Checklist (The Process of Writing an Essay)

Week 8. The Narrative Essay: Narrative organisation—Showing sequence in narrative essays: Time adverbs, etc.—Adding details—Practice: Several drafts with checklists

Week 9. The Descriptive Essay: Descriptive organisation—Prepositional phrases—Using adjectives in descriptive writing—Order of adjectives—Similes—Practice: Writing with time limit

Week 10. The Comparison and Contrast Essay: Comparison and contrast organisation—Comparison connectors—Contrast connectors—Using comparatives in comparison and contrast essays—Practice: Students write several drafts and use checklists for peer editing

Week 11. The Cause and Effect Essay: Using cause expressions: Practice—Using consequence expressions—Outlining: Practice—Drafting and editing: Practice

Week 12. The Opinion Essay: Opinion organisation—Fact and opinion—Counter-argument and refutation—Using connectors to show support and opposition—Practice: Drafting and editing

Appendix 3: Course Description GUIDELINES (Univ.2)

Composition 2: S3 (Semester 3)

1.1. Objectives of the module: The purpose of this course is to enable students to read complex texts with understanding and to write prose of sufficient richness and complexity to communicate effectively with mature readers. Students should be encouraged to place their emphasis on content, purpose, and audience and to allow this focus to guide the organisation of their writing. This course is designed to provide a guide for the development of critical thinking and analytical skills.

Composition 2 Week Description

Week 1. Review: Paragraph structure: Types of topic sentence—Supports—Details—Conclusion—Unity and coherence

Week 2. Types of sentences: Clauses: Dependent/independent—Simple sentence—Compound sentence—Complex sentence—Compound/complex sentence.

Week 3. Sentence: Sentence problems—Sentence fragments—Choppy sentences—Parallelism

Week 4. Essay structure: 5 paragraph-essay—The seven steps of process writing:

Week 5. Brainstorming and outlining: Types of brainstorming: (1) Listing, (2) mapping, (3) free-writing. Practice—Types of outlines—Practice

Week 6. Introduction and Conclusion—Elements of introduction—Types of introductions

Week 7 Elements of conclusion Cycle Licence 64/145 2014—Practice and peer-editing
Week 8. Thesis Statement: Structure of thesis statement—Types: divided/undivided—Problems
Week 9. Cause/Effect essay: Block organisation—Chain organisation—Signal words and phrases—Practice: Process writing
Week 10. Comparison/Contrast Essay:
Week 11. Process Essay: Understanding process—Outlining—Chronological order—Transition signals
Week 12. Argumentative Essay: Understanding argumentation—Outlining—Arguments and counter-arguments—Logical fallacies—Practice: Drafting and editing

References

Abouabdelkader, H., & Bouziane, A. (2016). The teaching of EFL writing in Morocco: Challenges and realities. In A. Ahmed & H. Abouabdelkader (Eds.), *Teaching EFL writing in the 21st century Arab world*. Basingstoke: Palgrave Macmillan.

Astin, A., & Antonio, A. (2012). *Assessment for excellent: The philosophy and practice of assessment and evaluation in higher education* (2nd ed.). Lanham, MD: Rowman & Littlefield.

Bouziane, A. (2017). Why should the assessment of literacy in Morocco be revisited? In S. Hidri & C. Coombe (Eds.), *Evaluation in foreign language education in the Middle East and North Africa*. Springer.

CEFR. (2017). *Common European Framework of Reference for language teaching and assessment*. Language Policy Unit, Strasbourg. Retrieved May 7, 2017, from www.coe.int/lang-CEFR

Dahbi, M., & Britten, D. (1989). Improving the reliability of composition scoring: A research-based recommendation. *Proceedings of the 10th National MATE Conference*, pp. 43–50.

Deygers, B., Van den Branden, K., & Peters, E. (2017). Checking assumed proficiency: Comparing L1 and L2 performance on a university entrance test. *Assessing Writing, 32*, 43–56.

Ennaji, M. (1987). Strategies for testing and scoring Composition. *Proceedings of the 11th MATE Annual Conference*, pp. 51–61.

Ezzroura. (1993). Teaching literature and culture: An anti-linguistic approach. *Proceedings of the Third Conference of the Moroccan Association of Teachers of English (MATE)*. Printed by the Institu d'Etudes et de Recherche pour l'Atabisation.

Hidri, S., & Coombe, C., (Eds.), (2017). *Evaluation in foreign language education in the Middle East and North Africa*. Second Language Learning and Teaching. Basel, Switzerland: Springer International Publishing.

Huot, B. (2002). *(Re)articulating writing assessment for teaching and learning*. Logan, Utah: Utah State Press.

Johnson, R. C., & Riazi, A. M. (2016). Validation of a locally-created and rated writing test used for placement in a higher education EFL program. *Assessing Writing, 32*, 85–104.

Mcewan, D. J. (2016). Toward a capacity framework for useful student learning outcomes: Assessment in college foreign language programs. *The Modern Language Journal, 100*(1), 377–395.

Oppenheimer, D., Zarombb, D., Pomerantzc, J. R., Williams, J. C., & Park, W. S. (2017). Improvement of writing skills during college: A multi-year cross-sectional and longitudinal study of undergraduate writing performance. *Assessing Writing, 32*(2017), 12–27.

Ouakrime, M. (1986). *English language teaching in higher education in Morocco: An evaluation of the Fez experience*. Unpublished Ph.D. thesis, Institute of Education, London.

Raddawi, R., & Bilikozen, N. (2017). ELT professors' perspectives on the use of e-rubrics in an academic writing class in a university in the UAE. In A. Ahmed & H. Abouabdelkader (Eds.), *Assessment practices of EFL writing in the 21st century Arab world: Revealing the unknown*. Basingstoke: Palgrave Macmillan.

Rakedzon, T., & Baram-Tsabari, A. (2017). To make a long story short: A rubric for assessing graduate students' academic and popular science writing skills. *Assessing Writing, 32*, 28–42.

Richardson, V. (2003). Constructivist pedagogy. *Teachers College Record, 105*(9), 1623–1640.

Staub D. F. (2017). Quality assurance and foreign language programme evaluation. In S. Hidri and C. Coombe (Eds.), *Evaluation in foreign language education in the Middle East and North Africa*. Second Language Learning and Teaching. Basel, Switzerland: Springer International Publishing.

Torrance, M., Thomas, G. V., & Robinson, E. J. (2000). Individual differences in undergraduate essay-writing strategies: A longitudinal study. *Higher Education, 39*(2), 181–200.

Turner, C. E., & Purpura, J. E. (2015). Learning oriented assessment in second and foreign language classrooms. In D. Tsagari & J. Baneerjee (Eds.), *Handbook of second language assessment*. Boston: de Gruyter Mouton.

Weigle, S. C. (2002). *Assessing writing*. Cambridge: Cambridge University Press.

Soufiane Abouabdelkader is a doctoral student at the Ibn Tofail University, Kenitra, Morocco. He is interested in issues related to technology use in education. Soufiane is an active researcher; he has participated in several conferences and conducted many workshops on the importance of grammar and vocabulary in EFL writing.

5

The Impact of Self and Peer Assessment on L2 Writing: The Case of Moodle Workshops

Abdelmajid Bouziane and Hicham Zyad

Introduction

In recent years, higher education practices have witnessed a series of major transformations that have had a tangible impact on the learning process. An outstanding transformation has been the shift in the conceptualisation of assessment from an end-product measurement phase to a decisive and pervasive determinant of students' learning. In the context of L2 writing, an extensive body of literature offers supportive evidence on the potential of peer feedback as a formative assessment tool capable of enhancing students' composition skills. According to this strand of research, peer feedback is an integral component of the writing process, allowing students to write multiple drafts based on the recursive sub-processes of revising and editing until a polished version is eventually produced. Peer response practices have also been considered useful in consolidating and transforming students' interlanguage knowledge. In

---

A. Bouziane (✉) • H. Zyad
The School of Humanities, Hassan II University, Ben M'Sik, Morocco

what has come to be known as languaging, the peer feedback discussions that L2 students hold enable them to develop meta-cognitive skills so essential for life-long autonomous learning (Swain, 2006). Research has also demonstrated that students invest more efforts in the writing process, knowing that their drafts will be subject to evaluative scrutiny by their peers (Baker, 2016). Moreover, researchers have found that feedback givers benefit more substantially than feedback receivers irrespective of the quality of the feedback they receive (Cho & Cho, 2011; Lundstrom & Baker, 2009).

Empirical investigations have uncovered benefits of peer review other than the enhanced quality of students' writing performance. Undoubtedly, one of the prime objectives of the educational enterprise is to foster in students an advanced level of independent performance. Correspondingly, peer assessment enables learners to become skilled self-assessors. The association between peer review and self-assessment is justifiable from a theoretical perspective. The socio-cultural perspective embraces the belief that higher mental functions initially develop in the interpersonal sphere before they emerge in the intrapersonal sphere (Vygotsky, 1978). The cognitive strategies that students develop as they actively engage in peer assessment enable them to become critical thinkers who can step outside of themselves to peruse their drafts with the goal being to improve their quality. Empirically, several studies have been conducted to explore the effects of self-assessment on students' learning. To exemplify, Fahimi and Rahimi (2015) found that self-assessment based on training sessions had a marked impact on students' capacity to self-assess their own work and on their writing performance. Andrade et al. (2009) reported that self-assessment positively affected students' self-efficacy in writing and contributed to their writing skills development.

The empirical documentation of the effectiveness of peer and self-assessment suggests that they are major contributors to the learning process, particularly in college-level writing courses. However, very little research has been conducted in the Moroccan context to examine the effects of an instructional procedure based on a combination of peer and self-assessment in an online learning management system. Besides, most of the studies conducted worldwide with regard to the potential of peer and self-assessment utilised holistic or analytic scoring rubrics to measure

L2 writing development. Although this type of measurement can help identify the development of students' writing ability, it may not be equally adequate to detect minute changes over shorter periods of times. In this vein, some studies did not report any progress in their participants' writings, which calls for research using other means of measurement to capture the possible change. With this in mind, the present study employs more objective measurement tools to gauge growth in students' composition skills. More specifically, measuring growth in terms of *t*-unit-based indices of complexity and accuracy, the present study aims to investigate the effects of a blended writing course on a cohort of semester two students' writing development and the nature of the feedback they exchanged with one another in Moodle. To achieve this, the study set out to answer the following couple of questions:

1. Are there any statistically significant differences between the control and experimental groups in terms of complexity and accuracy as a function of exposure to online peer and self-assessment procedures?
2. In what ways do online peer and self-assessment influence the nature of students' comments?

Review of the Literature

Peer and Self-assessment from Socio-cultural and Activity Theories

In L1 and L2 writing research contexts alike, peer and self-assessments have received widespread theoretical support from two influential, albeit related, theories of learning and human development, namely socio-cultural and activity theories. A common denominator of these two theoretical traditions is the special emphasis they place on the social and situated nature of learning (Asghar, 2013). Advocates of socio-cultural and activity theories argue that peer interaction and collaboration enable learners not only to become responsible for their own learning but also to act as facilitators in scaffolding their peers' learning (Schunk, 2014). Assigning students to collaborative groups and pairs, it is hypothesised, defuses learners' apprehension and increases their motivation to learn (Harris, Graham, & Mason, 2006). The meta-discourse that transpires among the learners during the interactive meaning-making and problem-solving episodes is believed to develop in learners' critical and metacognitive skills (Swain, 2006).

Among the concepts in socio-cultural theory that have had wide-ranging influence on psychology, and particularly educational research, are regulation and the zone of the proximal development (henceforth, ZPD). Experts or skilled individuals are capable of operating at higher levels of autonomous mental functioning. However, non-experts and unskilled individuals lack such autonomy and thus require the guidance of more capable members of society to help them appropriate new knowledge and skills. This usually takes place through collaborative dialogue, which serves as scaffolding that gradually decreases until self-regulation takes over (Wood, Bruner, & Ross, 1978). According to Vygotsky (1978), the ideal domain where learning can optimally occur is the ZPD. This concept refers to the distance between what a learner can do independently and what he or she can do only with the assistance of more knowledgeable others. The added value of the ZPD is that it not only characterises the current level of cognitive functioning, but it also incorporates levels of performance that can prospectively be attained with appropriate scaffolding. Lantolf and Thorne (2015) maintain that '[I]n this sense, ZPD-oriented assessment provides a nuanced determination of both developments achieved and development potential' (p. 206).

As pointed out earlier, the present study is also framed within an offspring of a sociocultural theory known as activity theory. Activity theory espouses most of the tenets of sociocultural theory and has developed into different models over time (Engestrom, 1999; Leont'ev, 1978). The model that informs the present study is visually represented in Fig. 5.1.

A closer examination of Fig. 5.1 readily demonstrates that the strength of the model comes from the ways in which it depicts the components of activity systems as they continuously interact with one another. Subjects (ELT learners) collaboratively work towards the achievement of an object (learning of writing skills) relying on a variety of socio-culturally mediating artefacts (e.g. material: pen, paper, computers, the Internet, dictionaries, books, multi-media files, etc.; symbolic: language). The

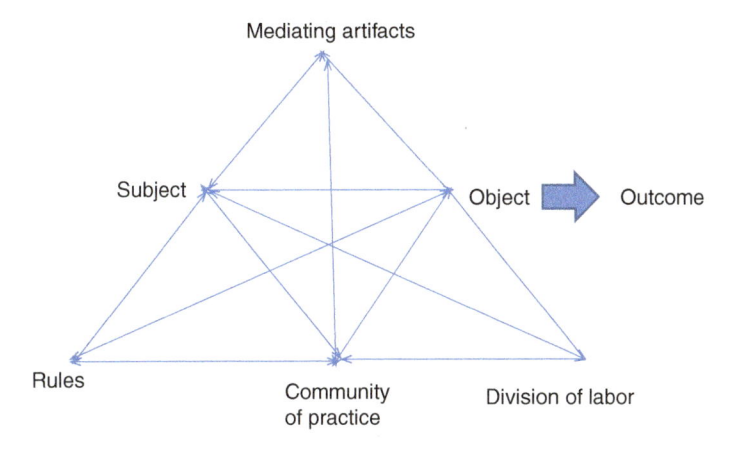

Fig. 5.1 An ELT writing peer and self-assessment activity system (adapted from Engestrom, 1999, p. 31)

school setting is regulated by numerous rules; some are related to the area being studied (grammar, style, rhetoric, genre, mechanics, etc.) while others have to do with interpersonal interactions (e.g. teacher-student and student-student relationships). Because ELT learners in a writing course are assembled in the classroom for a common objective, namely improving their writing ability, they form a community of practice characterised by a division of labour that should evenly be distributed among the learners to help them benefit maximally from experience.

It must be emphasised that sociocultural theory together with activity theory offers an array of key constructs that can serve as a highly pertinent framework in support of peer and self-assessment. As has been indicated above, collaborative interactions between and among learners as they actively engage in the exchange of feedback provide them with multiple opportunities to increase their awareness of their language problems. On the importance of collaborative dialogue, Swain and Lapkin (1998) argue that '[T]he co-construction of linguistic knowledge in dialogue is language learning in progress' (p. 321). Inspired by the Vygotskian socio-cultural perspective, Swain (2006) uses the term 'languaging' to overcome the limitations of other related words such as 'output' and 'verbalising'. 'Languaging' also makes it possible to portray interactive dialogues between learners as cognition-shaping activities based on problem solving and meaning making. She contends that 'languaging about language is one of the ways we learn a second language to an advanced level' (p. 96). The scaffolding, be it oral or written, that learners receive from their instructors and peers enables them to expand their ZPD to the next levels of independent performance and self-regulation.

Peer Assessment

Support from socio-cultural and activity theories has revitalised interest in the potential of peer assessment for learning. Empirically speaking, researchers have observed that peer assessment can more effectively improve students' writing performance if they are more actively engaged in the construction of criteria-based rubrics. Such observation has been the driving rationale for Becker (2016), who investigated the effects of involving students in constructing and/or applying a rubric on their writing performance. One class of students helped develop and apply a rubric, another class only applied the rubric, and still, another only saw the rubric while the fourth class served as a control group. On the basis of a summary writing task, the results demonstrated that the students who either co-created and/or applied the rubric performed more effectively than those who did not use the rubric. It was also found that the students who participated in developing the rubric had better scores than those who only applied the rubric.

If Becker (2016) provided evidence for the usefulness of involving students in developing the rubric they would use in assessing their peers' written work, Altstaedter (2016) highlighted the importance of peer feedback, be it with or without training. Through a quasi-experimental study, Altstaedter investigated the impact of trained as compared to untrained peer feedback on written comment types and writing quality. Both groups were given a set of guidelines that tapped on macro-level issues of organisation, development, content, and style. However, the experimental group also had a 30-minute session of training including modelling and how to use the guidelines to provide effective peer feedback. The peer feedback experience that involved training in how to use the feedback guidelines had a significant impact on the types of comments produced. While the untrained group focused more on local issues of writing, their trained counterparts were more concerned with global issues of organisation, development, content, and style.

Some researchers have shifted away from studying the outcomes of peer assessment with regard to learning towards focusing primarily on the nature of the process of peer feedback per se. In this vein, Baker (2016) examined the effects of structured peer feedback on the process itself, the nature of the comments, and the final draft. He reported that allowing the students more time (four weeks in his study) for the assignment enabled approximately all of them to submit complete papers. Moreover, the students provided their peers with formative feedback. They not only identified weaknesses but also suggested ways to improve their peers' writing. As for the outcome of the review process, an examination of final papers revealed that almost all students added more than 50% of the new material in response to the feedback provided. It was also observed that the greatest part of the changes that the students made was meaning-oriented.

Furthermore, empirical investigations on the utility of peer feedback for learning have raised other related questions such as whether peer assessment is more beneficial to the reviewer or the receiver of peer feedback. To illustrate, Lundstrom and Baker (2009) conducted a study to determine the beneficiary of peer assessment in terms of improved writing quality. As befits the nature of the study, one group of participants reviewed their peers' papers without receiving feedback while the comparison group received feedback without reviewing papers. The researchers found that L2 learners taught to give feedback benefitted more substantially than learners taught how to deal with peer feedback. This was attributed to the fact that the peer review activities enabled the learners to transfer the skills they learnt to self-evaluations of their own writing. Such was not the case with the learners who were taught how to improve their writing by effectively using the feedback they obtained from their peers.

Self-assessment

The viability and usefulness of alternative assessment methods such as self-assessment in L2 writing instruction have been driven by the growing recognition that students' learning can measurably be enhanced if they are increasingly involved in the assessment of their own compositions. In this regards, Fahimi and Rahimi (2015) investigated the relationship between self-assessment as a learning strategy and ELT students' writing performance. Over a four-week treatment period, the students were instructed on how to assess their own written assignments on the basis of predefined criteria. The study also sought to examine the students' attitudes towards self-assessment. It was found that the students' writing ability markedly improved in a number of areas over time. Additionally, the students' capacity for assessing their own assignments was comparatively enhanced. All the students reported their positive attitudes towards the role of self-assessment in improving their writing skills.

Similarly, Chelli (2013) explored the impact of portfolio-based self-assessment on ELT students' writing ability in terms of accuracy, grammatical complexity, and organisation. The inclusion of portfolios was motivated by the assumption that single-occasion assessment of writing ability cannot adequately provide a fuller picture of a students' true level of writing proficiency. On the basis of a semi-structured interview, Chelli also evaluated students' attitudes before and after the treatment. The results indicated that a significant difference existed between the students' pre-test score gains and those of their post-tests, particularly in accuracy and organisation. Grammatical complexity did not improve in response to the instructional treatment utilised. Attitudes towards portfolio-based self-assessment were found to be positive.

On the understanding that self-efficacy is a strong driver of increased engagement in writing, which in turn leads to improved writing proficiency, a line of research has examined the effects of self-assessment on self-efficacy and writing ability. As a case in point, Andrade et al. (2009) conducted a study on the effects of long-term and short-term rubric use (including self-assessment) on students' self-efficacy with regard to ELT writing. Out of the three times of collecting data on self-efficacy in the two conditions, it was reported that self-efficacy was the same on the first two occasions. In the third phase of data collection, however, the treatment group outperformed the comparison group in terms of average writing self-efficacy scores. While writing self-efficacy results for girls were higher than boys in the first administration of the instrument, they approached statistical significance in the third administration. On the second occasion of measurement, no statistically significant results were reported in terms of gender differences.

However, not all studies have reported positive results about the role of self-assessment in developing self-efficacy and writing ability. To exemplify, Covill (2012) explored the effectiveness of rubric-supported self-assessment in enhancing college-level students' writing self-efficacy and writing performance in a psychology class. Assigning the participants to two treatment conditions, the researcher found that self-assessment rubric-users did not exhibit any significant differences from non-rubric-users in terms of writing performance. This was explained by the fact that once students have reached university in an L1 context, they have already accumulated enough knowledge of writing assignment criteria. In an ESL or EFL context, the situation is different as students in college are still in need for training in how to use criteria-referenced self-assessment to acquire and improve their writing skills. Moreover, the use of a rubric did not affect the students' writing self-efficacy.

Another related strand of research has empirically examined the effects of involving students in the generation of criteria for self-assessing their written productions (Andrade, Du, & Mycek, 2010). This study addressed two closely intertwined questions. The first question is whether students' co-creation of a rubric can positively affect the quality of their writing. Assuming that such is the case, the second question ascertains whether this relationship is mediated by gender, time spent writing, grade level, prior rubric use, and previous achievement. Data analysis revealed that involving students in examining model papers to generate criteria for a writing assignment and self-assessing their first drafts by means of a rubric bears significantly on students' writing quality. Although gender relatively predicted writing quality, no statistically significant relationship was uncovered. Grade level, writing time, and previous achievement were all identified as predictors of students' writing quality.

Methods and Materials

Setting and Participants

The study was simultaneously conducted at Hassan II University and Chouaib Doukkali University, the Faculties of Letters and Humanities. Being a quasi-experimental study including a between-groups pre test-post

Table 5.1 Participants' demographics

Demographic		Class 1	Class 2	Class 3	Total
Condition	Experimental group (Hassan II University)	7	5	12	24
	Control group (Chouaib Doukkali University)	6	13	5	24
Gender	Males	5	9	7	21(43.75%)
	Females	8	9	10	27(56.25%)

test research design, the intervention started in the second week of February and continued up to the second week of May 2016. The participants were 48 undergraduate students enrolled in a writing course. This cohort of students participated in the present study after they had completed semester one. The writing course in semester one was named paragraph writing and aimed to help the students improve their skills and competencies at writing well-structured, coherent and unified narrative paragraphs. The writing course in semester two was designed to build on the skills acquired in the previous semester by studying essay structure.

For both groups, the sampling technique used to select the participants was convenience sampling, which is the most frequently used sampling technique in educational research conducted in naturalistic settings. However, the researchers in the present study believe that the sample is representative to an important degree. That is, the groups were intact in the sense that they were assigned to three classes in each faculty without any proficiency placement test or pre-determined criteria. To increase the representativeness of the sample, out of the three classes in each faculty, a given number of students were randomly selected for participation in the study as Table 5.1 below illustrates.

Instructional Procedure

To begin with, the instructional procedure centred on a blended writing course that included a face-to-face component and an online component. It should be mentioned that the main course teachers (three in each university) were in charge of the face-to-face mode. A typical face-to-face lesson opened with a lecture-based discussion on a given writing issue. These issues range from micro-level writing aspects such as spelling, punctuation, capitalisation, grammar, and vocabulary to macro-level concerns such as development, content, organisation, and rhetorical patterns. Instead of leaving students' questions to the end of the lecture, the teachers usually allowed the students to interrupt them on different occasions for more clarifications and illustrations.[1] In the second part of the lesson, the teacher provided the students with a writing topic to develop into an essay. The students were encouraged to form groups of collaborating peers to help one another.

As regards the online component of the course, the researchers were responsible for constructing and maintaining the online, Moodle-hosted platform. This included creating the online writing course and uploading relevant materials for the students to consult at their convenience. The researchers also created the rubric that constituted a cornerstone in the design of the present study. Each writing assignment was scheduled to be completed on a bi-weekly basis. It was deemed necessary to allow the students plenty of time to compose the essay and publish it online in Moodle. The two weeks' time span was also required for the students to read their peers' papers, offer formative feedback, rewrite the essay, and publish the revised version online again. The researchers were tasked with monitoring the students' feedback by preventing highly critical comments and encouraging less active participants to show more commitment to the peer and self-assessment processes.

An intriguing feature in a Moodle workshop is the assessment procedure. First, the researchers constructed a criterion-based rubric drawing on the relevant literature for the students to utilise in self-assessing their work as well as the work of their peers (see discussion below). Second, the students could write their essays offline using Word Office and later upload them onto Moodle. Alternatively, they could directly write their essays online in Moodle using the inbuilt word processor. Third, each student had to begin by assessing his or her own piece of writing and assigning a grade. Incidentally, the researcher divided the 24 participants into groups of four peers prior to the intervention. After they had completed the self-assessment task, they had to read their group-mates' writings and assess them by offering formative feedback and assign a grade. The final phase is for the researchers to read the students' work and assign a grade for each, offering general comments to help them improve their writings in future assignments.

Instrumentation

Rubric

As pointed out earlier, the researchers constructed a criterion-based rubric on a Moodle workshop for the students to use as a yardstick to assess their essays as well as those of their peers. The construction of the rubric was informed by studies from the literature, namely Paulus (1999), Lundstrom and Baker (2009), Andrade, Du and Mycek (2010), and Altstaedter (2016). However, several changes were applied to the rubrics proposed in these studies to meet the objectives of the present inquiry. To elucidate, since the rubric was designed for ELT students to use for peer and self-assessment and since the objective underpinning, the use of such a rubric was formative rather evaluative, it was deemed necessary to simplify it in terms the language used, the number of criteria and the levels of performance for each criterion. As regards the language, a special effort was made to avoid wording that might distract the students' attention or confuse them. The number of criteria was reduced to five. Criteria such as cohesion (Paulus, 1999) and tone of voice (Andrade et al., 2010) were removed because they lied outside the purview of the present study. Unlike the other empirical investigations, the rating scale included five levels of performance in descending order of quality with a weighting and a descriptive label for each. The rubric included two macro-level criteria (organisation and development) and three micro-level criteria (grammar, vocabulary, and mechanics). The labels and their weightings for the levels of performance were as follows: excellent (5), very good (4), good (3), fair (3), poor (2), and very poor (1).

Activity Reports: Students' Comments

The data pertaining to peer-feedback were collected from Moodle activity reports. Qualitative content analysis was used for the analysis of the data.

When the experimental intervention was over, all the comments were copied from Moodle to Microsoft Word for coding and analysis. Prior to the implementation of the current study, a coding scheme was devised on the basis of relevant research from the literature (Altstaedter, 2016; Baker, 2016; Paulus, 1999). The coding scheme included three major categories, each having further subcategories. The first major category incorporated comments that were regarded as unhelpful. Unhelpful comments can be defined as comments that do not help the feedback receiver to take action by way of ameliorating his or her essay. This category included highly critical comments and those that are incomprehensibly ambiguous. Highly critical comments were perceived as unhelpful because of their counterproductive effect on the receiver's motivation and self-esteem. By ambiguous comments, reference is made to the indecipherable wording used to describe a given issue in the peer's written product.

The two remaining major categories are surface-level comments and meaning-level comments. All the changes and modifications that occurred at the intra-sentential level were subsumed under surface-level feedback. These include suggestions for grammar error correction, vocabulary (e.g. word choice), and mechanics. The last type of comments designates feedback-targeting issues that lie outside the scope of the sentence. Meaning-level feedback is two-fold. Comments that suggest alterations in the semantic relationship between close-by sentential units are labelled micro-meaning feedback. By contrast, comments that propose modifications across paragraphs affecting the structure of the whole essay are dubbed macro-meaning feedback.

Data Analysis Tools

Regarding the assessment of the progress students make at the level of writing proficiency, researchers customarily use either analytic scoring rubrics or objective indices of complexity, accuracy, and fluency (Norris & Ortega, 2009). For the purposes of the present study, improvement in the students' writing proficiency was operationalised in terms of the constructs of complexity and accuracy. Prominent among the local measures employed to determine growth in these two constructs is the minimal terminable unit (*t*-unit). Hunt (1970) defined the *t*-unit as 'one main clause plus any subordinate clause or non-clausal structure attached to or embedded in it' (p. 4). Since the *t*-unit was introduced, numerous applications of the *t*-unit have been carried out. This unit of measurement also had its critics, leading to the emergence of several *t*-unit-based variants as well as other indices proposed as better candidates for characterising language performance, proficiency, and development. To measure growth in complexity, the present study utilised mean length of *t*-unit (MLTU), the mean number of *t*-units (MTU), and a number of clauses per *t*-unit (C/T). Additionally, a number of error-free *t*-units (EFT) and the ratio of error-free *t*-units to the total number of *t*-units (EFT/T) were used to assess growth in accuracy. It is worth mentioning that both descriptive and inferential statistics were used to present the results and test for significance. The descriptive statistics used were measures of central tendency and dispersion while the *t*-test, ANOVA, and Cohen's *d* were used as inferential statistics.

Results

Effects on Complexity and Accuracy

The first research question that the study attempted to answer is whether the instructional procedure based on online peer and self-assessment had any significant effects on the writing performance of semester two EFL students in a tertiary education setting. To answer this question, a paired *t*-test was employed to compare within-group mean differences from the pre-test to the post-test. Cohen's *d* was used to compute the effect size of the progress made by the two groups of participants. Table 5.2 below presents the relevant descriptive statistics including means and standard deviations:

As Table 5.3 indicates, the control and experimental groups improved in a number of complexity and accuracy measures. As for complexity, MLTU (M = 1.03, $p < 000$) and MTU (M = 0.87, $p < 0.05$) significantly increased in the control group. It can nonetheless be observed that the

Table 5.2 Pre-test-post-test descriptive statistics for the experimental and control groups

	Control group		Experimental group	
	Pre-test	Post-test	Pre-test	Post-test
MLTU	9.96 (1.04)	10.68 (.91)	10.30 (1.15)	11.27 (.78)
MTU	30.21 (1.12)	31.09 (1.42)	31.09 (1.16)	30.93 (1.31)
C/T	1.46 (0.85)	1.49 (0.65)	1.46 (0.07)	1.56 (0.06)
EFT	11.04 (0.96)	10.88 (0.71)	10.88 (0.94)	12.81 (1)
EFT/T	0.74 (0.17)	0.53 (0.06)	0.97 (0.32)	1.69 (0.92)

control group did not show as much growth in measures characterising complexity (C/T) and accuracy (EFT; EFT/T). Notably, their scores dropped at the level of accuracy measures from the pre-test to the post-test (EFT = −0.16; EFT/T = −0.21). By contrast, the experimental group scored significantly higher on all the tested measures. Out of the six indices of complexity and accuracy examined in the present study, three were statistically significant at a level of confidence set at $p < 0.000$ (C/T; EFT; EFT/T) and the remaining two indices at $p < 0.05$ (MLTU; MTU).

As pointed out earlier, Cohen's d was used to evaluate the magnitude of the difference between pre-test and post-test score gains. It should be mentioned that Cohen (1988) regarded a value of $d \leq .2$ as a small effect size, $d \leq .5$ as moderate and $d \leq .8$ as large. Table 5.4 shows that the effect size in the control group ranged from moderate to large except for EFT, which was non-significant. The table also reveals that the experimental group had large effect sizes for the measures in focus except for the number of MTU.

Moreover, Levene's test of equality of variances did not produce any significant result, indicating that the null hypothesis is to be rejected. Therefore, a t-test for equality of means was utilised to explore post-test mean differences between the two groups of participants. The results showed that the experimental group outperformed the control group in all the measures except for MTU ($t = 0.40, p < 0.05$). Examining Cohen's d for the magnitude of the differences in means between the two groups, it was found that all the measures had a large effect size except for MTU ($d = 0.11$) as Table 5.5 below demonstrates.

Table 5.3 Within-group mean differences from the pre-test to the post-test

	Measures	Mean	Std. deviation	Std. error mean	t
Control group	MLTU	0.72**	1.17	0.23	3.03
	MTU	0.87*	1.68	0.34	2.55
	C/T	0.00	0.06	0.01	0.17
	EFT	0.16	1.07	0.21	0.75
	EFT/T	0.21	0.11	0.02	9.58
Experimental group	MLTU	0.96**	1.32	0.26	3.58
	MTU	0.94*	0.41	0.01	2.29
	C/T	0.09***	0.01	0.25	4.71
	EFT	1.89***	0.25	0.24	7.48
	EFT/T	0.71***	0.61	0.12	5.71

*$p < 0.05$; **$p < 0.01$; ***$p < 0.000$/df = 23

Table 5.4 Effect size of the progress made by the two groups as measured by Cohen's d

	Effect size (Cohen's d)				
	MLTU	MTU	C/T	EFT	EFT/T
Control group	0.73[c]	0.68[c]	0.03[a]	−0.18[a]	−1.64[c]
Experimental group	0.98[c]	0.12[a]	1.53[c]	1.98[c]	1.04[c]

[a]Small; [b]moderate; [c]large

Table 5.5 Between-group mean differences from the pre-test to the post-test

	F	t	Mean difference	Std. error difference	Cohen's d
MLTU	0.94	−2.35**	−0.58	0.24	0.69
MTU	0.77	0.40	0.16	0.39	0.11
C/T	0.13	−5.60***	−0.10	0.01	1.66
EFT	4.98	−7.68***	−1.93	0.25	2.22
EFT/T	25.19	−3.57**	−0.71	0.20	1.04

*$p < 0.05$; **$p < 0.01$; ***$p < 0.000$/df = 46
$d \leq 0.2$, small; $d \leq 0.5$, moderate; $d \leq 0.8$, large

Effects on the Nature Students' Comments

The second research question aimed to address the extent to which online peer and self-assessment influenced the nature of students' feedback comments. It should be remembered that an a priori taxonomy of students' comments was established on the basis of the relevant literature. This

Table 5.6 Descriptive statistics of the students' comments

		M	SD	N	Per cent
Unhelpful comment	Highly critical	10.66	3.71	256	8.93
	Ambiguous	9.70	2.54	233	8.13
Surface-level Comments	Grammar	33.87	5.43	813	28.38
	Vocabulary	15.95	2.66	383	13.37
	Mechanics	23.50	6.93	564	19.69
Meaning-level Comments	Mirco-meaning	15.60	2.68	374.5	13.07
	Macro-meaning	10.02	2.66	240.5	8.39

M mean, *SD* standard deviation

taxonomy served as a useful tool to quantify and categorise the students' comments to examine the ways in which peer and self-assessment affected the students' capacity to offer formative feedback.

Table 5.6 presents the descriptive statistics pertaining to the various categories of the students' feedback. Over the treatment period, the students made 2864 comments of all the categories combined. Out of 2864 comments, unhelpful comments constituted 17.06% (M = 10.18, SD = 3.12). Taken together, surface-level feedback comments had the highest mean (M = 11.04, SD = 5), standing for 61.44% of all the comments made. Besides, 21.46% went to meaning-level comments with a mean of 12.81 (SD = 2.67). In light of these figures, it can be observed that the students were conspicuously more concerned with surface-level issues of writing at the neglect of local and global semantic units of composition. It can also be noted that the students had some difficulty in expressing their suggestions for their peers in ways that would enable them to understand the feedback given and revise their drafts accordingly.

To better understand the ways in which the students' feedback was influenced by the instructional procedure under study, a one-way ANOVA was employed at three different intervals over the semester. This was carried out by collecting data on the students' comments from the first assignment, the third assignment, and the last assignment. Comparing the means of the two categories of unhelpful comments, a downtrend can be detected from the beginning to the end of the study. This downtrend is statistically significant for both uncritical and ambiguous comments as suggested by an F (2, 49.833) = 19.92, significant at $p < 0.000$ and F

Table 5.7 Developments in the nature of the students' feedback across three time intervals

	First assignment	Third assignment	Last assignment	F	Partial eta squared
Highly critical	2 (1.10)	0.91 (0.82)	0.5 (0.51)	19.92***	0.366
Ambiguous	1.45 (1.21)	1 (0.93)	0.5 (0.78)	5.59**	0.140
Grammar	6.04 (1.23)	6.70 (1.54)	7.12 (1.32)	3.78*	0.099
Vocabulary	5.20 (1.69)	6.20 (1.47)	6.75 (1.64)	5.67**	0.141
Mechanics	5.91 (1.71)	7.04 (1.70)	7.54 (1.86)	5.34**	0.134
Micro-meaning	1.08 (0.71)	2.75 (0.79)	3.73 (0.72)	80.71***	0.701
Macro-meaning	0.54 (0.50)	1.83 (0.81)	3.29 (0.69)	97.20***	0.738

Mean (standard deviation); $*p < 0.05$; $**p < 0.01$; $***p < 0.000$/df = 2

(2, 67.958) = 5.59, significant at $p < 0.01$) respectively. As for effect size, partial eta squared suggested that highly critical comments accounted for 36.6% of the between-subjects variance while ambiguous comments accounted for 14%. Additionally, a comparison of the means of the three subcategories of surface-level comments yielded a slight, albeit significant, increase over the semester. This increase explains 9.9%, 14.1%, and 13.4% of the variance for grammar, vocabulary, and mechanics respectively. Most notable above all was the remarkable increase in meaning-level subcategories with a large effect size indicated by $\eta_p^2 = .70$ for micro-level and $\eta_p^2 = .73$ for macro-level meaning comments (Table 5.7).

Discussion

Initially, it should be recalled that the objective of this study was to empirically investigate the effects of an online ELT writing instructional procedure based on peer and self-assessment on a cohort of semester two students' writing development and their capacity to offer useful formative feedback. Writing development was measured by a host of *t*-unit-based indices of complexity and accuracy. As for the students' comments, development was measured by means of a taxonomy that was generated on the basis of the relevant literature.

Effects of Peer and Self-assessment on Writing Development

To evaluate the effects of peer and self-assessment on the students' writing development, it was deemed useful to explore within-group mean differences by comparing pre-test and post-test score gains. The results of a paired *t*-test showed that the control group improved in a couple of complexity measures, namely MLTU ($t = 3.03$, $p < 0.01$) and MTU ($t = 2.55$, $p < 0.05$). It was nevertheless found that C/T did not increase in the students' writings. A plausible explanation for this finding is that the students achieved complexification of their *t*-units by means other than the number of clauses per *t*-unit. It could be the case that instead of increasing the number of clauses in each *t*-unit, they enlarged their *t*-units by embedding more words and phrases. Besides, it was reported that the control group did not improve at the level of accuracy measures.

However, the paired *t*-test results indicated that the experimental group enhanced their written products on all the measures under study. Unlike the control group, the experimental group seems to deploy more advanced linguistic resources to achieve complexification. That is, the statistically significant increase in C/T suggests that the lengthening of *t*-units occurred at the level of clauses rather than words and phrases. It must be pointed out that MLTU and C/T are tightly related so that an increase in C/T presupposes an increase in MLTU but the other way around does not hold. This is why it was observed that although the control group had a significant increase in MLTU, it did not have an impact on C/T. Because phrasal complexification is outside the scope of the present paper, it is not clear whether or not the experimental group used more words and phrases in addition to more clauses. Moreover, the experimental group scored higher on the measures associated with accuracy. More specifically, EFT had a statistically significant increase from the pre-test to the post-test ($t = 7.48$, $p < 0.000$). Again, an increase in EFT must have an impact on the ratio of error-free *t*-units to the total number of *t*-units ($t = 5.71$, $p < 0.000$).

However, it was not until an independent *t*-test was run that an understanding could be established as to whether or not there were statistically significant differences in the means of the two groups together with the effect size of such differences. Except for MTU, the experimental group outperformed the control group on all the other measures. Such outperformance was corroborated by large effect sizes as suggested by the following Cohen's d values: MLTU, $d = 0.69$; C/T, $d = 0.1.66$; EFT, $d = 2.22$; EFT/T, $d = 1.04$.

These findings suggest that ELT writing students can enhance their composition skills by transferring the skills and knowledge they acquire from engagement in online peer and self-assessment using a criteria-based rubric. Theoretically speaking, socio-cultural and activity theories lend support to this suggestion. The combination of peer and self-assessment instantiates Vygotsky's (1978) fundamental contention, which holds that cognitive functions appear on the inter-psychological plane before they appear on the intra-psychological plane. The scaffolding that each student obtains from his or her peers appears to have a sizeable effect on the development of the major writing development constructs, namely complexity and accuracy. It is also noteworthy that assigning students to heterogeneous groups with different ZPDs seems to have benefits for both high-achieving and low-achieving students. Low achievers benefit from the feedback they receive from their more capable peers and high achievers benefit by consolidating their understanding of problematic writing issues. Moodle workshops offered the students a valuable opportunity to form a community of collaborating individuals with a common goal, which they jointly strove to achieve.

Empirically speaking, several other studies examining the effects of peer and self-assessment on L2 writing performance reported results consistent with the results of the present study. A case in point is Becker (2016), who found that the students who developed and/or applied a rubric had better writing scores. Although the students in the current study did not participate in developing the rubric, the process of giving and receiving feedback seems to have increased the students' noticing ability and gave them helpful insights into major writing issues and how they can be resolved. From another perspective, some studies reported that the students who gave feedback benefitted more substantially than those who received it (Lundstrom & Baker, 2009). Correspondingly, the improvement in complexity and accuracy measures reported in the current study can be construed as emanating from the combination of assessing their own work as well as giving and receiving peer feedback.

Effects on Peer and Self-assessment on the Students' Feedback

The second research question aimed to illuminate the nature of the influence that peer and self-assessment had on the comments the students exchanged with one another. The data suggested that the students had major difficulties in expressing formative feedback that could be used to enhance their peers' writings. This difficulty appears to be diminishing over time as unhelpful comments started out at M = 1.72 on the first assignment and dropped to M = 0.5 in the last. The second finding on the development of the students' feedback was the emphasis they placed on providing comments related to surface-level issues of writing. Although comments on grammar, vocabulary, and spelling slightly increased over time, the small effect size for each of these surface-level areas was not statistically significant. Another noteworthy finding was the sizeable increase in student's meaning-level comments. It seems that the students did not accord this area of writing much importance as they did with surface-level issues at the beginning of the study. However, the upward trend yielded significant differences across the three occasions of data collection (micro-meaning: F = 80.71, $\eta_p^2 = .70$; macro-meaning: F = 97.20; $\eta_p^2 = .73$).

Interestingly, the peer and self-assessment online instructional procedure affected not only the students' writings but also the nature of the peer-response process. Before they were introduced to the Moodle-hosted, criteria-based rubric, they focused most heavily on grammar, vocabulary and spelling. This focus may also have had a negative impact on the quality of their compositions in terms of inadequate organisation and development of content. However, the collaborative exchange of feedback and the constant guidance of the researchers in the online platform seem to have drawn their attention to issues of coherence, cohesion, organisation and development. In addition, the clarity and simplicity of the rubric may have brought them to recognise that writing quality is contingent on a concrete set of criteria. Such criteria can help the students improve their own drafts through self-assessment and the drafts of their peers through the comments they suggest.

It must be indicated that the present study did not attempt to examine whether or not the students applied the suggestions they received from their peers as Paulus (1999) did although it can surely be an insightful addition. Several studies reported that the students who give feedback benefit more substantially than those who receive it. For instance, Lundstrom and Baker (2009) found that feedback givers improved the quality of the comments they offered to their peers and had higher score gains for writing quality. Cho and Cho (2011) reported that student reviewers gained higher scores for their final drafts and their capacity to express formative feedback palpably improved. The fact that the participants in the present study had fewer and fewer unhelpful comments and increasingly more meaning-level comments is suggestive of the benefits they reaped from actively engaging in collaborative online peer and self-assessment.

Conclusion and Implications

To sum up, the present study was an attempt to examine the effects of a blended writing course based on peer and self-assessment on semester two students' writing ability and the nature of the feedback they collaboratively exchanged with one another. Regarding the first question, the control group had some significant progress in certain aspects of complexity, namely MLTU and MTU, except for C/T. They did not show any progress with regard to accuracy measures (EFT and EFT/T). By contrast, the experimental group scored significantly higher on all the measures in question. The comparison of the post-test scores of both groups revealed that the experimental group outperformed the control group with large effect size values except for MTU. As for the second question, the analysis of the feedback exchanged among the experimental group students showed that they had difficulties in expressing such feedback clearly and focused most noticeably on surface-level issues of writing at the expense of meaning-level aspects. It was nonetheless observed that unhelpful comments gradually decreased and more attention started to be geared towards meaning-level aspects.

On the basis of the findings obtained, peer and self-assessments have once again been found to contribute significantly to L2 students' learning. Such findings have several implications for the teaching of writing in college-level, L2 contexts. Teachers should make sure that their students are active participants in peer review activities. Moodle can serve as a useful platform for students to extend their contact with one another and their instructor well over class time. Additionally, they should be made familiar with the process of peer review through rubric-based training sessions. Although the present study did not explore the effects of training in how to use rubrics, the intervention began with a training session on how best to review one's peers' work. Most importantly, the instructor has an important role to play in monitoring the students' feedback and offering guidance on how to suggest a balanced assessment that taps on local and global aspects of writing. Another important implication is for peer assessment to be combined with self-assessment. Such combination is crucial as it serves to give students a chance to apply the skills they have learnt to their own work. It is also a vital means of assuring that students will achieve a level of independent, self-regulated behaviour.

Notes

1. Information about the face-to-face instructional procedure was garnered based on informal discussions with the main course teachers.

References

Altstaedter, L. L. (2016). Investigating the impact of peer feedback in foreign language writing. *Innovation in Language Learning and Teaching*, 1–15. https://doi.org/10.1080/17501229.2015.1115052

Andrade, H. L., Du, Y., & Mycek, K. (2010). Rubric-referenced self-assessment and middle school students' writing. *Assessment in Education: Principles, Policy & Practice, 17*(2), 199–214.

Asghar, M. (2013). Exploring formative assessment using cultural historical activity theory. *Turkish Online Journal of Qualitative Inquiry, 4*(2), 18–32.

Baker, A. (2016). Peer review as a strategy for improving students' writing process. *Active Learning in Higher Education, 17*(3), 1–14.

Becker, A. (2016). Writing student-generated scoring rubrics: Examining their formative value for improving ESL students' writing performance. *Assessing Writing, 29*, 15–24.

Chelli, S. (2013). Developing students' writing abilities by the use of self-assessment through portfolios. *Arab World English Journal, 4*(2), 220–234.

Cho, Y. H., & Cho, K. (2011). Peer reviewers learn from giving comments. *Instructional Science, 39*(5), 629–643.

Cohen, J. (1988). *Statistical power analysis for the behavioral sciences*. Hillsdale, NJ: Lawrence Erlbaum.

Covill, A. E. (2012). College students' use of a writing rubric: Effect on quality of writing, self-Efficacy, and writing practices. *The Journal of Writing Assessment, 5*(1), 1–9.

Engestrom, Y. (1999). *Perspectives on activity theory*. Cambridge, MA: Cambridge University Press.

Fahimi, Z., & Rahimi, A. (2015). On the impact of self-assessment practice on writing skill. *Procedia: Social and Behavioral Sciences, 192*, 730–736.

Harris, K., Graham, S., & Mason, L. (2006). Improving the writing, knowledge, and motivation of young struggling writers: Effects of self-regulated strategy development with and without peer support. *American Educational Research Journal, 43*(2), 295–340.

Lantolf, J. P., & Thorne, S. L. (2015). Sociocultural theory and second language learning. In B. V. Patten & J. Williams (Eds.), *Theories in second language acquisition* (2nd ed., pp. 201–224). New York: Routledge.

Leont'ev, A. N. (1978). *Activity, consciousness, and personality*. Englewood Cliffs, NJ: Prentice-Hall.

Lundstrom, K., & Baker, W. (2009). To give is better than to receive: The benefits of peer review to the reviewer's own writing. *Journal of Second Language Writing, 18*(1), 30–43.

Norris, J. M., & Ortega, L. (2009). Towards an organic approach to investigating CAF in instructed SLA: The case of complexity. *Applied Linguistics, 30*(4), 555–578.

Paulus, T. M. (1999). The effect of peer and teacher feedback on student writing. *Journal of Second Language Writing, 8*(3), 265–289.

Schunk, D. H. (2014). *Learning theories: An educational perspective*. New York: Pearson College Division.

Swain, M. (2006). Languaging, agency and collaboration in advanced language proficiency. In H. Byrnes (Ed.), *Advanced language learning: The contribution of Halliday and Vygotsky* (pp. 95–108). London: Continuum.

Swain, M., & Lapkin. (1998). Interaction and second language learning: Two adolescent French immersion students working together. *The Modern Language Journal, 82*, 320–337.

Vygotsky, L. S. (1978). Mind in society: The development of higher psychological processes. *Mind in Society The Development of Higher Psychological Processes, Mind in So, 159*. https://doi.org/10.1007/978-3-540-92784-6

Wood, D., Bruner, J., & Ross, G. (1978). The role of tutoring in problem solving. *Journal of Child Psychology and Child Psychiatry, 17*, 89–100.

Abdelmajid Bouziane is a professor at Hassan II University of Casablanca, School of Letters and Humanities Ben Msik, Casablanca, Morocco. He has published chapters of books, books, articles, reports reviews of books and websites on different areas of ELT and EFL.

Hicham Zyad is a doctoral student in the Moroccan-American doctoral studies program run by Hassan II University, the School of Humanities in Ben M'Sik. His research interests are ELT, writing pedagogy, and educational technology. He has publications in the *International Journal of Instruction, the International Journal of English and Education and the International Journal for 21st Century Education* (in press). He has participated in several national and international conferences and his contributions have been published in these conferences proceedings. He is an ELT professional in state-run secondary education with 12 years' experience.

6

English Writing Assessment and the Arabic Speaker: A Qualitative Longitudinal Retrospective on Arabic-Speaking Medical Students in Qatar

Alan S. Weber

Introduction

The teaching of writing began at Weill Cornell Medicine—Qatar (formerly the Weill Cornell Medical College in Qatar) in 2004, two years after the founding of the institution. The original physician-in-training cohorts scored highly on standardised international tests of English and writing was not originally viewed by administrators as a critical skill in the biomedically based curriculum. However, administrators soon recognised the value of the writing courses taught on the main campus of Cornell in Ithaca, NY, supervised by the John S. Knight Institute for Writing in the Disciplines in teaching critical/analytical thinking skills fundamental to medical diagnosis, as well as the role of writing in providing practical skills such as writing clear patient histories, preparing research manuscripts, and exploring topics in the medical humanities such as communication, doctor-patient relations, identity formation,

A. S. Weber (✉)
Premedical Department, Weill Cornell Medicine, Ar-Rayyan, Qatar

and professionalism. As originally conceived, the Qatar curricula, now moving to a six-year integrated program, consisted of a 2-year pre-medical basic sciences program followed by a 4-year postgraduate medical program identical to the one offered at Cornell's medical school in New York City. Normally in American medical education, students proceed to a graduate medical school after receiving a four-year bachelor's degree. Thus WCM-Q's 2-year Premedical Program represented a highly compressed course of study created by removing non-science electives, including humanities offerings, except for a medical ethics module taught using primary literature. WCM-Q was originally invited to set up its campus in Doha to help diversify Qatar's resource-based economy into a high-skills knowledge economy (Weber, 2014).

Additionally, WCM-Q expanded and diversified its programs shortly after its founding to include students with less preparation and proficiency in languages and specifically English language skills. A Foundation Program was established in 2007 to teach basic skills such as English, Chemistry, and Mathematics to compensate for the under-preparation in the government schools, which had undergone sweeping changes under the Education for a New Era program for the K-12 system developed by Rand Corporation in 2002 (Zellman et al., 2009).

Through ten years of practical experience, The Writing Program and its assessment practices based on American university models evolved to respond to both L1 Arabic-speaking and L1 Hindi-, Malayalam-, and Urdu-speaking student populations from regional schools with educational paradigms based historically on the oral transmission of knowledge, teacher-centeredness, and memorisation. Six of the ten Education City universities are affiliated with American institutions and hence employ American models of writing pedagogy.

The Traditional Qatari Educational System and the Qatari Writing Student

A brief review of Qatar's history and educational system is necessary to contextualise writing instruction in Qatar. The State of Qatar is located in the Persian Gulf on the Arabian Peninsula bordering Saudi Arabia and is a major gas and oil producer (EIA, 2014). The State of Qatar through its Qatar Foundation for Education, Science, and Community Development has established an education consortium called Education City with eight international and two local branch campuses, six of them branch campuses of American institutions (Cornell University, Carnegie Mellon University, Georgetown University, etc.). Qataris only make up about 9% of the total population of 2.6 million, which consists primarily of expatriate male workers on short-term contracts from Nepal, Philippines, Pakistan, and India. Qatar enjoys a high human development index with an HDI rank of 32 and a total score of 850 in 2014 (UNDP, 2015, p. 212). The Qatari society was traditionally made up of nomadic Bedouin tribes, settled Arabs (*hadar*) engaged in pearling and fishing, former slaves from Africa, and trading families from India, Persia, and Balochistan (Rahman, 2005; Zahlan, 1998).

Qatar was part of a British maritime protectorship called the 'Political Residency' from 1916–1971 and gained independence in 1971. Thus, the English language and British culture have exerted a strong influence on the country since the late nineteenth century because of the presence of the British Political Agents, Anglo-American oil companies, and the British Council office established in 1972. English has become an increasingly common language in the Gulf, with Qatari schools instituting English language classes in the public schools from an early date. However, there have been periodic backlashes against the increasing ubiquity of English, since it has become a *lingua franca* among expatriate populations from different language groups originating from areas of former British colonisation—India, Pakistan, Kenya, Yemen, Egypt, Sudan, and so on—eclipsing Arabic in some countries in education and business contexts (Weber, 2011).

In early Islam, the preference for the oral transmission of knowledge over the written word was an important intellectual current, possibly related to the still prevalent custom in the Gulf of doing business in person. In establishing truthfulness and accuracy of information, Arabs often establish a personal trust relationship with an information source. Also, many Muslims believe that the Prophet Muhammad who is revered as one of the wisest of men could not read and that he received divine revelation aurally. Thus there is not necessarily a link between knowledge of reading and writing and wisdom in Muslim traditions.

According to Seyyed Hossein Nasr, 'the revelation of the Qur'an was auditory before becoming crystallised in a written text. The Prophet first heard the term *iqra'* and only later recited the first revealed verses on the basis of their audition. The whole experience of the Qur'an for Muslims remains to this day first of all an auditory experience and is only later associated with reading in the ordinary sense of the word. There is an ever present, orally heard, and memorized Qur'an in addition to the written version of the Sacred Text, an auditory reality which touches the deepest chords in the souls of the faithful, even if they are unable to read the Arabic text' (quoted in Atiyeh, 1995, p. 57). Later, when false sayings of the Prophet Muhammed were proliferating after his death, scholars such as Al-Bukhari and Abu Dawood attempted to identify and record in writing his true utterances in part by following the oral chain of transmission (*isnad*) and establishing the veracity of the transmitters. This process closely resembles western models of 'writing as learning,' as the hadith scholars assembled and weighed evidence (variants) using linguistic and literary analytical techniques to determine style, chronological date, and word meanings.

In certain areas of the Islamic Caliphates, primarily the former Sumerian/Babylonian cultures, urbanised Eastern Mediterranean (Levant) regions and Egypt, which had a lengthy pre-Islamic tradition of literacy from Pharaonic times, writing and reading skills were widespread enough to support book production and intellectual culture, including the translation movement during the early Abbasid period (Hanna, 2007, pp. 175–193). However, the Gulf littoral region was isolated from these urban centres of learning until the modern era, and knowledge transmission was often by word of mouth. These traditions may explain the difficulties in explaining the concept of audience to the Gulf writing student. As orality theorist Walter Ong has noted, writing is an artificial process, unlike oral utterance, which is the default natural form of linguistic exchange (Ong, 1982, p. 82). Writing inhabits a space of relatively 'context-free' forms of language: both Arabic language and culture are often classed as 'high context', where unsaid and unwritten norms are communicated in subtle ways such as the social situation, dress, age, etc. (Weber, 2013, p. 16). Qatari students often adopt this high context form of discourse in writing, employing 'we' and 'our' when discussing topics that are unique to their culture and religion, not taking into account the instructor and other potential readers as a possible audience in the multicultural makeup of Doha.

The Masjid and Majlis were the original educational institutions in the early Islamic period and additionally employed primarily non-written forms of education such as recitation. According to Makdisi, 'the mosque, Masjid, was the first institution of learning in Islam. The term Majlis gives philological evidence to this effect. It was used in the first century of Islam to designate a hall in which the teaching of the hadith took place…it was also used to designate the lesson or lecture itself' (1981, p. 10). In the still popular tradition of the Majlis in Qatar, national and neighbourhood news, stories, and religious instruction are shared orally: over 80% of Qataris engage in some form of Majlis (Al Thani, 2016).

The definitive history of writing in the Islamic world has yet to be written. In the pre-oil era in addition to learning in the mosques, schooling in the Arabian Gulf was primarily carried out in the Kuttab or Maktab schools by a Muttawa or Mulla who would teach mixed groups of boys and girls in the basics of Arabic language, Quran, and reading and sometimes writing. Advanced courses could include mathematics and Arabic literature and were dependent on the educational background of the teachers, some of whom were semi-literate, but experts in religious learning. The Kuttabs employed memorisation and were generally teacher-centred, with students expected to listen to the instructor and not engage in the dialectical methods of discussion and debate (*disputation, dialectic*) common to the medieval scholastic heritage of western education. Group instruction was favoured. Discipline was strongly enforced: 'while their teaching methods were extremely simple and primitive, their methods of discipline were rather harsh', which contrasts today with some local schools in Qatar that experience high rates of absenteeism and a lack of discipline (Al-Misnad, 1985, p. 30). Students, therefore, learning in schools with the traditional strict discipline and teacher-centred practices in Qatar may be diffident about questioning authority, raising questions to further their understanding, or offering alternative interpretations in class discussions that clash with the teacher's ideas (Weber et al., 2015, pp. 81–82).

Ten Kuttabs could be found in Qatar in 1890, and the religious Al-Athariya school was established in 1913 (Torki, 1992). In the Maktab/Kuttab, there was a focus on religion and the memorisation and recitation of Quran, which could be transmitted to students entirely orally. There was no pressing need among pastoral nomads (*beddu*) for written literacy, and for settled trading Arabs, writing had a functionalist purpose for keeping accounts and transacting business with remote partners. These historical patterns may be impacting current Qatari student perceptions of the value of mastering writing as a skill, which many students probably view as a purely technical skill to accomplish tasks, similar to computer skills in the workplace. However, throughout the Arabic-speaking world in the postcolonial period beginning in the 1960s, a dramatic increase in literacy occurred: rates of literacy doubled in almost all of the Arab-speaking countries in the period 1960 to 1995 with most of the gains among males, and literacy itself became a marker of status (Akkari, 2004). As a very traditional society, Qatar has lagged behind other Arab countries in literacy and education.

A modern system of schooling was organised from 1947 to 1956 in Qatar with full public attendance not achieved until the 1960s. Only one advanced school (*madrasah*) in Qatar existed in this era where proper Arabic writing was stressed: 'with the exception of a semi-modern, but advanced Islamic school called Madrasah Al-Sheikh Al-Mani, the remainder of education in Qatar was of the Kuttab type before 1952. Madrasah Al-Sheikh Al-Mani was founded by Muhammed Abdelaziz Al-Mani, an eminent scholar who had received his education at Nejd and was a student of the reformer Muhammad Abduh of Egypt and of the scholar Al-Alusi of Baghdad. The school continued from 1918 to 1938 and was not only well known in Qatar but also in other parts of the Gulf because of Al-Mani himself. The school was for adult males only, and the teaching covered broad areas of Islamic studies including knowledge of the Quran, Islamic theology, jurisprudence, Prophet's traditions and Arabic language and literature. The school was closed in 1938 when Al-Mani left Doha to go to Saudi Arabia' (Al-Misnad, 1985, p. 35).

When oil wealth entered Gulf societies and advanced technological and management skills were needed, especially after the nationalisation of the western oil companies, Gulf students were sent abroad in increasing numbers not only to institutions such as Al-Azhar University, University of Cairo, American University of Beirut, and Damascus University, but also to British and American Universities. Female students in Qatar were not sent abroad for higher education until 1967/68 (Al-Misnad, 1985, p. 231). In the next stage of Gulf educational development, national universities appeared first in Saudi Arabia, including King Saud University in 1956, and Qatar University, Qatar's national university, in 1977, which originated as a teachers' college. These national universities were structured along very practical lines and were created to prepare citizens for employment in government offices; hence there was 'little room for academic and political freedom. Universities were created by the governments to perform a particular job: to prepare citizens for employment in the expanding bureaucracy' (Bahgat, 1999). Thus, again writing instruction in both Arabic and English in the Gulf was often framed as a technical skill rather than a means of discovery and learning, or as a creator of literacy and knowledge, which are two important functions of writing in American higher education.

The evolution of writing instruction and general education for girls in the Gulf reveals further culturally specific attitudes towards women's position in society and female education. Amina Mahmud's all-girls Kuttab was one of the few educational opportunities for women in the pre-oil era in Qatar and faced some opposition as many locals thought that female education was forbidden by the Quran (Al-Kobaisi, 1979; Al-Misnad, 1985). However, Amina Mahmud received government support to expand her Kuttab into a government school in 1956. According to Al-Misnad: 'one main objection to the education of girls in the Gulf area was that through education girls would learn how to write. The training of girls to write was considered a moral danger to those people who suggested to the Sheikh of Qatar that girls should be taught only reading and not writing. The underlying reason for this opposition was the fear that the ability to write would enable girls to communicate with the outside world from the seclusion to which they were normally confined. Typical arguments were that if the girls learned to read and write, what was to prevent them from receiving letters from men without their parents' knowledge' (Al-Misnad, 1985, p. 38).

Attitudes towards women in education have altered dramatically in recent years in part because of Sheikha Moza bint Nasser's (the wife of the former Emir of Qatar) promotion of women's education and business ownership. However, the number of fully socially acceptable professions for Qatari women is still small as the Bedouin culture historically has not allowed women to interact with males outside of their immediate tribal units. Also, very similar arguments to the early opposition to teaching women writing were raised about women's writing with the appearance of social media in the Gulf in the last decade, the fear that unregulated messaging on the Internet between females and males would encourage illicit relationships.

Additional writing issues arise with bilingualism as many students in the Gulf may not be mastering writing in Arabic, a skill that requires many years of disciplined study, because of inadequate textbooks and training of teachers. Gulf Arabs speak the *Khaliji* dialect, and formal writing (*Fus'ha* or Modern Standard Arabic) must be learned by instruction similar to a foreign language as it contains different lexical items and a different grammar from spoken dialectical Arabic. In teaching Arabic speaking, reading, and writing skills in Oman, Al-Ajmi noted: 'Although I used various materials to encourage [students] to talk and to write, most of their written texts were unstructured, comprising of no more than three or four lines. In addition, they were full of linguistic mistakes (i.e. spelling, grammar and punctuation errors), which meant that the students in Oman had critical problems in Arabic writing in both compositional, (generating ideas, imagination, and structuring the written text) and transcriptional (spelling, handwriting and punctuation) aspects' (Al-Ajmi, 2007, p. 7). The Arab Bureau of Education for the Gulf States (ABEGS) has recommended more focus on writing and reading skills in Arabic, as part of the functionalist goal of illiteracy reduction (ABEGS, 2016). Due in part to cultural heritage preservation projects carried out by Qatar National Library, Supreme Education Council (reading programs), and Qatar Museums Authority, advanced Arabic reading and writing skills are now being promoted as part of cultural heritage, which is adding prestige to the skill of writing.

Writing Assessment at WCM-Q and Writing in the Disciplines at Cornell University

Writing assessment in the First-Year Writing Seminars (FYWS) of the Writing Program at WCM-Q–which are the same courses taught in the undergraduate programs at Cornell University in Ithaca, New York–is coordinated by the John S. Knight Writing Institute for Writing in the Disciplines. The Knight Institute uses a practitioner model of assessment grounded in Writing in the Disciplines (WID) and Writing Across the Curriculum (WAC) pedagogies and sets up a framework of shared values for writing that should theoretically cover all disciplines. This assessment philosophy, as well as its practical application, is set out in the *Indispensable Reference for Teachers of First-Year Writing Seminars* published by the Knight Institute and is issued to all teachers of the First-Year Writing Seminar. The shared writing goals were developed from the 1960s to the present time through a process of research, committees, dialogue, and workshops in collaboration with university administrators and representative departments across the Cornell University campus.

Individual instructors develop their own rubrics and assessment methods based on their specific disciplinary and departmental practices—engineering, chemistry, philosophy, mathematics, etc. The assessment practices can be defined as a practitioner-based model rather than a set of standardised rules or protocols for teaching writing. This model places a high degree of trust in individual instructors. As an Ivy League school, Cornell can hire the most qualified and most highly trained instructors. Cornell professors are expected to be well-published scholars and respected leaders in their areas of expertise and to keep current with international best practices in their fields. Graduate student instructors who teach writing are drawn from the department's top candidates as well. On WCM-Q's Qatar campus, the majority of writing instructors hold terminal degrees from PhD granting research institutions in which they were specifically trained in classroom pedagogy, and all have undergone teaching apprenticeships.

An important distinction must be made between the First-Year Writing Seminars, which focus on critical and analytical skills and not basic

English language skills *per se*, and the Foundation Program English courses, which are more skills-based (English oral, written, and reading skills). The Foundation Program also uses holistic scoring, similar to the Writing Program, but also quantitative methods of assessment such as quizzes and multiple-choice examinations. However, in practice, this dichotomy between basic skills instruction in the Foundation Program and critical/analytical skills in the Writing Program is fuzzy, as clarity of expression is a key feature of all persuasive writing at all levels and often depends on mastery of both word denotation and connotation (word choice), correct grammar and spelling, and other linguistic features that are generally taught in EFL/ESL and English for Academic Purposes (EAP) courses.

The Writing in the Disciplines (WID) model, which shares many philosophical commonalities with the Writing Across the Curriculum (WAC) approach, teaches students how discourse operates in a particular field and introduces students to the writing norms of that discipline, taught by instructors who are both experts in their fields and enthusiastic about introducing undergraduates to their field of study. The late James Slevin once remarked that one of the primary strengths of the Knight Writing Institute was the intellectual excitement of the faculty (Slevin, 2003, p. 203). In addition, Nesi has pointed to the WAC paradigm and the importance of discipline-specific discourse in the instruction process: 'the writer's choice of text structure, grammar and lexis is governed by his or her own role and purpose, and the context and audience for which the text is produced. This means that writing tutors should always customise their advice according to the situation of the individual writer, bearing in mind that even slight changes in writing purpose and context will affect the way in which a socially-successful text unfolds. While it is true that student writers are developing as individuals, and need to learn to produce prose that "has a voice" or "sounds like a person" (Elbow, 2007, p. 7), students also need to learn to write like members of their own discipline, reflecting the particular values and conventions of their discourse community' (2012, p. 55).

Harrington additionally discusses how writing within a particular discipline must be grounded in the epistemological framework of that field, not simply in its formal rules of composition and presentation, since writing should be constructed as a fundamental act of knowledge production in the university: 'Through writing, and opportunities to practice writing, students learn not only to recognise the conventions used in the disciplines they are studying but also, more fundamentally, they learn how these conventions reveal and contribute to creating the epistemological orientation and knowledge-making practices at play in the disciplinary fields they are beginning to inhabit themselves. It is helpful, therefore, to conceptualise writing as an essential part of the processes of thinking and learning, rather than, for example, as the translation of already-formed thought into the appropriate written forms of a certain discipline' (Harrington, 2011, p. 48). Harrington's philosophy of writing represents a significant departure from both 'banking' models of education (accumulation of facts) and the formalism of the composition approach which views correct writing as the mastery of modular skills—as an example, thesis statements—and paradigms such as the five-paragraph essay. To illustrate the limited applicability of the composition approach, although all theses in all fields must be supported by evidence, different fields formulate theses (hypotheses) in very different ways, such as the sciences and social sciences, for example—which have a distinct logical paradigm of hypothesis construction and validation based on inductive and deductive logic.

Through the practitioner model, departmental autonomy is maintained, including assessment techniques, and yet all courses taught under the umbrella of the Knight Institute must meet the general criteria established for First-Year Writing Seminars detailed below and hence are reviewed by the Director before they can be entered into the university course catalogue. In this approach, expert practitioners (professors and graduate students) model knowledge production skills for beginning writers. The learning goals (objectives) and how these goals are assessed should be formalised as a written rubric or embedded within assignment sheets and additionally conveyed orally to students in class discussions. On the Ithaca campus, training is provided for instructors (primarily graduate students) who are first-time teachers of the FYWS through the 7100 course, which teaches the basics of rubric construction. The Course Director reviews the rubrics, and all syllabi are kept on file in the Knight Institute, which additionally houses a fully resourced centre of assignment sequences, syllabi, and recent books on writing pedagogy in its print library and eCommons Digital Repository.

In Qatar, the Ithaca FYWS Course Director visits once a year to review the rubrics of all the instructors and methods of assessment and additionally carries out a classroom observation. The Director discusses the observation with the instructor and provides feedback on both classroom performance and the written course materials. The historical development of the Knight Writing Institute provided below as it evolved into a program to instil humanistic learning campus wide in all programs will illuminate the writing instruction practices, approaches, and philosophies (including assessment) practiced on the Qatar campus of Cornell, since the Weill Cornell Medicine-Qatar campus mirrors practices on the main campus of Cornell in Ithaca, New York. The writing goals and assessment are consistent with the overall mission of Cornell to create well-rounded citizens capable of expressing themselves clearly, taking positions of responsibility in their communities, and being prepared to engage in social, political, and economic developments as critical thinkers in a democratic society.

Evolution of the John S. Knight Institute for Writing in the Disciplines

The foundations of a campus-wide independent writing program grew out of the Freshman Humanities Program established in 1966, which evolved into the Freshman Seminar Program in 1974. After the preparation of the 1965 'Report of the Faculty Committee on the Quality of Undergraduate Instruction', administrators recommended that writing seminars become the responsibility of departments across the Cornell campus, not just the English Department. According to an early administrator of the Cornell writing programs Katy Gottschalk, 'the idea received enthusiastic support from departments such as history of art and philosophy, which, while they saw writing seminars as excellent forums in which to target future majors, also saw writing as integral parts of their own disciplines' (Gottschalk, 2011, p. 24). From this report arose the Freshman Humanities Program in 1966 with 30 seminar subjects administered by nine departments.

In 1986, the John S. Knight Writing Program was fully funded and became the current John S. Knight Institute for Writing in the Disciplines in 2000. A seminal guiding text used by administrators in the training of faculty and graduate students in effective writing instruction was *Teaching Prose: A Guide for Writing Instructors* (1984), edited by Frederic V. Bogel and Katherine K. Gottschalk, who assisted in administering the programs. As former Knight Writing Institute Director Jonathan Monroe has pointed out about the adoption of the Writing in the Disciplines paradigm for the program: 'bringing the rich potentialities of Cornell's multidisciplinary approach into practice more effectively required some significant revising. Above all, we came to understand the importance of cultivating more extensively and incorporating more inclusively the discipline-specific experiences, insights, practices, and authorities of Cornell faculty representing a wide range of disciplines' (Monroe, 2003, p. 5).

The development of the Knight Institute came at a time when writing pedagogy was moving away from a focus on the end product and skills (*techne*) towards a process-based instructional model. Since writing tasks vary so greatly according to audience and purpose, it was theorised that instruction should focus on common process-oriented skills such as peer review, revision, multiple drafts, and dialogue and debate in constructing arguments and defending them with evidence. From this new understanding of writing that developed during the post-WWII-period grew the paradigms of Writing as Learning and Writing as Discovery, i.e. the idea that writing is in and of itself a learning modality useful for clarifying and organising thought. According to former Knight Institute Director Jonathan Monroe:

> ...in 1966, with the social pressures of the day inflecting academic work and academic writing in new directions...Cornell moved away from a form-based, 'composition' approach housed exclusively in the English Department, to the content- and discipline-based model that has continued to evolve at Cornell over the past three decades, and that now involves participation from some thirty departments each semester across all levels of the curriculum (Monroe, 2003, p. X).

Thus the development of the Writing Across the Curriculum (WAC) model started early at Cornell–in the 1960s–and evolved over decades to encompass more and more departments that had previously viewed the teaching of writing skills as the exclusive provenance of the English Department.

Writing Goals and Writing Assessment at WCM-Q

The overarching learning goal of the First-Year Writing Seminar (FYWS) at all Cornell campuses is 'through introductory work in a particular field of study help students learn to write good English expository prose—prose that, at its best, is characterized by clarity, coherence, intellectual force, and stylistic control' (Knight Institute, 2016, p. 3). The FYWS assumes that students are beginning writers, and not necessarily possessing or cognizant of (if they do enter the classroom with a formalised series of steps for essay writing) a writing process to achieve their final product. Although the FYWS additionally transmits introductory disciplinary knowledge, the focus is on writing skills and 50% of the class activities must be focused on writing instruction. Course readings are generally kept to 75 pages per week and should be integrated directly into the writing instruction.

Each FYWS should assign five to eight formal essays on new topics, comprising 25 pages of final revised prose. Three of the course essays must be written using a multiple draft and revision process through guided instruction. Techniques for mentoring students in their prose can include: written comments on the drafts (both responding to ideas, structures, and arguments, but also written and oral Corrective Feedback (CF) on language and grammar issues), an individual conference with the instructor or a designated trained peer tutor, individual or group work in class (such as small, timed writing exercises), formalised peer review using written peer review sheets, reading responses posted to electronic bulletin boards (asynchronous chat) for brainstorming and developing content, reflective writing journals, or a formalised portfolio process, etc. Some informal contrastive analysis can sometimes be helpful in identifying patterns of error in Arabic speakers' L2 English writing. For example, infrequent use of the copula in Arabic sometimes appears as student sentences constructed in English without the verb 'to be'. Also, a common Arabic writing format is to build evidence towards a final conclusion, placing more important information last, while many academic, popular and scientific writing genres in English use an inverted pyramid structure, such as news articles or the abstracts of scientific papers. Students are required by Knight Writing Center rules to meet with their instructor at least two times outside of class for one-on-one instruction, normally to revise a draft under guided conditions.

Writing assessment in the FYWS is designed to be primarily formative—focusing on a process (habits of successful writers)—but simultaneously summative, since the final grades on the 5–8 required essays form the bulk of the final grade for the course. This approach arises from a constructivist view of writers as individuals who are entering and learning to speak to new discourse communities, as Newell emphasises: 'a constructivist sees learning in context–how knowledge develops within particular instructional contexts when students are actively engaged, such as, for example, when they take positions on topics and issues presented by others. This view of teaching and learning is compatible with some of the motives underlying process-oriented approaches to writing instruction, and it offers, in a principled way, a description of effective teaching and learning' (Newell, 2006, p. 236). The constructivist view expands writing instruction beyond mere skills acquisition and focuses on developing a mind-set of reflective critical thinking and debate throughout the writing process. This process is recursive and fluid and is aligned with creativity, expression and innovation (construction of new knowledge). In the field of medicine, where 'best practices' and following established evidence-based protocols are important considerations, this cognitive model is sometimes viewed by students as antithetical to their core biomedical training. However, the reflective practitioner model (a feedback loop of action and reflection by the physician in his or her daily routines, often aided by writing journals and diaries) is a well-established medical practice discussed in the medical education literature.

Learning Outcomes of the First-Year Writing Seminar and How They Are Assessed

The Learning Outcomes expected in all First-Year Writing Seminars are listed below along with a detailed explanation in Table 6.1.

Table 6.1 Expected first-year writing seminar goals

FYWS Goal	Explanation
'Writing that is suitable for the field, occasion, or genre in its use of theses, argument, evidence, structure, and diction'	This statement encompasses the Writing in the Disciplines and Writing Across the Curriculum paradigms. It recognises that argumentative structures and what counts as evidence are highly field-specific, ranging from qualitative textual data in the humanities and social sciences to statistics and experimental interventions in the natural sciences. It also acknowledges the subtle rules of specific writing genres.
'Writing that is based on competent, careful reading and analysis of texts'	Writing and reading are closely inter-related as academic discourse is communicated primarily by textual means. Students should learn through writing that engages external authorities that discourse communities extend beyond their immediate peers and classmates and that experts communicate in writing in a specific mode and style.
'Appropriate, responsible handling of primary and secondary sources, using a style such as MLA or APA'	All academic fields set down similar rules for the ethical use of texts and authorities. Students should not only be aware of the rules of citation, copyright, and ownership of written intellectual property, but they also need to learn the philosophical and cultural principles behind these rules. This set of concepts has been particularly difficult for Qatari students, since one of their primary exemplars of knowledge is the Qur'an, which is a public revelation, available to everyone. Thus the private ownership of a series of words is a difficult, culturally bound concept to comprehend.
'Effective use of preparatory writing strategies such as drafting, revising, taking notes, and collaborating (the latter might be demonstrated in peer review, conferences with the instructor, consultations in the Writing Walk-In Service)'	Developing a writing process is a key skill taught in the FWYS instead of a focus on a final product. A concern only with the final product can lead students to rely too heavily on support from peers, tutors, or the professor, or in extreme cases they may pay ghost writers (a known and widespread problem in Qatar) to complete their papers. By learning and following a concrete writing process, students gain confidence in developing their own work and ideas and becoming autonomous learners instead of panicking and seeking inappropriate outside assistance.

(continued)

Table 6.1 (continued)

FYWS Goal	Explanation
'Final drafts of essays that have been effectively proofread for correctness of grammar, punctuation, and mechanics'	Papers written in the FYWS must first and foremost advance novel and well-supported and well-argued knowledge, but mechanical issues such as problems with spelling, grammar, and punctuation can render individual sentences meaningless and impair understanding of the author's main points. Thus, these mechanical issues, which normally can be fixed by simple proofreading techniques such as reading out loud or reading paragraphs backwards, are framed within the concept of 'clarity' or 'clearly articulated prose'.
'Individual instructors may wish to include statements about achievements in regard to the subject content of the course, presentations, and/or participation in discussion'	This goal again reinforces the WAC paradigm in that disciplinary content is not simply superfluous material for learning to master writing, but that writing is a cognitive process inseparable from developing mastery of a subject field. In the earlier 'Composition Model' of American writing still used in some high schools, topics are arbitrarily introduced to teach such skills as writing a 5-paragraph essay, not to explore a subject area.

Source: *Knight Institute* (2016, p. 5).

All of the goals detailed above are designed to teach students to eventually achieve mastery of knowledge in that discipline according to each field's particular rhetoric, technical lexicon, use of language, and norms of weighing and assessing evidence. The FYWS introduces students to the writing techniques that they will use throughout their major course of study and later graduate study as well.

A sample generic rubric from one of the author's courses is provided in Table 6.2 below. The rubric covers all of the papers in the course; however, additional writing objectives are presented in the individual assignment sheets since the general rubric cannot cover all the various genres used in the course (for example, an Expository Writing essay would not necessarily use external sources or evidence). Writing objectives are additionally explained by the instructor orally, by reviewing each individual goal and skill and engaging the class in a 'big picture thinking' discussion on how the assignment fits into not only their expected development as

Table 6.2 Sample general rubric from the author

GENERAL GRADING RUBRIC FOR PAPERS

GRADE	A to A+	B	C	D	F
CHARACTERISTIC	These papers have clear thesis statements, and are clearly written with few mechanical or language concerns. Allowance is made for non-native use of English, such as use of articles "the", "a", "an." Arguments are logically stated and the full range of logos, pathos, and ethos varieties of argumentation are present in the paper. The paper uses evidence to support its claims, either from secondary sources, interviews, or students' own experience. Anecdotes are acceptable and effective but should be backed up with other kinds of evidence. "A" papers generally are new and interesting, with the author developing a unique perspective instead of repeating other writers' arguments. MLA citation format is used correctly. A to A+ papers are the result of a multi-week rigorous writing process involving reflection, multiple drafts, peer review, expert review, editing and proofreading.	The B paper, which is a competent paper, has the basic strengths of the A paper: clear thesis, recognizable arguments and counterarguments, clearly written, use of evidence, logical structure with transitions. B papers, however, normally do not fully execute the features of the A paper, or use these features in a confusing or clumsy manner. For example, the paper may have a thesis statement, but the thesis may be trivial (self-evident, doesn't need to be argued since most would agree to it). There may be punctuation or grammatical concerns that prevent the reader from fully understanding the writer's ideas.	C and D papers share many similar qualities. They are usually underdeveloped, the result of lack of multiple drafts or work that was completed the previous night. There are numerous grammatical problems, un-edited sentences, and misuse of individual words which cause confusion in the reader. Arguments are weak and not well thought out. The paper may lack sufficient counterarguments. The paper may have serious disorganization, i.e. there is not a logical sequence of ideas or arguments, or these ideas may not be connected with transitions, causing shifts in the discussions that may confuse the reader (leaps of logic, or non-sequiturs). There are serious citation problems – quotes are not adequately referenced, or there are missing references or the works cited page is missing important information.	Please see the comments for the C grade. The professor rarely awards this grade since papers in this range normally sit at the tails of the C-F distribution. Sources may not be used, or they are unreliable (that is, not authoritative). Motivation becomes an important factor in this range of papers: if a student hands in a paper of D quality, with little evidence of interest in the course, topic, or improvement of writing skills, the grade will fall towards the F range. However, if a student is seeking assistance, participating in class writing activities, and genuinely would like to improve his or her writing skills, then the grade will move into the C range.	The paper is off-topic (does not respond to the assignment adequately). F papers can also be unacceptably short, for example, 1 page written for a 4-5 page assignment. Also, there is no argumentative structure and little understanding of the use of persuasive argument. An F will also be awarded for papers never turned in to the professor. Papers written by another person (ghost writing) or submitted for another course (simultaneous submission) will also receive an F and may result in Academic Integrity charges against the student.

writers, but also their academic career within the medical college. The author awards a single holistic score (letter grade) for each paper assignment; however, other FWYS instructors use analytical scoring, such as variations on the 6+1 Trait System developed by the Northwest Regional Educational Laboratory and still used in high schools, or a points system using checklists of 10 to 25 items. Items in the checklist may include thesis development, transitions, use of evidence, grammar, punctuation, voice, and so on. These quantitative assessments must eventually be converted to letter grades (A–F) for the final course grade reported to the registrar.

One area of concern with holistic grading from the perspective of the student is the apparent subjectivity of the process since many higher level cognitive features of student writing are difficult to quantify on mathematical scales. The author devotes 15–20% of his course grade to 'Class participation and behaviours', which represents the instructor's overall observations of the student as a developing writer (both in the classroom and using the student's handed in written work as a proxy for their out of class writing behaviours) during the entire semester's work: do they exhibit the behaviours expected of all professional and academic writers, i.e. demonstrate a developed writing process, make use of all the writing resources available to them, complete assignments and exercises on time, ethically use sources, and so on? This constructivist approach creates *engaged writers*, not *written products*.

Further learning outcomes of the Writing Seminar, many of which cannot be easily measured directly by any known assessment method outside of the reflective judgement of the instructor based on experience (which itself is a strong argument for holistic grading), include:

- Students emerge with *confidence* in their writing ability and in their ability to continue to learn to write; they emerge convinced of the importance of writing well. (*This outcome is measurable only indirectly, through students' self-reporting on end-of-semester evaluations.*)
- Students understand that *writing can help them to learn*; they have experienced that process through various kinds of preparatory writing work in and out of the classroom, in work that helps them to explore a subject and that prepares them for their essays. (*Students might*

demonstrate through preparatory or other informal writing the learning that writing has helped them achieve.)
- Students realise how what they have learned about writing applies (or does not apply) to other writing situations. *Their knowledge should be transferable.* In a best case scenario, after taking two seminars, students learn through experience and discussion that the demands of a particular subject, purpose, audience, or voice, can cause necessary variations in such matters as style, structure, content, and argument and that therefore one type of writing cannot be suitable for all purposes or all occasions. (*In a seminar, students might demonstrate the ability to adjust style or structure according to the demands of a particular genre or audience.*)
- Students perceive that *they must continue to investigate 'how to write'* in new disciplines and situations after their First-Year Writing Seminars in order to write clearly and well. (*One demonstration of transferable knowledge might be that students can describe, with appropriate terminology, what they have learned about writing, perhaps in a final reflective essay or in 'author's notes' on individual essays.*)
- Students develop what some researchers have called a *"growth mindset" in relation to writing'* (Knight Institute, p. 4).

Thus, although some aspects of student writing performance are clearly difficult to assess, the triangulation of a variety of assessment techniques recommended by the Knight Institute can provide an accurate picture of a beginning writer's progress and proficiency: (1) self-reported statements from the students themselves, (2) the submission of detailed portfolios documenting each stage of the writing process (to demonstrate they have learned an effective process), (3) direct querying of students in a private conference, (4) instructor observations, (5) end-of-semester written evaluations (qualitative and quantitative questionnaires), (6) written end product as demonstration of skills mastery, and (7) other kinds of proxy instruments.

Some error correction in assessment is necessary when working with L2 English writers: written corrective feedback can be offered by underlining problematic passages (grammar, spelling, and so on). Then, in individual conferences, students are asked to identify the problem and find a revision solution to clarify the sentence, passage, or idea. If unable to produce a correct sentence, for example, because of lack of knowledge of comma rules, students are referred to the Writing Centre for punctuation review or the instructor can provide instruction on the spot.

Thus, the majority of writing instructors within the WCM-Q Writing Program use a holistic grading system similar to the Graduate Record Examination (GRE) or AP English subject tests administered by the Educational Testing Service (ETS). The author was previously employed by the ETS in various capacities as a consultant, GRE question writer, and AP English Essay holistic test grader. Briefly, the ETS process awards a single numerical score to a paper based on sample anchor papers, which are scored according to the consensus of experts. Individual responses to a set of scored essays can be recorded, and the deviation from the expertly scored anchor papers is calculated. When individual responses vary too widely from the mean (grading 'drift') the individual(s) are retrained through debate and consensus with the expert graders until their scores match the anchor paper values within an acceptable margin of error (typically 1–2 standard deviations). Holistic grading can achieve high levels of reliability since there is currently no agreement on how to define the various sub-skills of writing by 'objective' quantitative analytical methods (Swain & Mahieu, 2012, p. 55). The holistic grading process basically seeks to achieve high inter-rater reliability on the scoring task and consensus about specific writing values established by expert practitioners.

Some professors at WCM-Q use a portfolio process in which they guide students in assembling examples of their best writing and then assist them in revising and reflecting on their work as a whole–this process encourages a self-reflective writing process that can be related to the reflective paradigm in medicine. In all assessment practices, both formative and summative, WCM-Q instructors endeavour to move students towards an autonomous paradigm of writing and knowledge production in which they receive feedback not just from the instructor (expert review), but also from peers as well as themselves (self-reflexivity) as they master the norms of their discipline. Thus, they move towards becoming experts in a field and begin to take personal ownership of knowledge. As Hortshoj advises beginning college writers, 'until you make this structure meaningful in your own terms, however, it will remain the structure of the text and will represent the author's knowledge, not yours. If you can explain the material to someone else, summarise it in your own words, or outline the structure, the knowledge is yours…' (Hortshoj, 2009, p. 141).

To ensure consistency within the Writing Program, the Writing Faculty engage in three separate calibration processes to ensure that instructors are grading within the Knight Institute guidelines and that individual instructor's grades do not vary substantially. First, as mentioned earlier, the FYWS Course Director visits the Qatar campus once a year and directs a rubric workshop in which selected anchor papers (exemplars) are discussed until consensus is reached. Second, the Writing Program also administers a Writing Diagnostic (45-minute timed interpretive essay) each year for placement of incoming premedical students. At first, a 5-point holistic scoring scale was used, and then a simplified 3-point scale (Below Average, Average, and Above Average) was adopted. The purpose of the diagnostic essay was to distribute students evenly according to their abilities so that strong and weak students were not grouped into the same class. Additionally, as a third means of calibration, the Writing Program Faculty publishes a one-volume anthology of the best student writing biannually, which again requires an anchor and calibration process involving agreement by debate and consensus to select the top essays. The number of submissions normally ranges from 60 to 120, and the selection process (blinded peer review) of reading and debating the merits of individual essays helps to reinforce and reaffirm the general Knight Institute rubric. These three methods ensure longitudinal consistency of grading practices and shared writing values among faculty.

Conclusion

The evolution of L2 English writer writing assessment at WCM-Q is embedded within recent trends in transnational education—since the institution is a satellite campus of Cornell's medical school in New York City—as well as American-style philosophies and pedagogies of writing instruction. Students in the First-Year Writing Seminars learn not just facility with the linguistic, rhetorical, and stylistic features of the English language in various genres, but also are expected to grasp the fundamental meaning of writing within the academy and various intellectual disciplines.

Since Writing as Learning and Writing as Discovery were not prevalent educational philosophies in Gulf education until recently, student misunderstanding of the function and potential of writing in the higher education classroom must be explicitly taught and modelled. Reflective discussion as well as asking students to reflect during individual sessions with the instructor aid in reinforcing these concepts. Holistic grading with periodic calibration with anchor texts is sometimes not easily explained to students nor welcomed by them in the medical school as they are conditioned to quantitative assessment in the sciences, such as multiple choice examinations, and points and percentage systems that they view as more objective, accurate, and reliable. However, in written feedback on essays and in individual conferences, a direct link between the course rubric and assignment sheet and the successes and deficits of a student paper can be readily demonstrated to the student by discussion and analysis of individual sentences and passages. Through the First-Year Writing Seminar, instructors endeavour to assist students in internalising the process of writing as a reflective, iterative practice of self-critique and peer feedback to become autonomous learners who create new knowledge through a discovery process.

The pedagogical implications of writing assessment are significant within any institution of learning. Students must not only be provided with tools and methods that help them to develop successful writing habits within a specific field, but they must also be confident that the system used to assess their progress and proficiency is fair, balanced, and has as its core goal student academic progress. The Writing Across the Curriculum and Writing in the Disciplines models employed at WCM-Q and many other American institutions aim to develop engaged writers and autonomous learners. One of the main challenges faced by the WCM-Q Writing Program in introducing new assessment models into the different educational paradigms of learning in the Arabian Gulf over the last decade has been to adjust these models to a new cultural context taking into account students' previous learning, and to educate students about the importance of writing to their later professional careers. The Writing Program has promoted through its assessment philosophy and procedures, its daily practice, and community outreach projects (literacy development), the concepts of 'writing as discovery' and as a means of clarifying thought, solving problems, and creating new knowledge.

References

Akkari, A. (2004). Education in the Middle East and North Africa: The current situation and future challenges. *International Education Journal*, 5(2), 144–153.
Al-Ajmi, M. H. (2007). *Teaching and learning Arabic writing to fourth grade students in the basic education schools in Oman*. Ph.D. thesis, University of Bath.
Al-Kobaisi, A. J. (1979). *The development of education in Qatar, 1950–1977 with analysis of some educational problems*. Ph.D. thesis, University of Durham.
Al-Misnad, S. (1985). *The development of modern education in the Gulf*. London: Ithaca Press.
Al Thani, N. (2016). Majlis participation and influence. *Qatar Foundation Annual Research Conference Proceedings, 2016*(1), SSHASP2415. Doha: QNRF.
Arab Bureau of Education for the Gulf States (ABEGS). (2016). Exploring the future of the educational work. Retrieved from http://www.abegs.org/eportal/about/plan5
Atiyeh, G. N. (1995). *The book in the Islamic world*. Albany: State University of New York Press.
Bahgat, G. (1999). Education in the Gulf monarchies: Retrospect and prospect. *International Review of Education, 45*(2), 127–136.
Elbow, P. (2007). Voice in writing again: Embracing contraries. *College English, 7*. Retrieved from http://scholarworks.umass.edu/eng_faculty_pubs/7
Gottschalk, K. (2011). Writing from experience: The evolving roles of personal writing in a writing in the disciplines program. *Across the Disciplines, 8*(1). Retrieved from http://wac.colostate.edu/atd/articles/gottschalk2011.cfm
Hanna, N. (2007). Literacy and the "great divide" in the Islamic world, 1300–1800. *Journal of Global History, 2*(2), 175–193.
Harrington, K. (2011). The role of assessment in "writing in the disciplines". In M. Deane & P. O'Neill (Eds.), *Writing in the disciplines* (pp. 48–64). New York: Palgrave Macmillan.
Hortshoj, K. (2009). *The transition to college writing*. New York: Bedford and St. Martin's.

The John S. Knight Institute for Writing in the Disciplines (Knight Institute). (2016). *Indispensable reference for teachers of first-year writing seminars*. Ithaca, NY: John S. Knight Institute.

Makdisi, G. (1981). *The rise of colleges: Institutions of learning in Islam and the West*. Edinburgh: Edinburgh University Press.

Monroe, J. (Ed.). (2003). *Local knowledges, local practices: Writing in the disciplines at Cornell*. Pittsburgh, PA: University of Pittsburgh Press.

Nesi, H. (2012). Writing in the disciplines. In C. Hardy & L. Clughen (Eds.), *Writing in the disciplines: Building supportive cultures for student writing in UK higher education* (pp. 55–74). London: Emerald Group Publishing Limited.

Newell, G. (2006). Writing to learn: How alternative theories of school writing account for student performance. In C. A. MacArthur, S. Graham, & J. Fitzgerald (Eds.), *Handbook of writing research* (pp. 35–47). New York: Guilford Press.

Ong, W. J. (1982). *Orality and literacy: The technologizing of the word*. Florence, KY: Routledge.

Rahman, H. (2005). *The emergence of Qatar: The turbulent years 1627–1916*. London: Kegan Paul.

Slevin, J. (2003). *Introducing English: Essays in the intellectual work of composition*. Pittsburgh, PA: University of Pittsburgh Press.

Swain, S. S., & Mahieu, P. L. (2012). Assessment in a culture of inquiry: The story of the national writing projects analytical writing continuum. In N. Elliot & L. Perelman (Eds.), *Writing assessment in the 21st century: Essays in honor of Edward M. White* (pp. 45–68). New York: Hampton Press.

Torki, A.-A. (1992). *Education in the state of Qatar in the 20th century* (I. M. Mohammad, Trans.). Doha: State of Qatar.

U.S. Energy Information Administration (EIA). (2014). Total petroleum and other liquids production 2014. Retrieved from http://www.eia.gov/beta/international/rankings/#?prodact=53-1&cy=2014

United Nations Development Program (UNDP). (2015). *Human development report 2015*. Geneva: United Nations.

Weber, A. S. (2011). Politics of English in the Arabian Gulf. In A. Akbarov (Ed.), *FLTAL 2011 proceedings* (pp. 60–66). Sarajevo: Burch University Press.

Weber, A. S. (2013). Literacy development in an Arab Gulf country. In N. Bakić-Mirić & D. Gaipov (Eds.), *Building cultural bridges in education*. Cambridge: Cambridge Scholars Press.

Weber, A. S. (2014). Education, development and sustainability in Qatar: A case study of economic and knowledge transformation in the Arabian Gulf.

In A. W. Wiseman, N. H. Alromi, & S. Alshumrani (Eds.), *Education for a knowledge society in Arabian Gulf countries* (pp. 59–82). London: Emerald Group Publishing.

Weber, A. S., Golkowska, K., Miller, I., Sharkey, R., Rishel, M. A., & Watts, A. (2015). The first-year writing seminar program at Weill Cornell Medical College–Qatar: Balancing tradition, culture, and innovation in transnational writing instruction. In D. S. Martins (Ed.), *Transnational writing program administration* (pp. 72–92). Salt Lake City: University of Utah State Press.

Zahlan, R. S. (1998). *The making of the modern gulf states: Kuwait, Bahrain, Qatar, The United Arab Emirates and Oman.* Reading: Ithaca Press.

Zellman, G. L., Ryan, G. W., Karam, R., Constant, L., Salem, H., Gonzalez, G., et al. (2009). *Implementation of the K-12 education reform in Qatar's schools.* Santa Monica, CA: RAND Corporation.

Alan S. Weber, Ph.D., teaches writing, the medical humanities, philosophy, and medical ethics at Weill Cornell Medicine in Qatar, a satellite campus of Cornell University in the Middle East. He has also taught at Cornell University, The Pennsylvania State University, and The State University of New York. He is an expert on Arabian Gulf education and is frequently interviewed by such international news outlets as *The New Republic, Al Fanar Media, Public Radio International,* and *Global Finance Magazine* on educational issues in the Gulf.

7

Investigating Assessment Literacy in Tunisia: The Case of EFL University Writing Teachers

Moez Athimni

Introduction

The last three decades have witnessed an unprecedented interest in language testing. Taylor (2009, p. 22) states that language testing and assessment 'have undoubtedly moved from periphery to centre stage in recent years'. The interest in this field can be explained by the role it plays in education, in general, and language teaching, in particular. She adds that today, testing is considered as an essential component in language teaching. In most countries, public and private educational bodies deploy considerable resources and efforts to improve the quality of the tests they administer to their learners. In addition to accountability concerns, this interest mainly stems from the desire of these bodies to align their assessment practices with the best practices recommended in the testing literature and with the internationally accepted standards and practices. For

---

M. Athimni (✉)
Department of English Language and Linguistics, The Higher Institute of Languages of Tunis (ISLT), Tunis, Tunisia

these educational organisations, alignment with international standards is a gateway to an international recognition of the quality of the education they offer. 'In today's globalised environment there is sometimes an additional aspiration to align local or indigenous assessment frameworks with internationally accepted standards or recognised benchmarks' (Taylor, 2009, pp. 21–22).

The growing interest in language assessment can also be related to the changes that have taken place in the structure of many societies around the world. Stansfield (2008, p. 321) explains that most western countries have recently witnessed massive waves of legal and illegal immigrants from different regions of the world who are 'simply looking for a job and a better future for themselves and their families'. This fact has transformed the societies in the host countries into multilingual and multicultural communities. To accommodate these immigrants and better integrate them in their societies, these countries have developed various educational programmes to help these newcomers learn the languages used in the host communities. This new context has created a demand for new language tests to assess the degree of integration of these immigrants and measure the effectiveness of the language programmes provided (Spolsky, 2008). Stanfield (2008, p. 321) expects that, in the future and as a result of immigration, '[t]here will be a need for tests of language proficiency in more languages, and tests of language skills for different situations. There will be a need for tests of proficiency in the national language for children in the schools. There will be a need for more LSP[1] tests'.

Today, language testing is more referred to as an independent profession. Taylor (2009, p. 3) states that the work performed by language testers to define 'quality standards, ethical codes, and guideline for good testing practice' has resulted in an 'increasing professionalisation over recent years'. Spolsky (2008) even refers to it as a 'big industry'. He explains that in the field of public education, standardised tests are heavily used all over the world especially in university-entry examinations. He cites the Chinese College English Test as an example of a huge testing event that involves around seven million candidates per year. He adds that language testing has also become a profitable enterprise especially in the field of ELT. Several companies around the world provide computer-based tests of English for international students or professionals who are learning English for academic or specific purposes. Examples of these companies include the 'Educational Testing Service or the owners of the publishing companies in Asia and the USA who continue to find gold in testing' (Spolsky, 2008, p. 301).

However, this growing interest in the field of testing seems to be only restricted to professional language examiners, public education officials, and owners of testing and publishing companies. As far as teachers are concerned, and despite the role they play mainly as test developers and users, little interest and effort seem to be allotted to develop their knowledge about educational assessment or what is referred to in the literature as 'assessment literacy'. Popham (2009, p. 5) argues that, due to the little importance attributed to assessment literacy in teacher education, 'many of today's teachers know little about educational assessment. For some teachers, the test is a four letter word, both literally and figuratively'. He adds that '[r]egrettably, when most of the today's teachers completed their teacher-education programmes, there was no requirement that they learn anything about educational assessment'. In the same vein, Volante and Fazio (2007, p. 2) cite several research studies (e.g., Zhang & Burry-Stock, 2003; Mertler, 2003; Galluzzo, 2005) that have described the way teachers assess the performance of their students as 'incongruent with the recommended best practices'.

Assessment Literacy

The term assessment literacy has been recently used in the testing literature to refer to the knowledge that teachers should have about the principles of sound assessment (Inbar-lourie, 2008; Stiggins, 2002). Popham (2009) refers to assessment literacy as a key component in teacher education programmes, which relates to the knowledge of some 'measurement basics' that teachers need to be familiar with to be able to perform specific assessment tasks in the classroom. Taylor (2009, p. 24) explains that the term assessment literacy is often used to refer to the knowledge about assessment matters that teachers need when 'engaged in selecting, administering, interpreting, and sharing results of large-scale tests produced by professional testing organisations, or in developing, scoring, interpreting, and improving classroom-based assessment'. She adds that the concept of assessment literacy should not be limited to teachers. It should also be developed across other groups of stakeholders that are directly or indirectly involved in the educational process such as members of national examination boards, administrators, academics, students, parents, politicians, and even the general public.

Components of Assessment Literacy

Xu and Brown (2016, p. 150) define the components of assessment literacy as 'the appropriate content and standards of knowledge and skills needed by teachers to be considered as assessment literate'. Davies (2008a) divides these components into skills, knowledge, and principles. Skills involve the ability to perform certain assessment tasks related to the development of test items and the analysis and reporting of test results. Knowledge refers to the background that teachers should have in assessment and language as well as their knowledge of the context in which the testing tasks are performed. The third component, principles, refers to the ethical and professional aspects that are specific to the performance of assessment tasks.

Xu and Brown (2016) report that the first detailed description of the components of assessment literacy appeared in a document entitled *Standards for Teacher Competence in the Educational Assessment of Students* and jointly published by the American Federation of Teachers (AFT), the National Council on Measurement in Education (NCME), and the National Education Association (NEA) in 1990. The document prescribes that teachers should be skilled in seven competency areas, which include:

1. Choice of assessment methods appropriate for instruction oriented decisions,
2. Development of assessment methods appropriate for instruction oriented decisions,
3. Administration, scoring and interpretation of the results of internally or externally produced tests,

4. Use of assessment results to make decisions about individual learners or the component of the educational programme,
5. Development of valid test correction procedures,
6. Communication of assessment results to students, teachers, and other stakeholders, and
7. Recognition of unethical, illegal and inappropriate assessment practices and uses of assessment results.

Xu and Brown (2016) explained that this document had established the 'knowledge base' for assessment literacy. The standards have been extensively used as the major reference for subsequent studies on the development of different instruments for the measurement of teachers' assessment literacy levels (e.g., Mertler, 2004; Plake, 1993). These standards, however, have been criticised on the ground that they provide a limited coverage of all facets of classroom assessment. Stiggins (1999b) argues that the standards do not provide a comprehensive picture of the realities that teachers face when performing their assessment tasks in the classroom. Today, and despite this criticism, the standards remain a major reference for the definition of the assessment literacy knowledge base. DeLuca, Klinger, Pyper, and Woods (2015) consider them as a solid foundation for research in assessment literacy. In the present study, these standards were used as a blueprint for the development of a questionnaire to investigate the assessment literacy level of Tunisian EFL university writing teachers.

Assessment in Tunisia

The review of the relevant literature about assessment in Tunisia has revealed that EFL teaching in Tunisia suffers from various deficiencies regarding assessment practices. Major limitations can be easily perceived especially at the level of test construction. Daoud (1999) posits that language assessment is the least developed aspect of English teaching in Tunisia. He attributes this to the dearth of research and expertise in this field; testing in the Tunisian English departments is often conducted in an extemporised way. In the same vein, Ghrib (2002, p. 55), in a study conducted to explore students and teachers' attitudes towards the EFL reading courses taught at the *Institut Supérieur des Langues des Tunis* (ISLT), explains that most of the teachers and students who took part in her study suggested that reading courses at the ISLT should have a better assessment system by

> establishing criteria for both text selection and testing: reconsidering the choice of exam tests and questions; choosing shorter and less difficult texts similar to those dealt with in class texts that would assess comprehension, strategy use and degree of assimilation of the various skills.

The recent years, however, have witnessed a growing interest in the area of language testing and assessment. At the level of research, several studies have been conducted in the area of test construction (e.g., Athimni, 2017a; Hidri, 2012), pragmatics testing (e.g., Labben, 2016), test-takers' attitudes and beliefs (e.g., Maaoui, 2016), and alignment between assessment and curriculum (e.g., Athimni, 2017b). Testing and assessment have also been the main topics of several academic events recently organised in some higher education institutions. Lately, some language testing and assessment associations have appeared such as the Tunisian Association for Language Testing and Assessment (TALTA) and the Tunisian Association of Language Assessment and Evaluation (TALAE).

Despite this growing interest, assessment practices in Tunisia could still be described as not up to date with the international standards or the best practices recommended in the literature. The absence of testing courses for undergraduate students in most English departments in the Tunisian higher education institutions and the dearth of training programmes in language testing and assessment for university or high-school teachers make most of the testing practitioners poorly equipped in terms of the knowledge and skills they need to perform their regular classroom assessment tasks. Considerable efforts need to be deployed, first, to provide a complete description of assessment practices in Tunisia and, second, to take the necessary measures to make testing practitioners in Tunisia more assessment literate.

The Study

The present study is undertaken to explore the level of assessment literacy of a sample of Tunisian university EFL writing teachers. More specifically, it investigates the way these teachers construct, administer, and mark their tests and how they interpret and communicate the results they obtain from those tests. The following questions guided the study:

1. What assessment competencies do Tunisian EFL writing teachers have?
2. To what extent are Tunisian EFL writing teachers assessment literate?

Method

The present study relied on a questionnaire designed to collect information about the participants' knowledge and beliefs about assessment, their ability to perform certain assessment tasks, and their knowledge about testing principles. To ensure the validity of this questionnaire, the items were formulated based on the seven assessment competencies listed in *Standards for Teacher Competence in the Educational Assessment of Students* in 1990 (see Table 7.1, below). Each competency was operationalised into specific components, which were used to generate the questionnaire items. For example, the first competency listed in the standards, namely 'the choice of assessment methods appropriate for instruction oriented decisions', was operationalised into two specific components that included (1) the ability to identify clear purposes for the writing tests and (2) the ability to relate those tests to the instructional decisions. The questionnaire items designed based on those components were:

(a) What is/are the purpose(s) of the writing tests you administer to your students?
(b) Are there differences between the purposes of the writing progress tests and the purposes of the writing final examination tests to your students? If yes, what are the differences?

Table 7.1 Classification of the questionnaire items according to the assessment standards

Assessment literacy standards	Questionnaire items
1. Choosing assessment methods appropriate to instruction decisions	a. What is/are the purpose(s) of the writing tests you administer to your students? b. Are there differences between the purposes of the writing progress tests and the purposes of the writing final examination tests you administer to your students? If yes, what are the differences?
2. Developing assessment methods appropriate to instruction decisions	c. What are the main steps you follow to produce your writing tests? d. Do you have specific guidelines you and your colleagues follow to produce your writing tests? e. What are the characteristics you take into consideration when choosing a topic for your writing tests? f. How do you decide on the number and type of items/topics you select to include in your writing tests? g. What are the criteria you use to ensure that each writing test is appropriate to the level of the students you teach in terms of length and difficulty?
3. Administering, scoring, and interpreting the results of internally or externally produced tests	h. Do you pilot the writing tests before giving them to your students? If yes, how? i. Do you write the score allotted to each item on the test paper?
4. Using assessment results to make decisions about individual learners or about the components of the educational programme	j. What are the different uses you make of the results you obtain from the writing progress tests? k. What are the different uses you make of the results you obtain from the writing final examination tests?
5. Developing valid grading procedures	l. What are the main criteria you take into consideration when scoring the students' writing tests?

(*continued*)

Table 7.1 (continued)

Assessment literacy standards	Questionnaire items
6. Communicating assessment results to various stakeholders	m. Do you give the writing tests to the students after scoring them? n. Do you provide your students with feedback on their performances in each test? If yes, how?? o. Do you correct each test in class and explain some of the writing problems that you judge serious? p. Do you communicate your results to other teachers?
7. Recognising unethical and illegal assessment practices	q. Does your students' behaviour in class, whether good or bad, affect the way you score their tests? r. If a student informed you that s/he was in danger of failing, would that affect the way you score his/her test?

The questionnaire (Appendix 1) is divided into two sections. The first section includes six demographic questions about the respondents' gender, affiliation, teaching experience, and training in language assessment. The second section consists of 18 open-ended questions. The choice of this type of questions was motivated by the quality of data they provide. Dornyei and Taguchi (2009, p. 36) contend that:

> [I]n spite of this inherent limitation of the questionnaire as a research instrument…open-ended questions still have merits. Although we cannot expect any soul-searching self-disclosure in the responses, by permitting greater freedom of expression, open-format items can provide a greater "richness" than fully quantitative data.

To avoid some of the limitations often attributed to open-ended items in written questionnaires about the load they put on the respondent and the researcher, the items included in the second section of the questionnaire only consisted of short-answer questions. These questions do not require long responses as they guide the respondent to specific pieces of information. They are also suitable for the studies in which the researcher explores a specific issue or is interested in the collection of qualitative descriptions of a specific process or phenomenon. Dornyei and Taguchi (2009, p. 38) assert that '[s]hort-answer questions involve a real exploratory inquiry about an issue; that is, they require a more free-ranging and unpredictable response…'.

The questionnaire was piloted with two writing teachers. The teachers' comments were used to revise the wording of some questions and the layout of the questionnaire. Based on this feedback, the decision was also made to delete one question about the criteria that writing teachers use to check the validity and reliability of their writing tests. It was judged very complex as it requires specific theoretical knowledge about assessment.

Before the administration of the questionnaire, each participant was informed that the study would be conducted for research purposes. The data to be collected would only be used to provide information about the assessment practices of the Tunisian writing teachers. Each participant was also informed that the findings of the study would be published in an academic article from which s/he would be allowed to obtain a copy. S/he was also told that s/he can withdraw at any time and that his rights to confidentiality and anonymity would be respected as no reference to his/her name or identity would be made when reporting the study findings.

Participants

The questionnaire was administered to ten university EFL writing teachers from three different higher education institutions. Table 7.2 shows that most of these teachers can be considered as experienced. Three teachers had more than 15 years of teaching experience; four had between 10 and 14 years, and only three had less than 5 years. At the level of a teaching position, the sample included six secondary school teachers working in higher education institutions, three lecturers, and one assistant professor. Regarding background in assessment, only three teachers had university courses in language testing.

Table 7.2 General profile of the participants

	Gender		Teaching experience				Position			Background in assessment	
	Male	Female	<5	5–10	10–15	>15	PES[a]	Lecturers	Assistant professor	University courses	Training courses
Number of participants	1	9	3	0	4	3	6	3	1	3	0

[a]PES: Stands for 'Professeur d'Enseignement Secondaire', which means in English secondary school teacher. These teachers are generally trained as high school teachers but they are recruited by the Ministry of Higher Education for a specific period of time.

Analysis

The participants' responses to the questionnaire items were coded in accordance to the seven literacy assessment competencies listed in Table 7.1. Responses to each question were first scrutinised in terms of the general trends that appeared in the respondents' answers. To build a complete picture about the mastery of each competency, these responses were then grouped with the participant's responses to the other questions about the same competency. The same process was repeated with the questions about each of the seven competencies. Participants' level of assessment literacy was then estimated based on their mastery/non-mastery of those competencies.

Results

Teachers' General Background in Language Assessment

The analysis of the responses to the questions included in the first section of the questionnaire revealed that the majority of the teachers had little background knowledge about language assessment. Out of ten participants, only three mentioned that they had had testing courses in their undergraduate studies. None of the participants reported that they had had a training course in language assessment as an EFL teacher. This indicates that despite their long experience as EFL teachers (see 4.3, above) most of these teachers had no formal training in assessment as pre/in-service teachers. It is then legitimate to ask how these teachers performed their regular assessment tasks without having any formal exposure to the knowledge and the skills needed to perform those tasks. To answer this question, more information is needed about the assessment competencies of these teachers. More specifically, more information is required about the way they constructed, administered, and marked their tests and how they interpreted and communicated the results they obtained from those tests.

Teachers' Assessment Competencies

The description of the teachers' assessment competencies was based on their responses to the questions included in the second section of the questionnaire. Their accounts on the way they performed their regular assessment tasks were used to draw a general profile about their mastery of the seven assessment competencies listed in *Standards for Teacher Competence in the Educational Assessment of Students* (see Table 7.1).

a. *Choosing writing assessment methods appropriate to instruction decisions*

This competency relates to teachers' ability to identify clear purposes for the writing tests that they develop and relate them to the instructional decisions they make. In response to this question, the participants provided a variety of answers. Some referred to general purposes that do not necessarily relate to the skill in question such as '*to assess the students' skills or abilities*' or '*evaluate the students' competence in mastering the language*'. Other teachers, however, related the purposes of the tests to the objectives of the courses they taught. They reported that they designed tests to '*check if they have achieved the objectives of the lessons*' or '*measure the students' capacity to meet the objectives of the course*'. The third category of respondents referred to specific purposes which relate to the assessment of some writing skills or techniques taught in class such as '*to assess their ability to write an essay*' or '*to measure their ability to write an argumentative essay in response to written text*'. Only one teacher failed to identify the purposes of the writing tests she administered to her students. Her response consisted of a listing of the course objectives such as '*to write an argumentative essay, to write various types of essays and to respond to an argumentative essay*'.

In reference to the teachers' ability to relate the tests they administer to the instructional decisions they make, the analysis of the participants' responses revealed that the majority of these participants were able to identify different purposes for the progress and final examination tests they produced. Eight teachers reported that while they administered progress tests to have an idea about their students' development or progress in writing, they administered final-examination tests to assess their students' overall achievement in the course. Some of them even referred to the differences between these two types of tests using some technical terms such as '*formative*' for the progress tests and '*summative*' for the final examinaiton tests. Only two teachers failed to perceive the differences between the purposes of two types of tests. One teacher mentioned that no differences exist between the purposes of the progress and the final exam tests and another teacher mentioned that she was '*not used to give progress tests to [her] students because it is supposed to be a final exam*'.

In summary and in relation to the ability to choose testing methods appropriate to instructional decisions, the analysis showed that most teachers who participated in the study were able to (1) identify clear purposes for the tests they produced and (2) differentiate between test types based on their instructional decisions. Certain variance, however, was perceived in the teachers' ability to identify the purposes of the tests. While some teachers were able to identify clear purposes relative the measurement of the writing skill, other teachers provided either very general or very specific purpose. Differences were also perceived at the level of the teachers' knowledge about the use of measurement in instruction. While some teachers seemed to have extensive knowledge about the difference between summative and formative assessment methods, other teachers seemed to have a very limited knowledge or even failed to perceive the difference.

b. *Developing writing assessment methods appropriate to instructional decisions*

This competency relates to the ability to design writing tests appropriate to instructional decisions. More specifically, it includes the teachers' knowledge about (1) test construction, (2) test-content selection, and (3) appropriateness of test content. In terms of knowledge about test construction, particpants seemed to have limited knowledge about the steps followed and the guidelines used to design writing tests. In response to the question about the steps followed to design their writing tests, most respondents referred to the choice of topic as the only step. Most of their responses consisted of detailed descriptions of the criteria they used for topic selection. Only three respondents provided a broader description of the test-construction process. Their responses consisted of lists of three or four steps, which mainly included:

- Deciding on the method of development/genre of the essay
- Choosing the appropriate topic,
- Generating ideas about the topic to check its accessibility to the students, and
- Checking the clarity and the correctness of the assignment

In reference to the use of test specifications, the respondents provided different lists of specifications. Four teachers provided lists that were only limited to the characteristics of the test input such as students' accessibility to the topic or the alignment of the test activities to the course content and objectives. Four other teachers, however, provided guidelines that focused on the characteristics of students' expected responses such as '*the structure of the essay or the paragraph*', '*the coherence between the ideas*' or '*the use of cohesive devices*'. Only two teachers reported that they had no guidelines and that they only relied on samples of writing tests previously designed by their colleagues or downloaded from the Internet.

Regarding the selection of test content, the study participants reported that they used different criteria to help them decide on the number and the characteristics of the items they included in their writing tests. When asked about how they decided on the number of items they included in each test, five respondents mentioned that the decision was made based on students' level. They explained that first-year writing tests often consisted of separate items related more to the application of some theoretical notions in writing; second and third years writing tests, on the other hand, consisted of one single topic that the students had to develop in an academic essay form. Four other respondents mentioned that the decision about the number of items was based on the number of topics discussed in class. One of them explained, '*if we taught three types of essays we give them three topics according to the types taught. The students then choose one topic and develop it*'. A close examination of these responses, however, revealed that the respondents were not referring to the number of items included in each test, but the number of topics included in each test item. The teachers' decisions about the characteristics of the items or the topics they included in their writing tests were also made according to certain criteria. Five respondents reported that the choice of the test items was related to the degree of students' familiarity with the topic. They explained that the topics included in the tests were similar to the ones taught in class. Four other respondents mentioned that the main criterion for the selection of items for the writing tests was topic relevance and originality. They mentioned that the topics had to be '*interesting*' and '*contemporary*'.

With regard to the criteria of the appropriateness of test content, seven respondents reported that to ensure the appropriateness of their tests to their students' level, they selected contents that were familiar and activities that were practised in class. Some of them even pointed to students' familiarity with the testing method. They explained that to calibrate the difficulty level of their tests, they provided their students with enough practice on the same type of tests administered in the final examination. Two other teachers reported that they relied on a different measure as they sought feedback on the appropriateness of their writing tests from their colleagues. They explained that they '*check with the teachers of other subjects to know the familiarity of the students with the topics*'.

To summarise and in relation to the ability to develop writing assessment methods appropriate to instructional decisions, the analysis of the responses revealed that the participants in the study seemed to have little knowledge about the different steps to be followed in test design. In addition, the lists of specifications provided were to a certain extent limited as they did not cover the characteristics of the different components of the writing test. The analysis also showed that most respondents used different criteria when deciding about the number and the characteristics of the items included in their writing tests. These criteria are related to students' familiarity with test content and appropriateness of the content to the students' level.

c. *Administering scoring and interpreting the results*

This competency concerns the way teachers administer, score, and interpret the results of the writing tests they produce. More specifically, it relates to the piloting of the tests and allocation of scores to the test items. When asked about whether they piloted the writing tests before administering them to their students, nine out of ten participants reported that this practice was not common in their institutions. While some of them regretted this fact, others mentioned that they did the piloting by themselves. One respondent explained saying, *'I try to figure out all the possible plans that I can have out of the writing test I administer to my students'*. Other teachers mentioned that they tried to compensate for not doing the piloting through the administration of mock examinations. Only one teacher reported that she piloted the tests with her colleagues in the department.

Regarding the scoring of test items, eight participants mentioned that they wrote the score relative to each test item on the students' test papers. Most of them provided short answers to the question, such as '*yes*' or '*yes of course*', while others explained that writing the score helped their students have a detailed account of their performances. Two teachers, however, mentioned that they did not perform this task. They reported that the nature of the writing tests, in general, does not allow the allocation of the score for each test item since writing tests especially for advanced classes consist of one single item. Still, in relation to test scoring, all the respondents mentioned that they had criteria for marking students' writing performance. They provided lists of criteria that were content-focused for some teachers and language-focused for others.

In general, the analysis of the responses to the questions about this competency revealed that all participants did not pilot the tests they produced. Instead, most of them relied on other techniques such as the use of mock examinations or test 'self-administration'. At the level of test scoring, most participants provided detailed accounts of their students' performance based on some clear scoring criteria.

d. *Using assessment results to make decisions*

The questions related to this competency were meant to collect information about the way teachers used the results they obtained from the progress tests and the final examinations. Regarding the decisions made based on the results of the progress tests, the respondents provided a variety of answers. Eight teachers reported that these tests helped them identify the writing problems faced by their students. They explained that they used the results to *'do some remedial work so that students can learn from their mistakes and avoid them in the final test'*. Four of these eight teachers also referred to the improvement of course contents and instruction. They mentioned that the results of progress tests helped them tailor the course contents and the instruction and made them more responsive to their learners' needs. Only two teachers referred to the basic function of tests, which is to identify the students who passed and those who failed. One teacher explained that the progress test results helped her monitor the progress of her students' writing skills. She explained saying *'I keep track of these mistakes to contrast them with the mistakes made in the final exam test'*.

In reference to the decisions made based on the results of the final examinations, eight participants reported that they used the results to identify students' mistakes and improve the courses they had taught. Some of these participants mentioned that the results of the final examinations had the same use as those of the progress tests (i.e., to identify and correct the students' mistakes). Others, however, referred to some differences especially at the level of course improvement. They explained that the final examination results helped them evaluate and redesign the general aspects of the courses they had taught and not the specific aspects, as was the case with the progress-test results. Only two respondents mentioned that the tests helped them identify the students who passed and those who failed.

The analysis of the responses to the questions about this competency showed that the participants in the study seemed to have similar uses for the results of progress tests and final examinations. Some respondents, however, referred to some differences related to the nature of the changes implemented in the courses taught.

e. *Developing valid grading procedures*

This competency relates to the knowledge of grading and the ability to develop valid grading procedures. In response to the question about the main criteria they took into consideration when scoring students' writing tests, the respondents provided different criteria. Most of these criteria mainly focused on the form of students' writings as they included language components such grammar, vocabulary, and style and other criteria related to the structure or the organisation of the essay. Fewer criteria, however, were more content-focused as they mainly included criteria such as the quality and originality of the ideas as well as the unity and coherence between those ideas. Three respondents also focused on the criterion of accuracy. They explained that, as future English language teachers, their students should be able '*to produce error-free essays*'.

f. *Communicating assessment results*

This competency refers to teachers' ability to communicate assessment results. More specifically, in the present study, it relates to the ways used by the teachers to report the results of the writing tests to their students and other stakeholders. When asked about whether they returned the writing tests to their students after scoring them, the participants in the study provided different responses. Eight teachers mentioned that they only returned the progress tests. They explained that, according to the rules in their institutions, the final examinations should never be returned to students. Two teachers mentioned that they did not return any writing tests to their students because, according to the rules of their institution, even progress tests should never be returned to students.

In relation to the way teachers communicated the test results to their students, most teachers mentioned that, in addition to the score on the overall performance of each student, they provided written feedback on the students' test paper, which consisted mainly of general comments on the organisation, the ideas, and the style of writing. They also mentioned that they often underlined or corrected the students' language mistakes on the test papers. Six teachers added that they often organised in-class oral feedback sessions in which they marked the tests and focused on samples of students' mistakes. In reference to the teachers who were not allowed to return the test papers to their students, they explained that they made lists of students' errors and collectively discussed them with their students in class.

Regarding the communication of test results to other teachers, nine out of ten participants mentioned that they shared their results with other writing teachers. Most of them, however, mentioned that the communication of the results was oral, informal, and conducted for the purpose of *'exchanging ideas and impressions'*. Only one teacher reported that she did not share her test results with her colleagues.

In summary, the analysis of the responses revealed that the participants in the present study communicated the results of the tests they administered to their students in the form of written feedback on the test paper and oral feedback in class. They also communicated their results to their colleagues, but orally and informally.

g. *Recognising unethical or illegal assessment practices*

This last competency relates to the knowledge of assessment ethics. More precisely, it refers to the teacher's ability to recognise unethical assessment practices. Seven participants reported that the way they assessed the writing skills of their students was not affected by any other variables such as the students' behaviour in class. Only two teachers mentioned that they sometimes took the behaviour of the students into consideration especially when marking students' progress tests and when the students' marks were close to the passing mark. One teacher mentioned that the students' behaviour in the classroom *'would affect the way feedback would be given to him/her during classes'*.

In response to another question about assessment practices, seven participants mentioned that the assessment of their students' writing skills would not be affected if they were informed that one of their students was in danger of failing. They provided answers such as *'no way'* or *'never'*, which means that they classified the practice as unethical. Some of them explained that the procedures they followed especially in the marking of the final examinations did not allow them to identify students' names. Three teachers, however, reported that they sometimes took students' marks in other courses into consideration especially for students who had attended regularly and had actively participated in the classroom activities.

To sum up, the analysis of the responses showed that most participants rejected unethical or illegal practices such as being affected by the students' behaviour or performance when marking the writing tests. Few teachers, however, tolerated these practices, especially when marking students' progress tests.

Conclusions and Discussion

The present study set out to examine the assessment competencies of a group of Tunisian EFL writing teachers and investigate the extent to which these teachers are assessment literate. At the level of assessment competencies, the teachers' accounts on the assessment tasks revealed that most of them mastered, to a certain degree, the seven competencies stated in the *Standards for Teacher Competence in the Educational Assessment of Students*. They were able to choose assessment methods appropriate to instructional decisions, as they were able to identify clear purposes for the writing tests they produced and differentiate between the purposes of different types of writing tests. They were also able to develop writing assessment methods appropriate to instructional decisions since they identified the lists of specifications they used to produce the writing tests and used certain criteria when deciding about the number and the characteristics of the items they included in their writing tests. The teachers' account also showed that the majority of the participants were able to administer, score, and interpret writing test results as they managed to score the writing tests and provide detailed accounts of the performances of their students based on some clear correction criteria. They were also able to use assessment results to make decisions about the actions taken to address their students' writing problems and improve course contents and instruction. The study also revealed that these teachers were able to develop valid grading procedures based on clear criteria that they used while assessing their students' performances. The majority of these teachers were also able to communicate the results of the tests they administered to their students in the form of written feedback on the test paper and oral feedback in class. Finally, teachers' accounts also proved that most of them were able to identify unethical and illegal assessment practices such as being affected by the students' behaviour or performance when marking the writing tests.

These accounts, however, need to be read in relation to the teachers' general background in writing assessment, in particular, and language assessment, in general. As demonstrated above, despite their long experience in EFL teaching, most teachers who participated in the study had no formal training in assessment as either university students or in-service teachers. It is thus assumed that their ability to perform certain assessment tasks principally derived from their regular practice of the assessment activities they performed along with their careers as language teachers. When performing those activities, these teachers could have probably managed to fine-tune their assessment skills in terms of test construction, scoring and communication of results based the feedback they obtained from their students or their colleagues. In addition, they could have probably had the opportunity to learn from more experienced teachers and improve their assessment practices accordingly.

This conclusion is, to a certain extent, confirmed by the findings of the quality of the knowledge about assessment that these teachers possessed. The close examination of their responses to the different items in the questionnaire revealed that their knowledge about assessment seemed to be limited, superficial, and in most cases based on idiosyncratic definitions of certain assessment principles. For example, in relation to test construction, most participants were able to provide lists of the specifications they said that they had used when designing their writing tests. These lists, however, consisted of some simple criteria for topic selection and were not up to the level of the test specifications regularly used in test construction in higher-education institutions around the world. Regarding the communication of test results, the teachers reported that they communicated their results to other colleagues. However, the mode of communication, which was oral and informal, makes the whole task void of any academic purpose and reduces it to a friendly discussion between colleagues.

In summary, the results showed that the Tunisian EFL university writing teachers could be, to a certain degree, described as assessment literate. However, relating these results to the participants' background in assessment reveals that these teachers acquired their assessment abilities through regular practice of assessment tasks. In addition, their knowledge of certain assessment principles was shown to be limited and even superficial.

Appendix 1: Assessment Literacy of the Tunisian In-Service Writing Teachers

This questionnaire aims to collect background information about the way you assess the writing skills of your students in the writing course(s) that you teach. Your answers are very important and will be strictly confidential.

Please fill in the information requested.

This questionnaire includes 4 pages and may take about 15 minutes if you answer all the questions. Please return it to the person who gave it to you.

Thank You for Your Cooperation

Section A: Biodata

1- Gender: Female ☐   Male ☐

2- Institution (where you work): ---

3- Position : PES Détaché ☐ Assistant ☐ Maître assistant ☐ Maître de conférences ☐

4- Total number of years of experience as an EFL writing teacher: -----------------------.

5- Did you take courses in language testing during your university studies? Yes ☐ No ☐

6- As a teacher, have you ever had a training course in language testing? Yes ... No ...

If yes, please specify the place, focus, and length--------------------------------
----

Section B: Questions

1- What is /are the purpose(s) of the writing tests you administer to your students?

....
....
....

2- Are there differences between the purposes of the progress tests and the purposes of the final exam tests that you administer to your students? If yes, what are these differences?

....
....
....

3- What are the main steps you follow to design your writing tests?

....
....
....

4- Do you have specific guidelines or specifications that you and your colleagues follow to design your writing tests?

....
....
....

5- How do you decide on the number of items/ topics to include in your writing tests?

....
....
....

6- What are the characteristics you take into consideration when choosing the items / topic(s) to be included in your writing tests?

....
....
....

7- Do you write the score allocated to each test item on the test paper?

....
....
....

8- What criteria do you use to ensure that the tests you design are appropriate to the level of the students you teach in terms of length and difficulty??

....
....
....

9- Do you pilot the writing tests before administering them to your students? If yes, how?

....
....
....

10- What are the main criteria you take into consideration when marking your students' writing tests?

11- Do you give the tests back to your students after marking them?

12- Do you provide your students with feedback on their performances in each test? If yes, how?

13- Do you correct each test in class and explain some of the writing problems that you judge serious?

14- What are the different uses you make of the results you obtain from the writing progress tests?

15- What are the different uses you make of the results you obtain from the writing final exam tests?

16- Do you communicate you results to other teachers?

17- Does your students' behaviour in class, whether good or bad, affect the way you mark their tests.

18- If a student informed that he/she was in danger of failing, would that affect the way you correct his/her test?

Notes

1. LSP stands for Language for Specific Purposes.

References

Athimni, A. (2017a). *Development and validation of specifications for EFL reading tests*. Unpublished Ph.D. thesis. ISLT: University of Carthage.

Athimni, A. (2017b). Evaluating the Tunisian Baccalaureate: investigation of alignment between test content and curriculum. Manuscript submitted for publication.

Daoud, M. (1999). The management of innovation in ELT in Tunisia. In M. Jabeur, A. Manai, & M. Bahloul (Eds.), *English in North Africa* (pp. 121–137). Tunis: TSAS.

Davies, A. (2008). Textbook trends in teaching language testing. *Language Testing, 25*(3), 327–347.

DeLuca, C., Klinger, D., Pyper, J., & Woods, J. (2015). Instructional Rounds as a professional learning model for systemic implementation of Assessment for Learning. Assessment in education. *Principles, Policy & Practice, 22*(1), 122–139.

Dörnyei, Z., & Taguchi, T. (2009). *Questionnaires in second language research: Construction, administration, and processing*. New York: Routledge.

Galluzzo, G. R. (2005). Performance assessment and renewing teacher education: The possibilities of the NBPTS standards. *The Clearing House, 78*(4), 142–145.

Ghrib, M. E. (2002, May). *University students' and teachers' attitudes towards the EFL reading program*. Paper presented at the Fourth International Conference on Education, Athens, Greece.

Hidri, S. (2012). *Assessing static vs. dynamic listening: Validation of the test specifications*. Unpublished Ph.D. thesis. ISLT: University of Carthage.

Inbar-Lourie, O. (2008). Constructing a language assessment knowledge base: A focus on language assessment courses. *Language Testing, 25*(3), 385–402.

Labben, A. (2016). Reconsidering the development of the discourse completion test in interlanguage pragmatics. *Pragmatics, 26*(1), 69–91.

Maaoui, A. (2016). *Test taker beliefs, strategies and achievement in EFL reading*. Unpublished Ph.D. thesis. ISLT: University of Carthage.

Mertler, C. (2003, October). *Pre-service versus in-service teachers' assessment literacy: Does classroom experience make a difference?* Paper presented at the annual meeting of the Mid-Western Educational Research Association, Columbus, OH.

Mertler, C. A. (2004). Secondary teachers' assessment literacy: Does classroom experience make a difference? *American Secondary Education, 33*(1), 49–64.

Plake, B. S. (1993). Teacher assessment literacy: Teachers' competencies in the educational assessment of students. *Mid-Western Educational Researcher, 6*(1), 21–27.

Popham, W. J. (2009). Assessment literacy for teachers: Faddish or fundamental? *Theory into Practice, 48*(1), 4–11.

Stiggins, R. J. (1999). Evaluating classroom assessment training in teacher education programs. *Educational Measurement: Issues and practice, 18*(1), 23–27.

Stiggins, R. J. (2002). Assessment crisis: The absence of assessment for learning. *Phi Delta Kappan, 83*(10), 758–765.

Taylor, L. (2009). Developing assessment literacy. *Annual Review of Applied Linguistics, 29*, 21–36.

Volante, L., & Fazio, X. (2007). Exploring teacher candidates' assessment literacy: Implications for teacher education reform and professional development. *Canadian Journal of Education, 30*(3), 749.

Xu, Y., & Brown, G. T. (2016). Teacher assessment literacy in practice: A reconceptualization. *Teaching and Teacher Education, 58*, 149–162.

Zhang, Z., & Burry-Stock, J. A. (2003). Classroom assessment practices and teachers' self-perceived assessment skills. *Applied Measurement in Education, 16*(4), 323–342.

Moez Athimni is an assistant professor of English language and linguistics at the Higher Institute of Languages of Tunis (ISLT). His research interests include the areas of language testing and evaluation and English language teaching. Dr. Athimni holds advanced degrees in English language and linguistics.

8

EFL Assessment and the Construction of Positioned Writer Identities in Gulf University Students

Lelania Sperrazza

Introduction

Purpose of Study

This interpretive study explores the writer identities of three EFL students attending an intermediate-level writing course at a private American university in the UAE. It also explores the various ways teachers assess their students and the impact that those assessments have on the construction and reconstruction of students' writer identities. The results presented in the study are based on narrative responses and semi-structured interviews of three participants during a fall 2015 writing course. The narratives describe examples of student positioning by the participants' secondary school writing teachers and highlight various concerns students feel about how they are assessed according to their writing abilities in English; additionally, the interviews reveal other perspectives about the participants' writer identities that were not captured

L. Sperrazza (✉)
American University of Sharjah, Sharjah, UAE

in their written texts. Three themes emerged from the data in which the participants felt a lack of control in relation to their identities as writers, which, in turn, negatively impacted their identities as writers upon entering a freshmen-level writing course.

Based on these findings, I suggest that university-level educators in the Gulf engage in specific pedagogical and assessment practices to assist EFL students as they transition into using academic discourse at university. As such, the current study addresses a major gap in the literature on EFL assessment in the Gulf region and contributes to the growing body of knowledge on writer identity for secondary and university-level students. Within this context, my research questions are: (1) In what ways do EFL students perceive themselves based on the writing assessments of their secondary school teachers? (2) How are students interactively or reflexively positioned based on their secondary school teachers' writing assessments? (3) How do these assessments position students' writer identities once they enter a freshmen-level academic writing course at university?

Background Information

This study is located in an academic writing classroom of a private American university in the UAE, a region that has undergone massive economic and social change brought about by oil wealth after it achieved independence from Britain in 1971. While the national language is Arabic, 90% of the workforce consists of either Western expatriates or workers from South Asia, North Africa, or other parts of the Middle East (Findlow, 2006) as continuous demands for the country's rapid growth are met with foreign labourers. English is now the *lingua franca* of the region while over 60% of the country's student population receives its higher education in English-medium universities (Findlow, 2006). The decision to actively pursue western models of education in the Gulf is based on the belief that English instruction would further increase the region's development and help its citizens compete in a globalised economy for the twenty-first century (Dahl, 2010).

As a result, Western-style liberal-arts universities have flourished in the Gulf since the 1990s, attaching prestige to Bachelors' degrees that are mostly from American universities. According to Romani (2006), two-thirds of the western-style universities abundant in this region are American. EFL students, including Gulf nationals, other Arabs, and those from South Asia or North Africa, flock to these universities because they provide an American degree without having to reside in the United States, a benefit to those who do not want to study so far from home or cannot travel because of visa issues. These universities actively recruit faculty coached in Western pedagogy, they use English as the Medium of Instruction (EMI), and they emulate the curriculum and degree programmes of universities in the United States (Moughrabi, 2009). Most importantly, in relation to my study, these universities have adopted American-style academic writing programmes, commonly known as freshman composition in the US, in which all incoming students must learn rhetorical conventions, critical thinking skills, and the processes of writing academic papers. It is important to emphasise that these courses are required of all students, no matter their discipline, with the understanding that the introductory writing courses will 'prepare' students for the writing assignments they will later receive in their majors of study. As such, the university where I teach requires four academic writing courses, based on these core-curriculum standards, which students must pass to graduate with a bachelor's degree.

Research in the Gulf that examines students' perceptions of their academic writing in an English-speaking context reveals common difficulties that students face before they even enter university. For example, Picard (2007) found that secondary school students were labelled 'deficient' by their teachers if they could not appropriate the conventions of academic writing, and even students themselves appeared 'to have internalized a Discourse of deficit' (p. 279) based on their teachers' assessments and judgments. While some teachers could sympathise with the difficulties their students were facing, other teachers blamed them for their poor writing skills (Dahl, 2010) or perceived a lack of motivation (Hudson, 2013). In Sperrazza's (2016) longitudinal study in the Gulf, 59% of the 80 students surveyed had established negative feelings about their writing during secondary school, citing feelings of ridicule or shame for not being able to write a 'correct' academic essay. Zhou and Urhahne's (2013) study on teacher expectations highlights how consistently underestimating students and unfairly judging their abilities may lead them to believe, and therefore eventually perform, according to their teachers' expectations even years after their initial point of contact. In their longitudinal study (Zhou & Urhahne, 2013), the authors found that underestimated students performed more poorly on their achievement tests the succeeding year than overestimated students, even though both groups originally performed at the same level. While the above studies reflect some of the current issues EFL students in the Gulf are facing, they investigate the issue from teachers' points of view, reflecting on concerns such as teachers' pre-conceived notions of correct academic writing (Hall, 2011; Romanowski & Nasser, 2012), lack of motivation in their students (Dahl, 2010; Picard, 2007), or students' overall lack of academic writing experience before they enter the discourse community of an English-speaking university (Hall, 2011; Picard, 2007). However, I believe this study, by investigating EFL assessment and positioned writer identities from the participants' points of view, allows room for students to reflect on their linguistic experiences so that educators may become aware of how their writing assessments impact identity construction. Therefore, the purpose of my study is two-fold: to shed light on students' past experiences with writing assessment to understand their present writer identity positionings in a university-level writing course.

Literature Review

Academic Discourse

The theoretical framework I use in this study is post-structuralism, which supports the Vygotskian (1978) view that identities are socially, culturally, and historically constructed. Within the context of this study, academic discourse is a form of written language that is privileged, required, cultivated, or conventionalised, and, therefore, often exalted by instructors, institutions, and others in educational and professional contexts. It is normally introduced and instilled within academic communities such as elementary and secondary school, but it is especially initiated in university writing programmes. In the UAE, in particular, educational policies dictate either 'standard American' or 'standard British' curricula (Weber, 2011), which uphold the belief that native-English norms are the only acceptable standard of learning (Qiong, 2004). Duff (2010) describes this standardisation as a form of institutional ideology that both enculturates and positions students because they arrive with different types of prior experience, even when their home language is the same as that of their school. As such, I believe students in the UAE, who are often multi-competent language users, are being forced into a very one-dimensional 'native vs. non-native' role, especially when it comes to writing in English.

The merging of primary Discourses (one's social language of family or culture) and secondary Discourses (the institutional language of school) can be very problematic for students, especially those whose home language differs from that of the academy (Duff, 2002, 2003, 2007, 2010; Gee, 2000). Discursive issues and tensions, commonplace in academic writing, may be especially acute in sociocultural contexts in which local and global languages may differ; furthermore, the expectations of students producing academic discourse and those assessing it may be at odds because of different expectations (Reder & Davila, 2005). Institutions, as agents of these mainstream Discourses, typically do not value the primary Discourses from diverse student populations that differ from their linguistic norms (Duff, 2010; Seror, 2008). This is partly because institutionalised Discourses of the academy can differ considerably from the Discourses students are familiar with in their everyday lives or previous learning experiences (Canagarajah, 2006a, 2006b, 2013, 2014). It is also because students are often taught that the conventions of a written language (i.e. Standard English) take precedence over constructing a writer identity that allows them to use 'English in their terms' (Lin, Wang, Akamatsu, & Riazi, 2002, p. 295). Thus, creating a positive construction regarding one's writer identity is very difficult for students whose first language is not English (Hyland, 2002). As several educators currently argue (Canagarajah, 2006c, 2013, 2014; Fernsten, 2008; Hirano, 2009; Ivanič, 2004; Kumaravadivelu, 2003; Norton, 2000, 2001; Park, 2013), competency in academic English should not be equated with established native-speaker norms. EFL students are constantly shifting between different varieties and discourses depending on their context just as the act of writing is a shifting process that can embrace multiple identities, not only an idealised fixed one. What accounts for discoursal success, according to Canagarajah (2013, 2014), is the ability to practice and negotiate within a language, not adopt a single norm. Yet, academic writing in English continues to include or exclude EFL students based on their ability to write according to native-English norms.

EFL Students in a Global Context

When English is learned by millions of speakers as an additional language for international communication, the native-English pedagogical model is rarely attainable (Kirkpatrick, 2007). Research in second language acquisition has shown that relatively few learners can develop native-like competence in English, and even students who study English throughout their entire educations, but in a global context, will rarely attain native-like mastery (Kirkpatrick, 2007). As Davies (2008) explains, the criteria for native-like mastery involves grammatical intuition, a capacity for fluent spontaneous discourse, creative ranges of communication, and, most importantly, immersion with the language during childhood and beyond. Since global English is used as a form of international communication outside of the home, and most users learn it at different stages of their lives, the above criteria rarely apply to global students' linguist experiences. Thus, as Kirkpatrick (2007) emphasises, a native-English pedagogical model is simply impractical for today's students.

Scholars, such as Jenkins (2006), who are concerned about the 'native/non-native divide' in academia, are currently advocating alternate models of global English for their students that include local language communities. Many have adopted the position that English is a heterogeneous language with multiple norms and diverse systems that would benefit global English students in an educational context. Others, like Modiano (2004) and Jenkins (2003, 2006), have even proposed linguistic models that level the diverse varieties based upon McArthur's (1987) 'World Standard Auxiliary English' or Crystal's (2004) 'World Standard Spoken English', which would presumably be common to all language communities. Crystal (2004), as well, predicts that 'it may not be many years before an international standard will be the starting point, with British, American, and other varieties all seen as optional localisations' (p. 40). According to Llurda (2009), these optional localisations could be achieved by hiring more non-native English teachers who share the same multilingual experiences as their students, with the assumption being that their expectations, English standards, and pedagogical practices would be better suited for a diverse student population. Alternatively, as Scarino and Crichton (2008) argue, the 'intercultural' approach to teaching English as a *lingua franca* would allow both teachers and students to understand how they are shaped, positioned, and influenced by their respective languages.

However, language teachers themselves, who are actively teaching in a global context, still feel that their only option is to choose between British or American English (Harmer, 2008). In Jenkins's (2007) study on foreign language teachers, she found that while her participants accepted the notion of English as a *lingua franca*, it was the students themselves who desired and expected native English to be their standard of instruction. To exemplify, in Qiong's (2004) analysis of 1251 returned questionnaires from students in a Mainland Chinese university, she found that 100% of the respondents regarded British and American English to be the only two acceptable standards. She found that 'this belief has been inculcated into them, and their teachers before them, by all the language books that they use' (p. 31). While advocates of the *lingua franca* movement, such as Jenkins (2003, 2006, 2007, 2009), are providing hopeful alternatives to international language learning, which includes an acceptance of English varieties or even a more culturally encompassing linguistic model, it does not take into account the ingrained beliefs some EFL students hold regarding the prestige of native-like English. Kuo (2006), as well, after presenting the results of a small-scale study, concluded that a 'native-speaker model…would appear to be more appropriate and appealing in second-language pedagogy than a description of English which is somewhat reduced and incomplete' (p. 220). Kuo (2006) argues that it is precisely because English is now used extensively for international purposes that it is necessary to move beyond an anything-goes global intelligibility and strive for a standard that everyone can understand—global speakers and native speakers alike. Despite such conflicting views regarding the practices of English as a *lingua franca*, my belief is that the perspectives and interests of its users are rarely heard among the scholarly debates that surround the politics of native-English norms (Kirkpatrick, 2007).

EFL Students in a Gulf Context

In reality, EFL students who attend western-style universities are not given the opportunity to choose which English variety they prefer. The expectation that EFL students must read, think, speak, and write like natives prevails in universities throughout the world (Jenkins, 2009). Often, the discursive expectations for academic discourse are seldom fully explained, addressed, or taught as a 'new' subject to students from diverse cultural and linguistic backgrounds who enter university for the very first time (Pennington, 2013). Even when students do learn to use a form of academic discourse in elementary or secondary school, such discourses may not prepare them for the academic expectations at university. This is especially true for students in the Gulf who attend various public (Arabic-speaking) or private (mostly English-speaking) schools that operate at varying degrees of academic rigour. Based on Picard's (2007) study in the UAE, a major reason that students find difficulty adjusting to the academic discourse community of English-speaking universities is because their previous teachers used formulaic methods of academic writing, a common practice also highlighted in Ahmed and Myhill's (2016) study on formulaic teaching expressions used with Egyptian students in the EFL writing context. These methods may have allowed students to pass such examinations as the IELTS (International English Language Testing System) or TOEFL (Test of English as a Foreign Language) at the required level for university entry, but they do little to prepare students for the content-driven writing they will need after arriving at university. As Templer (2003) notes, the variety of English used in these standardised examinations does not represent authentic English usage to such a degree that he considers it an artificial form of English. Therefore, the disconnect between what students learn up to the secondary level and what they are expected to know at the university level is quite high when they enter private universities in the Gulf that follow the standards of American core liberal arts programmes.

Writer Identity and Writing Assessment

The post-structural understanding of writer identity as echoed by various researchers (Ivanič, 2004; McKinney & Norton, 2008; Norton, 2000, 2001; Norton & Toohey, 2011) views identity as a plural, dynamic concept that can be created through various writing contexts. However, it is important to realise that while identities may be socially constructed through language, writers are not able to effortlessly adopt any identity they choose within a sociocultural context. They must negotiate, manoeuvre, and re-position themselves as a result of individual discoursal experiences that can easily clash with those of dominant members of a discourse community. According to Ivanič (1998), discoursal constructions cause tensions during the act of writing depending on how they are adopted, adapted, or combined by the writer. If students are unable to master this discourse, even within the very institution that purports to teach them about its linguistic norms, then coercive power relations between those in dominant positions, such as teachers, and those in subordinate positions, such as students, can develop (Weedon, 1997). This fairly common, teacher-student relationship has influenced many researchers to examine the inter-related dynamics among teachers, students, academic discourse, and their combined effects on identity construction (Clark & Ivanič, 1997; Clarke, 2008; Ivanič, 1998; Kanno & Norton, 2003; Nelson, 2011; Norton, 2000, 2001; Pavlenko, 2003; Pavlenko & Norton, 2007; Varghese, Morgan, Johnston, & Johnson, 2005). As Garcia (2009) confirms about teaching practices in the Gulf region, 'The language choice available to learners and their parents, as well as the discursive practices that are encouraged and supported in school, have an important impact on [their] identity and their possibilities of developing agency or resisting' (p. 84).

According to Duff (2010), many writing instructors in tertiary or higher education do not provide explicit directions for it is commonly assumed that students are already familiar with the discoursal conventions of academia. These ideological concepts of correct writing are passed down as established values in schools and students are indoctrinated from early on as to what consists of acceptable, standard writing even as they feel ill-prepared to understand, replicate, and produce its discoursal conventions (Dowden, Pittaway, Yost, & McCarthy, 2013). Several studies on written feedback assessment (Dowden et al., 2013; Hattie & Timperley, 2007; Nicol & Macfarlane-Dick, 2006) have found that teachers often assume their students will fully comprehend their feedback and are capable of devising an appropriate course of action to improve future work. In a longitudinal case study on student responses to written feedback in a Gulf university writing course, Shine (2008) found that while students want written feedback they often do not understand what to revise or how to revise based on their teachers' comments. As a result, students often never learn the writing skills they are expected to know already (Hall, 2011).

Interactive and Reflexive Positioning

The possibilities that positioning holds as a window into the discoursal interactions within a classroom context are crucial for understanding identity construction, and, as such, it informs my study on writer identity. Specifically, Davies and Harré (1999) have formulated two types of positioning: 'interactive positioning', in which one person positions another, and 'reflexive positioning', in which one positions oneself. As previously mentioned, students will internalise the positions placed upon them, especially by those in dominant positions, such as their teachers, which affects their identity construction in the classroom (Fernsten, 2008; Hirano, 2009; Ivanič, 2007; Kanno & Norton, 2003; Norton, 2000, 2001; Picard, 2007; Park, 2013). To illustrate, in Vetter's (2010) study, she examined subject positioning by highlighting how a teacher used certain language to position students in the classroom. Vetter (2010) found, 'The ways teachers position students as readers and writers over time contribute to how students fashion their identities and become members of the classroom community' (p. 36). Other studies have found that the positioning of students in the classroom community can affect their 'identity investment and cognitive engagement' as well as how they position themselves as learners (Bernhard et al., 2006, p. 2387). This supports Norton's (2000) claim in her seminal post-structural study that students' desires to invest in their learning are not just intrinsic to the learner, but rather dependent on the complex, linguistic environment around them. While Yoon (2008) points out that a single occurrence of positioning in the classroom may not seriously impact the identities of students, repeated positionings within the classroom community, according to Nasir and Saxe (2003), could 'matter to later identity development' (p. 16). As identity theorists argue (Bruner, 1996; Fivush, Habermas, Waters, & Zaman, 2011), people tend to maintain their identities, even when they are negative, to sustain coherence and stability in their lives. In relation to writer identities, past failures will, therefore, predict future failures if students do not have an understanding of how their identities were positioned in the first place (Fernsten, 2008; Hirano, 2009).

The Study

Methodology and Methods

I used an exploratory, interpretive approach to my study in which the autobiographical narratives of my composition students were the main focus of my inquiry. This type of methodology works well within a poststructuralist framework because narratives capture the subjective, multiple perspectives of participants and how they position themselves in the world, highlighting the influence of culture and society in identity construction (Crotty, 1998; Pring, 2000; Vygotsky, 1978). Narratives also bring research to life, and, unlike generalised, scientific data, they can help researchers and readers fully comprehend the varied experiences of participants and how their identities were formed (Cohen, Manion, & Morrison, 2011), which is necessary for a study such as my own on writer identity. Since interpretivism specifically examines subjective realities, such as the various writing experiences of students, it is essential for my participants' views, along with my interpretations, to be embedded into the research. I adopted a 'selective focus' approach (Cohen et al., 2011) by choosing meaningful moments surrounding students' writing experiences that highlighted their awareness and response to the situation. Specifically, the narrative prompt I used explored my participants' past feelings and experiences in an academic writing context in English to understand the subject positions that shaped their writer identities before entering a freshman-level university writing course.

The second method I used to gather data was semi-structured interviews. All three interviews were conducted in my office on the university campus at the convenience of each participant. All interviews were audio-recorded and transcribed verbatim for the purpose of analysis. In a study such as mine, which explores the past and present experiences of its participants, the qualitative research interview also has the advantage of being able to investigate respondents' views, perspectives, or life histories (Wellington, 2000), which highlights the constructed nature of discourse and the interpretive nature of qualitative research, in general. According to Duff (2010), it is a common practice in language and identity research to combine narratives with interviews because both approaches 'provide a better sense of learners' actual abilities—and changes over time' (p. 18). With this in mind, I felt the interviews provided an additional layer to my participants' autobiographical narratives, which was enhanced by the pre-established relationship I had with them as their writing instructor. While Yin (2009) and Berger (2013) claim this can lead to subjectivity and bias on the part of the interviewer, I felt that my understanding and knowledge of the autobiographical narratives helped me ensure what Kvale (1996) considers 'directive' interviews: dynamic, reciprocal interactions between interviewer and interviewee that move the conversation further by asking open-ended questions, which allow for more flexibility and depth of responses.

Participants

I used a convenience sampling of three intermediate-level writing students from one of Fall 2015 academic writing courses. Participants were informed about the purpose of the study and signed a consent form before their voluntary participation in which they were informed of their rights to withdraw at any time. To ensure confidentiality and anonymity, pseudonyms were used in place of the participants' real names. I specifically chose the participants' narratives for my study, and their overall participation in my research, because their descriptions, feelings, and interpretations of their writing experiences reflected a 'negative' experience based on the writing assessments of their secondary school teachers.

Since my exploratory, interpretive research does not seek to generalise about a larger population but rather aims to provide insight into my students' subjective writing experiences, I believe this type of sampling is appropriate for my study. According to Bruner (1996), using the 'storied texts' (p. 14) of participants provides a rich, lived reality to the research and, as Gibbs (2007) adds, personalises what would otherwise be considered generalisations about the participants' experiences. Additionally, I felt it was necessary to use participants from my classroom because interpretive research necessitates a relationship between the researcher and participant (Cohen et al., 2011).

The three participants range in age between 17–18 years and are Jordanian, Sudanese, and Indian, respectively. They are fluent in at least two languages and have attended English-instruction schools since elementary or secondary school. While all three have varied abilities writing in academic English, they share similar experiences based on the negative writing assessments they received during secondary school. Their pseudonyms are as follows: Dana (Participant 1), Mumin (Participant 2), and Prashant (Participant 3).

Data Collection and Analysis

I triangulated my methods of data collection by using autobiographical narratives and semi-structured student interviews. According to Cohen et al. (2011), methodological triangulation consists of different data-collection methods used on the same participants, which is the most frequently used form of triangulation in educational contexts. By using multiple data sources, issues of validity and reliability are better addressed since the credibility of the data can be checked from different perspectives. I also sought to minimise the influence of personal bias and my subjective interpretations by adopting an 'exploratory content analysis' approach (Troudi, Coombe, & Al-Hamly, 2009), which involves an objective, systematic, and thematic method to analysing the data. Then, I combined data from the autobiographical narratives and interviews, looking for recurrent themes based on my research questions: (1) In what ways do EFL students perceive themselves based on the writing assessments of their secondary school teachers? (2) How are students interactively or reflexively positioned based on their secondary school teachers' writing assessments? (3) How do these assessments position students' writer identities once they enter a freshmen-level academic writing course at university?

The emerging themes were then categorised, classified, and compared using a 'constant comparison method' in which reading and rereading across participant responses was necessary for accuracy and validity (Lalik & Potts, 2001) when comparing results between the autobiographical narratives and interviews. Three themes emerged in response to my research questions that stemmed from the ways participants were positioned based on how they perceived their writing assessments, which impacted their writer identities before entering a freshmen-level academic writing course at university. The three themes, based on a lack of Perceived Academic Control (PAC), are: (1) feeling at fault for not knowing how to write academically, (2) feeling forced to write academically, and (3) feeling like the 'weakest' writer in class. While it is beyond the scope of this study to include all the findings, the coding system and major themes are presented and discussed below. I specifically used 'process coding' to help thematise my data as it represents 'observable and conceptual action in the data' (Miles, Huberman, & Saldaña, 2014, p. 75), which is commonly addressed in narratives and interviews (See Table 8.1).

Findings and Discussion

Lack of Perceived Academic Control (PAC)

PAC is defined as a student's belief in his or her capacity to influence and predict positive outcomes in the classroom in relation to examinations, assignments, or course grades (Pekrun & Perry, 2014). Fishman (2014) found that PAC had a positive influence on students' motivation and achievement because students who feel they are able to produce positive outcomes on classroom assessments are more likely to engage in effective learning strategies and take the initiative for their learning. For example, if students attribute an academic setback to something internal and

Table 8.1 Process coding: how lack of PAC (perceived academic control) positions writer identities

Main themes	Sub-themes	Data collection tools	Participants' names
FAFNK—Feeling at Fault for Not Knowing	NUTF—Not Understanding Teacher Feedback	SN—Student Narratives	Participant 1: Dana
FAFNK—Feeling at Fault for Not Knowing	WGM—Writing as Gatekeeping Mechanism	SN—Student Narratives	Participant 1: Dana
FAFNK—Feeling at Fault for Not Knowing	NTA—Needing Teacher's Approval	SN—Student Narratives	Participant 1: Dana
FAFNK—Feeling at Fault for Not Knowing	IPT—Interactive Positioning by Teacher	SN—Student Narratives	Participant 1: Dana
FAFNK—Feeling at Fault for Not Knowing	FDG—Feeling Disappointed by Grades	SN—Student Narratives	Participant 1: Dana
FAFNK—Feeling at Fault for Not Knowing	FLF—Feeling Like a Failure	SI—Student Interviews	Participant 1: Dana
FAFNK—Feeling at Fault for Not Knowing	LC—Losing Confidence	SN—Student Narratives	Participant 1: Dana
FFWA—Feeling Forced to Write Academically	RSAW—Resisting Systematic Approach to Writing	SN—Student Narratives	Participant 2: Mumin
FFWA—Feeling Forced to Write Academically	RPM—Reflexive Positioning by Mumin	SN—Student Narratives	Participant 2: Mumin
FFWA—Feeling Forced to Write Academically	RDRT—Resenting Dominant Role of Teachers	SI—Student Interviews	Participant 2: Mumin
FLWWC—Feeling Like the Weakest Writer in Class	WAE—Writing as an Act of Embarrassment	SN—Student Narratives	Participant 3: Prashant
FLWWC—Feeling Like the Weakest Writer in Class	IPT—Interactive Positioning by Teacher	SN—Student Interviews	Participant 3: Prashant
FLWWC—Feeling Like the Weakest Writer in Class	ATC—Accepting Teachers' Criticism	SN—Student Narratives	Participant 3: Prashant
FLWWC—Feeling Like the Weakest Writer in Class	RPP—Reflexive Positioning by Prashant	SN—Student Narratives	Participant 3: Prashant

controllable (such as not studying enough), then they are more likely to alter the cause (such as studying harder next time) to avoid a repetition of the outcome. In contrast, if the cause of the academic setback is perceived as being external and uncontrollable (such as being labelled 'weak'), students may feel there is nothing they can do to change the outcome next time (Collie, Martin, Malmberg, Hall, & Ginns, 2015). The following examples show how the participants felt a lack of control based on their teachers' writing assessments.

Feeling at Fault for Not Knowing (How to Write Academically)

When instructors present themselves as authoritative holders of knowledge and students are made to feel like outsiders (Looker, 2012), a dichotic 'us/them' relationship can occur in the classroom, which Bartholomae (1986) describes as a gatekeeping mechanism in his seminal essay 'Inventing the University'. Beaufort (1999) characterises this as 'keeping the aspiring writer from being "in the know"' (p. 170), which encourages students to try to figure out what their teachers 'want' as the only possible option to earn a satisfactory grade (Voller, 2015). For Dana, this occurred when her teacher wrote the following assessment about her writing: 'Your writing is underdeveloped. Thoughts are incoherent. Needs revision' (FAFNK-NUTF-SN-Dana). When Dana questioned her teacher's comments, she relayed the following, 'When I asked her why she didn't like my essay, she told me that I shouldn't take her comments to heart and that I should just do better next time' (FAFNK-WGM-SN-Dana). But this only resulted in the following response from Dana: 'I still didn't understand why she didn't like it. She didn't tell me why' (FAFNK-NTA-SN-Dana). According to Lillis (2003), 'The idea that students can't write is central to official, public and pedagogic discourse' (p. 21), which presents a view of students as outsiders and beginners whose poor writing skills must be improved before they can be inducted into their academic discourse communities as full members. This gatekeeping mechanism can influence students like Dana to internalise negative feelings about their writing, but even more important, it can make them believe they are the ones at fault for not knowing how to write academically (Fernsten, 2008; Voller, 2015).

Based on this experience, Dana felt that her writing would never improve, and in fact, she felt positioned as a 'B' student for the rest of her English course and upcoming writing courses, in general. After that," she says, 'my writings in school would always get a score of either "B-" or "B"' (FAFNK-IPT-SN-Dana). Interactive positioning, in this context, occurs when those in power, such as teachers, impose their labels on those who are less in power, such as students. According to (Alderman, 2013), labelling students, especially with maintained grades, can constrain their subject-positions because students feel helpless to change their situation. Dana admits, 'To some people, those grades might be considered really good, but I was personally never proud of what I got' (FAFNK-FDG-SN-Dana). Since academic discourse maintains such a powerful standard, it, therefore, represents prestige (Foucault, 1980), which Dana openly declares is important to her by striving for such high grades. However, her desire to master academic writing was a failure, at least in Dana's eyes, because she could never receive an 'A' for her writing (FAFNK-FLF-SI-Dana). According to Bartholomae (1986), to succeed as a writer, students must be able to communicate as 'academics' by acquiring their scholarly language and writing standards. This includes knowing the specific conventions of its linguistic style as well as the rules for when and how to employ them (Gee, 2000). For students such as Dana, who are instilled with the belief that correct academic writing is the only acceptable form, it can be demoralising when they feel incapable of achieving an 'A', which Dana describes in reference to her teacher's feedback,

> I felt hurt. Her comments made me feel like my writing would never be good enough. I believed that, because of that incident, I wasn't a confident writer at the beginning of the semester [in WRI 101]. (FANK-LC-SN-Dana)

Feeling Forced to Write Academically

The merging of primary and secondary Discourses (Gee, 2000) can be very problematic for students, especially those whose home language differs from that of the academy, because students may fear that their identification with a secondary Discourse means a complete loss of their primary Discourse (Duff, 2010; Canagarajah, 2014; White & Lowenthall, 2011). As Delpit (1995, 1998) once argued, students need to understand and practice certain Discoursal conventions if they want to find academic success at school, as was the case with Dana, and, according to House (2013), if academic English is just looked at as one of many forms of Discourse, issues of culture, power, or oppressed writing identities should not arise. Yet, in post-structural theory, language and identity cannot be separated; students make meaning based on their respective sociocultural experiences, their specific uses of a Discourse, and the power dynamics at play between those using the Discourses (Lakoff, 2008; White & Lowenthal, 2011).

For Mumin, the clash between his primary and secondary Discourses resulted, in large part, to what appears to be the very narrow view of what his teachers 'counted' as Academic Discourse. As Mumin states,

> Since 8th grade, I have gradually lost interest in writing because of the systematic approach that schools and teachers followed which, to a great extent, made me write forcefully to get good grades and satisfy my teachers' goals of writing properly. (FFWA-RSAW-SN-Mumin)

Thus, while Academic Discourse can be a tool for empowerment, it can also cause conflict and feelings of oppression based on the way it is taught and assessed. Simply forcing students into following the discoursal norms of academic English can easily create a dichotomous choice: adapt to using academic English and leave behind one's primary Discourse *or* resist adopting this form of secondary Discourse and reflexively position oneself, like Mumin, as 'less of a writer' in English (FFWA-RPM-SN-Mumin).

In Mumin's case, since he felt forced to follow his teachers' 'systematic approach' to writing academically in English, it seemed the only identity available to him was that of 'less of a writer'. When students are solely influenced by external, sociocultural obligations in the classroom, such as feeling forced to 'write properly', then there is little chance for them to reflexively re-position their identities. Coercive power relations between those in dominant positions, such as teachers, and those in subordinate positions, such as students, are often maintained when using powerful Discourses like academic writing so that the divisions remain inequitable (Cummins, 1996). Therefore, the process of renegotiating one's writer identity is difficult and complex (Hirano, 2009), and in many cases, a student's identity is maintained throughout his or her entire education, even negative ones shaped by the enforcement of a rigid set of institutional standards (Barab & Duffy, 1998; Bruner, 1996; Fivush et al., 2011). In the case of Mumin, his negative feelings regarding institutionalised writing standards, as imposed by his secondary school teachers, followed him to university, as he claims, 'On the first day in our writing 101 class I was scared not because of the tasks or of the assignments, I was scared because I had a lot of negative experiences with writing with my teachers' (FFWA-RDRT-SI-Mumin).

Feeling Like the 'Weakest' Writer in Class

Kearney, Hays, and Ivey's (1991) oft-cited study on 'teacher misbehaviour' signifies the shift in focusing on student misbehaviour as the sole form of conflict to examining teachers themselves as possible sources of conflict within the sociocultural context of the classroom. According to Kearney et al. (1991), any behaviour deemed aggressive or damaging by students, whether intentional or not, is considered teacher misbehaviour, and it falls into three categories: incompetence, indolence, and offensiveness. Students perceive incompetent teachers as not caring about them or the course; indolent teachers are judged to be apathetic about their teaching, but offensive teachers, who are viewed as mean, cruel, and insulting, are cited as having the most negative impact on students, including damaging criticism, embarrassment, and humiliation (Sava, 2002). Such deliberate embarrassment, in which a teacher consciously shames a student, can be debilitating to that student's self-esteem, motivation, and ability to perform in the classroom (Linnenbrink-Garcia & Pekrun, 2011; Romi, Lewis, Roache, & Riley, 2011), and often, the lasting effects mostly occur when teachers misbehave in front of primary and secondary school children who are more emotionally vulnerable than older students (Sava, 2002). As Prashant confirms, 'Most of my high school writing experiences contain embarrassing moments as I was blamed for my style of writing' (FLWWC-WAE-SN-Prashant), which relates to Vetter's (2010) claim that students fashion their identities over time based on the ways their teachers treat them as a member of the classroom community. While Dana, as well, was negatively impacted by the socio-emotional context of her classroom, in which she attributed her failure to who she was as a person rather than a task-based endeavour, she never once described a moment in which she felt her teacher tried to make her feel like a failure intentionally. In contrast, Prashant 'studied in schools where teachers would like to embarrass the students to teach them a lesson so that they don't repeat it and remember it forever' (FLWWC-IPT-SI-Prashant).

Such public embarrassment reflects how Prashant's teachers 'interactively' positioned him based on their judgments and criticisms, which in turn, made him dependent on his teachers' criticisms as a way to 'learn something very important from [his] mistakes' (FLWWC-ATC-SN-Prashant). While this, ostensibly, is a common practice among students as a result of their teachers giving written feedback with the assumption that they revise, rectify, and learn from their mistakes for future assignments, for Prashant, this appears to be his only effort at influencing his academic outcomes. In essence, he does not attempt to find his effective learning strategies to help guide him *through* the writing process. This relates to Fishman's (2014) distinction between 'internally accepted responsibility' and 'externally imposed responsibility' as the difference between 'feeling responsible' and 'being held responsible', respectively. Essentially, those who feel in control are more likely to take responsibility for their learning whereas those who do not helplessly accept the circumstances around them, such as waiting for a teacher to tell them what is wrong with their work. When maintained identities occur in the classroom, based on interactive positioning by teachers, students have the potential to 'reflexively' position themselves as well because, like Prashant, they have internalised their teachers' judgments. This is evident when Prashant depicts his writing experiences at the beginning of the semester in WRI 101 as a sustained series of weaknesses that 'follow' him around, almost independent of Prashant himself: 'My weakness in writing skills has been following me from elementary level to high school and even at the university level' (FLWWC-RPP-SN-Prashant).

Reflections on Student Responses

Based on my participants' responses, I was reminded of how we, as educators, need to acknowledge the greater power structure from which academic discourse arises. Teaching academic discourse to EFL students while ignoring the numerous power dynamics that take place in this discourse only serves to perpetuate inequality—as I believe was the case with Dana, Mumin, and Prashant. At the same time, the issue of agency is a complicated concept when my students are the participants of my study. It is often difficult for participants to separate the instructor from the researcher, especially for those conditioned to follow their teachers' expectations, and a desire to please the researcher (i.e. Hawthorne effect) can easily occur. While such ethical issues should be acknowledged, I do not want to detract from what I felt were genuine, powerful stories from my students. I tried, to the best of my ability, to provide a safe, writing space for their voices to be heard, and the 'truth' in these stories was a truth that was authored by my students, not me.

As a result, I feel that my own pedagogical practices have changed after listening to my students' needs, specifically regarding their perceived lack of control in the classroom. This has made me reflect on my own teaching methods and how easily we, as instructors, can forget how much power we wield over our students' lives. A thoughtless, critical comment regarding a student's essay, for example, can remain with that student from secondary school throughout the university, as was the case with Prashant, or, regarding Mumin, forcing students to write formulaic essays that are meaningless to their lives also encourages disinterest and resistance. Even more important, we need to remember to share our knowledge about academic discourse by demystifying its rules and regulations, which Dana so desperately wanted from her secondary school teachers. Once the mystery of academic discourse and the system it represents is lost, students are more likely to attempt to learn it, use it, and perhaps, at some point, embrace it.

Implications and Conclusion

Based on the research above, as well as upon my own practice in the field, I suggest that university-level educators in the Gulf engage in specific pedagogical and assessment practices to assist EFL students as they use academic discourse at the university. First, simply acknowledging the fact that the university *has* its own discoursal norms—and then examining some of those norms—can help prevent students from feeling powerless in the classroom. This can easily be achieved by providing specific examples of academic discourse, such as sample student essays, and allow ample time for review, questions, and discussion about content and form. Educators can also model appropriate uses of academic discourse while also explaining 'why and how' they are using this particular form of discourse. However, I believe educators must be willing to challenge and question the conventions of academic discourse (and their own use of it) for such lessons to resonate with students. Otherwise, students may be likely to resist appropriating or using this dominant form of communication (Ogbu, 2004). Finally, all students can benefit from detailed feedback on the quality of their written work. While we expect students to use academic discourse in their written work, all too often students receive feedback from their teachers that only confuses them further. (Comments such as 'underdeveloped' or 'incoherent' do little to clarify for students why or how they might improve, as was the case with Dana.) Thus, providing students with concrete suggestions on ways to improve their academic writing can help them develop stronger academic writing skills, such as using a 'writer's workshop' or 'process approach' to writing that encourages several stages of draft writing based on teacher feedback.

In conclusion, I believe that we, as instructors, must deconstruct the conventions of our own assessment practices so that students can better understand and appropriate academic discourse. This would allow students to stop blaming themselves for an embedded, institutionalised marginalisation that only recognises Standard English as the norm. For example, I emphasise how I want to promote my students' ownership of individual ideas, but at the same time, I often feel that I am not allowed to recognise their ideas as valuable if they stray from the academic rules and regulations of the western academy. In this way, by modelling to my students how my own views diverge from the dominant ones of the University (in regard to grading and assessment, for example), I am hoping to communicate that they can freely express their views—no matter how different those views are from mine—in a safe space that encourages diversity. If English-speaking instructors, such as myself, discuss our own role as 'gatekeepers' within the sociocultural context of the classroom, then our EFL students may be better equipped to understand why they feel at fault, resistant to, or weak when writing academic discourses in English, as was the case with Dana, Mumin, and Prashant, respectively. As Fernsten (2008) claims, it is possible for students to reconstruct their writer identities if they are made aware of their own subject-positionings based on the assessment practices of their teachers. Once this awareness is achieved, it is the first step for students to transition into academic discourse at the university.

References

Ahmed, A., & Myhill, D. (2016). The impact of the socio-cultural context of L2 English writing of Egyptian university students. *Learning, Culture and Social Interaction, 11*, 117–129.

Alderman, M. K. (2013). *Motivation for achievement: Possibilities for teaching and learning*. New York: Routledge.

Barab, S. A., & Duffy, T. (1998). From practice fields to communities of practice. In D. U. Jonassen & S. M. Land (Eds.), *Theoretical foundations of learning environments* (pp. 29–63). Mahwah, NJ: Lawrence Erlbaum Associates.

Bartholomae, D. (1986). Inventing the university. *Journal of Basic Writing, 5*, 4–23.

Beaufort, A. (1999). *Writing in the real world: Making the transition from school to work*. New York: Teacher's College Press.

Berger, R. (2013). Now I see it, now I don't: Researcher's position and reflexivity in qualitative research. *Qualitative Research, 15*(2), 219–234.

Bernhard, J. K., Cummins, J., Campoy, F. I., Ada, A. F., Winsler, A., & Bleiker, C. (2006). Identity texts and literacy development among preschool English language learners: Enhancing learning opportunities for children at risk with learning disabilities. *Teachers College Record, 108*(11), 2380–2405.

Bruner, J. S. (1996). *The culture of education*. Harvard: Harvard University Press.

Canagarajah, A. S. (2006a). Negotiating the local in English as a Lingua Franca. *Annual Review of Applied Linguistics, 26*, 197–218.

Canagarajah, A. S. (2006b). Toward a writing pedagogy of shuttling between languages: Learning from multilingual writers. *College English, 68*(5), 589–604.
Canagarajah, A. S. (2006c). World Englishes in composition: Pluralization continued. *College Composition and Communication, 57*(4), 586–619.
Canagarajah, S. (2013). *Translingual practice: Global Englishes and cosmopolitan relations*. New York: Routledge.
Canagarajah, S. (2014). In search of a new paradigm for teaching English as an international language. *TESOL Journal, 5*(4), 767–785.
Clark, R., & Ivanič, R. (1997). *The politics of writing*. London: Routledge.
Clarke, M. (2008). *Language teacher identities: Co-constructing discourse and community*. Clevedon: Multilingual Matters.
Cohen, L., Manion, L., & Morrison, K. (2011). *Research methods in education* (7th ed.). New York: Routledge.
Collie, R. J., Martin, A. J., Malmberg, L. E., Hall, J., & Ginns, P. (2015). Academic buoyancy, student's achievement, and the linking role of control: A cross-lagged analysis of high school students. *British Journal of Educational Psychology, 85*(1), 113–130.
Crotty, M. (1998). *The foundations of social research*. Thousand Oaks, CA: Sage.
Crystal, D. (2004). *The stories of English*. London: Allen Lane.
Cummins, J. (1996). *Negotiating identities: Education for empowerment in a diverse society*. Ontario, CA: California Association for Bilingual Education.
Dahl, M. (2010). *Failure to thrive in constructivism: A cross-cultural malady*. Rotterdam: Sense Publishers.
Davies, A. (2008). The native speaker in applied linguistics. In A. Davies & C. Elder (Eds.), *The handbook of applied linguistics* (pp. 431–449). Oxford: Blackwell Publishing.
Davies, B., & Harré, R. (1999). Positioning and personhood. In R. Harré & L. V. Langenhove (Eds.), *Moral contexts of intentional action* (pp. 32–52). Malden, MA: Blackwell.
Delpit, L. (1995). *Other people's children: Cultural conflict in the classroom*. New York: The Press.
Delpit, L. (1998). The silenced dialogue: Power and pedagogy in educating other people's children. *Harvard Educational Review, 58*(3), 280–298.
Dowden, T., Pittaway, S., Yost, H., & Mccarthy, R. (2013). Students' perceptions of written feedback in teacher education: Ideally, feedback is a continuing two-way communication. *Assessment & Evaluation in Higher Education, 38*(3), 349–362.

Duff, P. A. (2002). The discursive co-construction of knowledge, identity, and difference: An ethnography of communication in the high school mainstream. *Applied Linguistics, 23*(3), 289–322.

Duff, P. A. (2003). New directions in second language socialization research. *Korean Journal of English Language and Linguistics, 3*(1), 309–339.

Duff, P. A. (2007). Second language socialization as sociocultural theory: Insights and issues. *Language Teaching, 40*(1), 309–319.

Duff, P. A. (2010). Language socialization into academic discourse communities. *Annual Review of Applied Linguistics, 30*, 169–192.

Fernsten, L. (2008). Writer identity and ESL learners. *Journal of Adolescent & Adult Literacy, 52*(1), 44–52.

Findlow, S. (2006). Higher education and linguistic dualism in the Arab Gulf. *British Journal of Sociology of Education, 27*(1), 19–36.

Fishman, E. (2014). With great control comes great responsibility: The relationship between perceived academic control, student responsibility, and self-regulation. *British Journal of Educational Psychology, 84*(1), 685–702.

Fivush, R., Habermas, T., Waters, T. E., & Zaman, W. (2011). The making of autobiographical memory: Intersections of culture, narratives and identity. *International Journal of Psychology, 46*(5), 321–345.

Foucault, M. (1980). *Power/knowledge: Selected interviews and other writings 1972–1977* (C. Gordon, Ed.). New York: Pantheon.

Garcia, O. (2009). *Bilingual education in the 21st century: A global perspective.* West Essex, UK: Wiley-Blackwell.

Gee, J. P. (2000). Identity as an analytic lens for research in education. *Review of Research in Education, 25*, 99–125.

Gibbs, G. (2007). *Analyzing qualitative data.* London: Sage.

Hall, K. (2011). Teaching composition and rhetoric to Arab EFL learners. In C. Gitskaki (Ed.), *Teaching and learning in the Arab world* (pp. 421–440). New York: Peter Lang Publishing.

Harmer, J. (2008). *The practice of English language teaching* (4th ed.). Harlow, UK: Longman.

Hattie, J., & Timperley, H. (2007). The power of feedback. *Review of Educational Research, 77*(1), 81–112.

Hirano, E. (2009). Learning difficulty and learner identity: A symbiotic relationship. *ELT Journal, 63*(1), 33–41.

House, J. (2013). Pragmatics across languages and cultures. In A. Trosborg (Ed.), *The pragmatics of English as a lingua franca* (pp. 363–387). Berlin and New York: De Gruyter Mouton.

Hudson, P. (2013). *Tiptoeing through the minefield: Teaching English in higher educational institutes in the United Arab Emirates*. Ph.D., Canterbury Christ Church University, UK.
Hyland, K. (2002). Options of identity in academic writing. *ELT Journal, 56*(4), 351–358.
Ivanič, R. (1998). *Writing and identity: The discoursal construction of identity in academic writing*. Amsterdam and Philadelphia: John Benjamins.
Ivanič, R. (2004). Discourses of writing and learning to write. *Language and Education, 18*(3), 220–245.
Jenkins, J. (2003). *World Englishes: A resource book for students*. London: Routledge.
Jenkins, J. (2006). Global intelligibility and local diversity: Possibility or paradox? In R. Rubby & M. Saraceni (Eds.), *English in the world: Global rules, global roles* (pp. 32–39). London and New York: Continuum.
Jenkins, J. (2007). *English as a lingua franca: Attitude and identity*. Oxford: Oxford University Press.
Jenkins, J. (2009). English as a lingua franca: Interpretations and attitudes. *World Englishes, 28*(2), 200–207.
Kanno, Y., & Norton, B. (2003). Imagined communities and educational possibilities. *Journal of Language, Identity, and Education, 2*, 241–249.
Kearney, P., Plax, T. G., Hays, E. R., & Ivey, M. J. (1991). College teacher misbehaviors: What students don't like about what teachers say and do. *Communication Quarterly, 39*(4), 309–324.
Kirkpatrick, A. (2007). *World Englishes: Implications for international communication and English language teaching*. Cambridge: Cambridge University Press.
Kumaravadivelu, B. (2003). Problematizing cultural stereotypes in TESOL. *TESOL Quarterly, 37*(4), 709–719.
Kuo, I.-C. (2006). Addressing the issue of teaching English as a lingua franca. *ELT Journal, 60*(3), 213–221.
Kvale, S. (1996). *Interviews*. London: Sage Publishing.
Lakoff, G. (2008). *The political mind: Why you can't understand 21st-century American politics with an 18th-century brain*. New York: The Penguin Group.
Lalik, R., & Potts, A. (2001). Social reconstructivism as a framework for literacy teacher education. In C. M. Roller (Ed.), *Learning to teach reading: Setting the research agenda*. Neward, DE: International Reading Association.
Lillis, T. (2003). Student writing as 'academic literacies': Drawing on Bahktin to move from critique to design. *Language and Education, 17*(3), 192–207.
Lin, A., Wang, W., Akamatsu, N., & Riazi, M. (2002). Appropriating English, expanding identities, and re-visioning the field: From TESOL to teaching

English for glocalized communication (TEGCOM). *Journal of Language, Identity, and Education, 1*(4), 295–316.

Linnenbrink-Garcia, L., & Pekrun, R. (2011). Students' emotions and academic achievement: Introduction to the special issue. *Contemporary Educational Psychology, 36*(1), 1–3.

Llurda, E. (2009). Attitudes towards English as an international language: The pervasiveness of native models among L2 users and teachers. In F. Sharafian (Ed.), *English as an international language: Perspectives and pedagogical issues*. Bristol, UK: Multilingual Matters.

Looker, S. (2012). Rethinking roles, relationships and voices in studies of undergraduate student writing. *English Teaching: Practice and Critique, 11*(2), 113–127.

McArthur, T. (1987). The English languages? *English Today, 11*, 9–13.

McKinney, C., & Norton, B. (2008). Identity in language and literacy education. In B. Spolsky & F. Hult (Eds.), *The handbook of educational linguistics* (pp. 192–205). Malden, MA: Blackwell.

Miles, M., Huberman, A., & Saldaña, J. (2014). *Qualitative data analysis: A methods sourcebook*. Thousand Oaks, CA: Sage Publishing.

Modiano, M. (2004). Monoculturalization and language dissemination. *Journal of Language, Identity, and Education, 3*(3), 215–227.

Moughrabi, F. (2009). Moving toward a knowledge society in the Arab world. *Arab Studies Quarterly, 31*(4), 17–31.

Nasir, N. S., & Saxe, G. B. (2003). Ethnic and academic identities. A cultural practice perspective on emerging tensions and their management in the lives of minority students. *Educational Researcher, 32*(5), 14–18.

Nelson, C. (2011). Narratives of classroom life: Changing conceptions of knowledge. *TESOL Quarterly, 45*(3), 463–485.

Nicol, D., & Macfarlane-Dick, D. (2006). Formative assessment and self-regulated learning: A model and seven principles of good feedback practice. *Studies in Higher Education, 31*(2), 199–218.

Norton, B. (2000). *Identity and language learning: Gender, ethnicity, and educational change*. Essex, UK: Pearson Education.

Norton, B. (2001). Non-participation, imagined communities and the language classroom. In M. Breen (Ed.), *Learner contributions to language learning: New directions in research* (pp. 159–171). London: Longman–Pearson Education.

Norton, B., & Toohey, K. (2011). Identity, language learning, and social change. *Language Teaching, 44*, 412–446.

Ogbu, J. U. (2004). Collective identity and the burden of acting "white" in Black history, community, and education. *The Urban Collective, 36*(1), 1–34.

Park, G. (2013). Writing is a way of knowing: Writing and identity. *ELT Journal, 67*(3), 336–345.

Pavlenko, A. (2003). "In the world of the tradition I was unimagined": Negotiation of identities in cross-cultural autobiographies. *International Journal of Bilingualism, 5*(3), 317–344.

Pavlenko, A., & Norton, B. (2007). Imagined communities, identity, and English language learning. In J. Cummins & C. Davison (Eds.), *International handbook of English language teaching* (Vol. 11, pp. 669–680). New York: Springer.

Pekrun, R., & Perry, R. (2014). Control-value theory of achievement emotions. In R. P. L. Linnenbrink-Garcia (Ed.), *International handbook of emotions in education* (pp. 120–141). New York, NY: Routledge.

Pennington, M. (2013). Evolutionary trends in writing pedagogy: An early 21st century view. *Writing & Pedagogy, 5*(1), 1–22.

Picard, M. Y. (2007). *Academic literacy right from the start? A critical realist study of the way university literacy is constructed at a Gulf university.* Ph.D., Rhodes University, South Africa. Retrieved from http://eprints.ru.ac.za/907/

Pring, R. (2000). *Philosophy of educational research.* London: Continuum International Publishing.

Qiong, H. X. (2004). Why China English should stand alongside British, American, and the other 'world Englishes'. *English Today, 20*(2), 26–33.

Reder, S., & Davila, E. (2005). Context and literacy practices. *Annual Review of Applied Linguistics, 25*, 170–187.

Romani, V. (2006). The politics of higher education in the Middle East: Problems and prospects. *Crown Center for Middle East Studies, 36*, 1–8.

Romi, S., Lewis, R., Roache, J., & Riley, P. (2011). The impact of teachers' aggressive management techniques on students' attitudes to schoolwork. *The Journal of Educational Research, 104*(4), 231–240.

Romanowski, M., & Nasser, R. (2012). Critical thinking and Qatar's "Education for a New Era": Negotiating possibilities. *International Journal of Critical Pedagogy, 4*(1), 118–134.

Sava, F. A. (2002). Causes and effects of teacher conflict-inducing attitudes towards pupils: A path analysis model. *Teaching and Teacher Education, 18*(8), 1007–1021.

Scarino, A., & Crichton, J. (2008). Why the intercultural matters to language teaching and learning: An orientation to the ILTLP program. *Babel, 43*(1), 4–6.

Seror, J. (2008). *Socialization in the margins: Second language writers and feedback practices in university content courses.* Ph.D., University of British Columbia, Vancouver, Canada.

Shine, E. A. (2008). *Written feedback in a freshmen-writing course in the UAE: Instructors and students' perspectives on giving, getting, and using feedback*. Ph.D., Massey University, Palmerston North, New Zealand.

Sperrazza, L. (2016). Narrative of struggle: Understanding writer identity in the UAE. *International Journal of Bilingual & Multicultural Teachers of English, 4*(1), 15–24.

Templer, W. (2003). ELT in the "reconstruction" of Iraq. *IA TEFL Issues, 173*, 4–5.

Troudi, S., Coombe, C., & Al-Hamly, M. (2009). EFL teachers' views of English language assessment in higher education in United Arab Emirates and Kuwait. *TESOL Quarterly, 43*(3), 546–555.

Varghese, M., Morgan, B., Johnston, B., & Johnson, K. (2005). Theorizing language teacher identity: Three perspectives and beyond. *Journal of Language, Identity, and Education, 4*, 21–44.

Vetter, A. (2010). Positioning students as readers and writers through talk in a high school English classroom. *English Education, 43*(1), 33–64.

Voller, N. (2015). Value in academic writing: An inquiry into reader response. *Young Scholars in Writing, 12*(1), 54–66.

Vygotsky, L. (1978). *Mind in society*. Cambridge, MA: Harvard University Press.

Weber, A. (2011). Politics of English in the Arabian Gulf. *Proceedings of the 1st International Conference on Foreign Language Teaching and Applied Linguistics (FLTAL'11)*, 5–7 May 2011, Sarajevo, pp. 60–66.

Weedon, C. (1997). *Feminist practice and poststructuralist theory* (2nd ed.). London: Blackwell Publishing.

Wellington, J. (2000). *Educational research: Contemporary issues and practical approaches*. New York: Continuum International Publishing.

White, J. W., & Lowenthal, P. R. (2011). Academic discourse and the formation of an academic identity: Minority college students and the hidden curriculum. *Review of Higher Education, 34*(2), 1–47.

Yin, R. K. (2009). *Case study research: Design and methods* (4th ed.). Thousand Oaks, CA: Sage.

Yoon, B. (2008). Uninvited guests: The influence of teachers' roles and pedagogies on the positioning of English language learners in the regular classroom. *American Educational Research Journal, 45*(2), 495–522.

Zhou, J., & Urhahne, D. (2013). Teacher judgment, student motivation, and the mediating effect of attributions. *European Journal of Psychology of Education, 28*(2), 275–295.

Lelania Sperrazza is a senior writing instructor at the American University of Sharjah. Previously, she taught TESOL and Composition for the US Department of State at the University of Aden in Yemen and Al-Azhar University in Egypt. She has also taught Rhetoric at the American University in Cairo. Her areas of interest are language and identity, focusing specifically on the writer identities of Gulf university students. Currently, she is working on her PhD in TESOL Composition at the University of Exeter.

9

ELT Professors' Perspectives on the Use of E-rubrics in an Academic Writing Class in a University in the UAE

Rana Raddawi and Neslihan Bilikozen

Introduction

Testing and assessment are usually used interchangeably because writing assessments started off as testing in college to place students into appropriate courses (Reynolds, 2010). Assessment dates back to 1874 in Harvard (Connors, 1997), where students were divided based on their levels into different courses through placement tests. However, the earliest mention of writing assessment in its current form dates to the 1960s. This description prevailed with the emergence of testing initiatives such as CaMLA (formerly known as 'English Language Institute Testing and Certificate Division at the University of Michigan') in 1941 ('U-M LSA English Language Institute', n.d.), ELTB in the 1950s, and TOEFL in 1961 (Davies, 2007). At the same time when tests such as TOEFL and ELTS (1980) were developing to IBT TOEFL and IELTS (1989), and general IELTS (1995), the first wave of writing assessment development started from 1950–1970. Yancey (1999) describes writing assessment to have

R. Raddawi (✉) • N. Bilikozen
American University of Sharjah, Sharjah, UAE

undergone three waves of development. The first wave (1950–1970) consisted of when writing assessment was purely objective testing. The second wave (1970–1986) took the form of holistically scored essays, and the third wave (1986–1999) consisted of portfolio assessment and programmatic assessment. According to Yancey (1999), the waves overlap; practices prevailing in a period do not cease to exist right away but are integrated, developed, and, with time, taken over by the proceeding practices. During the early period, while educators decided what to teach, testing specialists decided where to place students. Later, these two spheres of influence merged, with administrators and educators taking on the responsibility for testing previously claimed by testing specialists.

Little literature has focused on the history behind how rubrics, or any other form of assessment methods, evolved (Cooper & Gargan, 2009; Phillips, 1658; Reddy & Andrade, 2010; Wolf & Stevens, 2007; Jonsson & Svingby, 2007). Studies mainly focused on either how to use such methods, explanations of what the methods entail, or the history of writing assessment in general as stated in the previous section. An exception of these methods is portfolios, whose development was explained by the transition to the third wave, but this is mainly because it was an integral part in the development of writing assessments generally, from objective testing to essay writing or direct assessment.

Although there has been massive literature with various perspectives on the use of rubrics in writing assessment, which will be explored in the following pages, research on the development of e-rubrics and their role in writing assessment compared to that of traditional essay writing rubrics remains scarce. The present study attempts to examine the use of e-rubrics in a series of required academic writing classes in an American University in the United Arab Emirates. The paper will focus on the effectiveness and practicality of these e-rubrics in providing feedback and improving students' writing skills.

Literature Review

Since the development of essay writing assessment and the use of portfolios (Yancey, 1999), the use of rubrics has become a very common way to examine a student's progress in English writing. According to Cooper and Gargan (2009):

The term "Rubric" is used widely in education. In the classroom, the rubric may mean a set of categories, criteria for assessment, and the gradients for presenting and evaluating learning. (p. 1)

The term rubric has been used in English since the 1400s. Phillips (1658) says that a rubric is 'a noted sentence of any Bookmarked with red letters'. Rubrics have been considered an efficient way to categorise behaviour that could be used to evaluate academic performances. A conventional rubric used in most educational institutions around the world shows the levels of work needed to achieve a certain performance. It could be said that the introduction of rubrics has made life easier for students as well as instructors. For an instructor, a rubric is a great way to make the requirements and expectations of an assignment clear, transparent, and objective. Students from both graduate and undergraduate schools have valued rubrics, as they can clarify the targets for their work very well while allowing students to keep a check on their progress (Reddy & Andrade, 2010). Similarly, the process of following the guidelines of an assignment and getting the expected grade becomes much easier for a student. Unlike in the past, there is currently a common set of criteria to conclude on the quality of work and the performance of a student (Cooper & Gargan, 2009). Some scholars believe that using rubrics adds to the quality of assessment (Jonsson & Svingby, 2007; Wolf & Stevens, 2007). However, this has not necessarily always been the case.

The kind of rubrics that are used, i.e., when a paper is graded based on its overall standard in relation to the scale on the rubric is called 'holistic grading rubrics' ('Writing@CSU', n.d.; DePaul University Teaching Commons', n.d.). Holistic grading prevailed during the second wave, however not necessarily under the mention of rubrics. AP and SAT examinations use this in writing assessment ('Writing@CSU', n.d.).

Rubrics' most valuable product is the one at the end (Jonsson & Svingby, 2007), whereas portfolios consider the whole process before judgment. After the third wave, the emergence of portfolios that is, a new writing assessment form prevailed: Writing Across the Curriculum (WAC).

Assessment, according to Dochy et al. (2006) (cited in Jonsson & Svingby, 2007), has lately been changing from testing of knowledge to 'assessment for learning' itself. This is where and why Writing Across the Curriculum emerged. The latter consists of testing and teaching writing not only in writing classes but also across the full course of study including major-related courses (Reynolds, 2010). Hence rubrics developed to enhance the assessment of learning as the writing component began to be introduced across the curriculum.

Some recent research studies have shown that the use of rubrics in writing assessment could promote learning and achievement in higher education. At Texas A&M University, Leggette, McKim, and Dunsford (2013) conducted a case study of using electronic self-assessment rubrics in a core curriculum-writing course. The study results revealed that students became more comfortable in assessing their writing when using an e-rubric and assigning themselves a score. De Silva (2014), from the Open University of Sri Lanka, conducted a study about the use of rubrics for assessment and their effects on English as a second language (ESL) students. The research was intended to find the extent of exposure rubrics had on ESL students' writing performances. The study was carried out on two classes. One class was given a rubric for a writing assignment, and the rubric was explained to them by their teachers, while the second class was only given the rubric without any explanations of how it worked or its purpose. At the end of the study, it was found that students who were provided with an explanation along with the rubrics were subjected to more of a positive change in their performance compared to the ones who were not given any explanations.

The use of rubrics in academia has also had its fair share of criticism. Rubrics are often lashed at for standardisation, decrement of interactions in a student-teacher relationship, and most importantly for reducing creativity. Once instructors comply strictly with the rubrics provided, this could, in turn, hamper students' capabilities to think differently and look at the problems in a different way (Kohn, 2006).

Research in the state of Illinois showed that the use of rubrics in assessing writing led to formulaic writing as well as simplification and homogenization of the writing process (Marby, 1999). Similarly, Chapman and Inman (2009) voice their concern regarding the use of rubrics by saying '[…] our concern is that the teacher is restricting students' problem-solving, decision-making, and creativity—traits needed in a democratic society for governance' (p. 198–202). Another major concern teachers must look into while using rubrics is the descriptive language used in those rubrics as students interpret the language in them differently from instructors (Li & Lindsey, 2015). When teachers examine students' writing, a rigid rubric could hamper accommodating different genres, voices, and styles of writing a student could offer. Rubrics have been created to save time, to increase the efficiency of teaching, and most importantly to make sure that the objectives of assignments are made clear to the students.

As Turley and Gallagher (2008) write, rubrics could be created for various purposes and in many contexts. What is important is examining their impact on the educator and the student instead of labeling all rubrics 'good' or 'bad'. One of the main objectives of a rubric would perhaps be not to lead to any negative standardisation or restrict the capabilities of a student.

With the rise of the digital age, standard rubrics have acquired their digital companions too, called Electronic Rubrics or e-rubrics. Just like any computer-assisted system, e-rubrics make the grading and assessing much simpler for an instructor as it reduces the time required to grade assignments. Furthermore, an e-rubric also increases the precision and legitimacy of the grading process, as an educator's stress or issues do not affect the grading process (Czaplewski, 2009).

The discussion of e-rubrics is very limited in the literature. When it is mentioned in research, only the outcomes about a specific stimulus are studied. An example of such articles is the 'Study of the impact on student learning using the eRubric tool and Peer Assessment' by Angulo and La Serna, who conclude that 'The eRubric methodology and technique applied to peer assessment poses a huge professional challenge for both students and teachers' (2011, p. 426).

However, technology, in general, has been gradually added to assessment techniques. The process did not happen at a specific time, but rather started being integrated simultaneously with the advancements of technology. For instance, a survey conducted by around 2500 Advanced Placement and National Writing Project teachers proves that the inclusion of technology had an impact on students' writing, mostly positive. Sharing writings with a wider audience, enforcing group work, enhancing creativity, and self-expression are examples of the impacts (Purcell, Buchanan, & Friedrich, 2013). Students, in general, were also capable of adapting fast to new assessment technologies such as e-rubrics (Angulo & La Serna, 2011).

A literature review reveals a certain dearth in the assessment of English writing in tertiary education using e-rubrics. To the best of our knowledge, no research has been conducted on the use of e-rubrics in the Gulf region although the region has made noticeable progress in modelling the education system as a whole. Places such as United Arab Emirates (UAE) have made bilingual education compulsory and have since then recorded several linguistic, academic, and socioeconomic benefits for students while also underlining some sociocultural challenges (Gallagher, 2011). Furthermore, research conducted in the UAE and Kuwait emphasised the teachers' roles and philosophies regarding assessment of English language education in the Gulf. Such studies have only found that a clear gap exists between the philosophies teachers hold regarding assessment and their practices of assessing (Troudi, Coombe, & Al-Hamliy, 2009). Self-assessment is also not seen to be widely used in the Gulf region. However, research from Iran reveals the existence of a general understanding among students about the benefits of self-assessment (Normand-Marconnet, 2012). Research in the Gulf States shows a clear lack of focus on formative assessment strategies in English language education (El Ebyary, 2013). Uncertainty about assessment in English language courses is clearly seen in the region. The present study attempts to fill this gap by examining the effectiveness of e-rubrics in assessing academic essays written by undergraduates enrolled in a series of required academic writing courses at an American university in the UAE.

Context

With globalisation being salient in the Gulf region, the influx of numerous immigrants mainly in the United Arab Emirates, and the fast development of the country after the oil boom, communication skills in English have become a necessity. Currently, English in the UAE is viewed as a symbol of power and success, modernism, liberalism, freedom, and equality as well as a departure from old-fashioned, inefficient, teacher-centred educational systems (Troudi & Jendli, 2011). According to Troudi and Jendli (2011), these wider socio-cultural, political, and educational factors contributed to the current language policy in the UAE. Indeed, Shaikh Nahyan Bin Mubarak Al Nahyan, former Minister of Higher Education and Scientific Research, confirmed these views when he pointed out: 'We will not deny our young generation the opportunity to interact with the outside world in English, today's language of science and technology' in response to a question regarding Federal National Council's (FNC) proposal to make Arabic the primary language of instruction in state universities ('Nahyan: English to stay as medium of instruction', 2009).

Since the country hosts more than 200 nationalities (Randall & Samimi, 2010), English has been used as a lingua franca in many fields. Furthermore, excellent competency in English has become a must as English is the medium of instruction in most tertiary-level institutions in the UAE. The mission statement of the university under scrutiny has subscribed, since its inception, to this strategy of developing students' four competencies in Shakespeare's language.

The Study: Description of Courses and E-rubrics

The present study was conducted at a local university situated in one of the Emirates. Founded as an independent, co-educational institution in 1997, today the university is considered one of the leading higher education institutions in the Gulf and serves approximately 6000 students from more than 90 different nations. It offers 26 majors and 46 minors at the undergraduate level and 14 master's degree programmes through four academic divisions (Fast Facts, 2017).

Newly enrolled students at this university who receive less than the required TOEFL/IELTS score but who otherwise meet the university's admission standards are required to complete a series of remedial language classes offered by the university's Achievement Academy Bridge Program (AABP). Having passed the AABP exit tests and scoring 76

(540) or above on the TOEFL or 6.5 or above on the IELTS, they are eligible to take the English Placement Test (EPT), a test developed and assessed by a group of professors in the department under scrutiny. Students are then placed in one of the three courses offered by the department depending on the score they receive on the EPT. The main objectives of the department under study include providing students with the academic language, critical thinking, and rhetorical foundations essential to writing and reading successfully in a university environment. It offers a series of three academic writing courses that all undergraduates are required to take either as a pre-requisite or a co-requisite for many of the courses they have to take to complete their degree programmes.

The curricula and syllabi for all the courses in the department under study are designed and regularly updated by the Department Curriculum Committee, whose members are appointed by the Head of the Department. While the use of e-rubrics on ilearn, a virtual course management system, was initiated and shared with the department as an alternative assessment tool by some professors in 2013, the adoption of e-rubrics as a common assessment method started in 2015. The goal was to standardise the various assessment tools and methods used by professors teaching the three courses offered by the department. This decision was taken to meet the requirements for common courses set by the University Undergraduate Curriculum Committee, which can be briefly stated as common syllabi, textbooks, assignments, and grading strategies.

To put this decision into action, the Department Curriculum Committee was asked to create a common rubric for each common assignment in all courses offered by the department, in consultation with faculty. These rubrics, created through ilearn, consisted of several assessment criteria and performance descriptors demonstrating progressively more sophisticated levels of attainment for each criterion and allowed feedback to be typed under each descriptor and/or in-text, using several-learn tools (see Appendix 1: A Sample student paper graded and provided feedback with the department's common e-rubric). This shift from more flexible assessment strategies to a standard form of assessment was met with mixed responses from the faculty, who had different levels of familiarity with and interest in online assessment platforms. The differences of opinion and conflicts revolved around the overall set-up of the grading criteria such as the weight assigned to each criterion, the number of criteria, the content of descriptors, and the technical issues associated with grading and providing feedback through e-rubrics. The perceptions and attitudes of the faculty in the department towards the use of e-rubrics, developed in 2015, will be explored in the following sections.

Research Questions Three broad research questions are proposed in this study to investigate the advantages, impacts, and challenges of using e-rubrics in writing assessment as perceived by professors:

1. What are the advantages of using e-rubrics in an academic writing class?
2. What are the impacts of these e-rubrics on students' advancement in the course?
3. What are the challenges facing ELT faculty while using e-rubrics in their academic writing classes?

Methodology

Informed by an interpretive framework of research, this study regards the individual as the centre of any understanding of social reality. Guided by the research questions, the current research is an exploratory case study in nature, using a mixed method research design for data collection and analysis. The purpose is not to make predictions or generalisations, but to understand how individuals in a given social and educational context interact to create meaning and to draw conclusions about pedagogy and language learning. Using multiple methods helps not only to portray a fuller picture of the phenomenon under investigation by providing rich and informative data but also to validate and triangulate the data by investigating the same issue through both quantitative and qualitative methods (Silverman, 2000).

The main data sources for this study are a survey sent to all faculty in the department and the follow-up semi-structured interviews conducted with three volunteers identified with the help of the survey (see Appendix 2: Survey and Appendix 4: Interview Questions). Hence, a two-phase mixed methods design is used, where the research team use 'qualitative data to help explain, or to build upon, initial quantitative results' and 'where the first-phase quantitative results guide the selection of subsamples for follow-up in-depth qualitative investigation in the second phase' (Punch, 2009, p. 296). In this study, the quantitative stage served as the starting point for a more detailed investigation process, that is, the qualitative stage of the in-depth interviews conducted with volunteers. The data collection procedures started in December 2016 and ended in February 2017.

There are various data analysis strategies used in qualitative research; however, the overall data analysis process can be conceptualised in three steps: preparing and organising the data for analysis, reducing the data into themes through coding and condensing the codes, and finally representing the data in figures, tables, or discussion (Creswell, 2007). This strategy was carefully followed in the present study.

All interviews were audio-recorded and fully transcribed. Following Radnor's (2002) approach to analysing semi-structured interviews in interpretive research, we prepared the data for analysis first by reading the whole transcribed data several times and noting down the topics that emerged from the data. Radnor (2002) calls this stage topic ordering. In addition to reading, we also listened to the recorded interviews several times to make sure we understand the transcribed spoken interaction as well as possible, as advised by Richards (2003). During the data analysis process, while the interview and survey questions gave access to some of the topics, we made sure to read the transcripts carefully to draw out any other topics that were embedded in the responses more implicitly. We made a list of the topics, giving a name and code (abbreviation) to each. We then read the transcripts very carefully one more time to draw out the categories within each topic. We listed these categories under each topic as subheadings. The next step was reading the transcripts for content, that is, going through the text one more time to highlight and code the main quotes that go under each category (see Appendix 5: Topics, codes, and categories identified in the data). These quotes were used to illustrate the participants' voices and viewpoints more clearly in the discussion of the findings.

We also followed the strategy of constant comparison of different data sources (i.e., the notes we took during and after each interview and survey results). In support of this approach, Richards (2003) notes that the relationship between the interview data and other data sources should never be disregarded and that it is the researcher's responsibility to make use of all available data sources to get the best possible fix on the information that is presented in the interviews.

Data Collection Phase 1: Survey

The research questions and the literature review informed the design of the survey and interview items. 'The questionnaire is a widely used and useful instrument for collecting survey information, providing structured, often numerical data, being able to be administered without the presence of the researcher and often being comparatively straightforward to analyse' (Cohen, Manion, & Morrison, 2011, p. 245). For the purposes of this study, the survey was designed to collect demographic information about the participants and to uncover the participants' general preferences regarding English writing assessment methods. The main objective was to examine the professors' perspectives on the effectiveness of the use of e-rubrics in providing feedback, the impact of e-rubrics on students' learning process, and finally the challenges and benefits of using these assessments methods in general. As flexible data collection instruments, surveys allow the researchers to use a variety of question types and 'gather a lot of, as well as a variety of information relatively quickly' (Mertler, 2009, p. 117). The survey items designed for this study included five-point Likert-scale questions: strongly agree, agree, neutral, disagree, strongly disagree, and open-ended questions, which fed into the later qualitative analysis of the data.

The survey was sent through an email to all full-time faculty in the department. Since one of the researchers conducting this study teaches in the department under study, the survey was sent to 21 out of 22 faculty members. The response rate was high, with 19 out of 21 instructors (90.47%) completing the survey.

Data Collection Phase 2: Interview

The quantitative phase of the data collection process led into the more in-depth qualitative phase, which involved interviewing the volunteers identified through the survey. According to Brown (2001), interviews have a 'high return rate, fewer incomplete answers, can involve realia, relatively flexible and personal' (p. 75). As Mertler (2009) states, 'interviews permit the teacher-researcher to probe further and ask for clarification in a participant's response to a given question' (p. 111). Thus, interviews give a researcher an advantage over surveys as they can get more details on vague answers and in-depth reasons for responding to such answers. Furthermore, with interviews, other observations can be made, such as analysing body language and facial expressions (Brown, 2001).

To protect the anonymity and confidentiality of the participants, we used pseudonyms. Moreover, records of the data collected (including transcripts and any audio recordings) were stored in a secure and safe place.

The first volunteer was William, who had a PhD in Rhetoric and Composition and had been teaching academic writing for about 20 years. He was from the USA and had been teaching in the UAE for nine years. The next professor who showed interest in a follow-up interview was Ali, who had an MA in TESL. Originally from Turkey, Ali had been teaching academic writing in the UAE for about four years, and was working towards his PhD in Linguistics. The third volunteer, Laura, had a PhD in Curriculum and Instruction and had been teaching academic writing for more than 25 years. Originally from the USA, she had been teaching in the UAE for about ten years. Table 9.1 below summarises the three interviewed faculty members' information.

Table 9.1 Summary of interviewed faculty information

Pseudonym	William	Ali	Laura
Gender	Male	Male	Female
Nationality	USA	Turkey	USA
Qualifications	PhD in rhetoric and composition	MA in TESL	PhD in curriculum and instruction
Teaching experience	20 years	4 years	25 years

When the volunteers expressed their interest in a follow-up interview by providing their contact details upon completing the survey, they were contacted via e-mail to set up the interview time. A semi-structured interview process consisting of a set of data collection questions that were thought to have the potential to engage the participants in conversations about their use of e-rubrics was used. Both researchers were present at two of the interviews while the last interview was conducted by one of the researchers because of time conflicts. All interviews were audio-recorded after obtaining the permission from the participants. In addition, detailed notes were taken during the interviews.

The present study was conducted following the strict ethical standards of the institute in which it was undertaken. These standards concern the ethical issues of informed consent, anonymity, and confidentiality. Along with the university policy, permissions from the Institution Review Board (IRB) were obtained before the data collection process. This procedure, which is required by several universities, is helpful in determining the levels of risk and reducing potential risk by adjusting the study while still clearly receiving answers to their questions (Schreiber & Asner-Self, 2011). Essentially, informed consent was an on-going process throughout the entire research process. Participants were ensured that they had the right to withdraw from the research at any given time and that data related to them would be destroyed if they so wished.

Research Findings and Discussion

Background of participants and their general preferences regarding assessment and feedback on student writing

Originating from various cultural backgrounds and countries such as the USA, UK, South Africa, India, Lebanon, Greece, and Turkey, the instructors had a master's or doctorate degree mostly from North American and British universities. Table 9.2 below describes the surveyed faculty's relevant information such as nationality, qualifications, and teaching experience.

Table 9.2 Surveyed faculty demographics

Gender	14 females
	7 males
Nationality/ethnicity	USA, UK, South Africa, India, Lebanon, Greece and Turkey
Qualifications	4 had a PhD
	15 had a master's degree in fields such as English, TESOL, Rhetoric and Composition, and Curriculum Development
Teaching experience	3 had more than 25 years
	1 had 20–25 years
	2 had 16–20 years
	6 had 11–15 years
	5 had 5–10 years
	2 had less than 5 years
Years of experience in using e-rubrics for writing assessment	5 had more than 5 years
	1 had 4–5 years
	10 had 3–4 years
	2 had 1–2 years
	1 had less than a year

Seventy-nine per cent of the faculty stated that they preferred using a computer/web-based medium of grading and giving feedback as opposed to 21% who preferred a paper-based medium. While 63% stated preferring analytic rubrics, 26% preferred holistic ones. More than half of the participants had been using e-rubrics for 3–4 years, which coincides with the time e-rubrics was adopted as a common assessment tool in the department (see Appendix 3).

Benefits of E-rubrics in Assessing Academic Writing

This section addresses the first research question on the advantages of e-rubrics in a writing classroom. The analysis of the data regarding this research question revealed three main themes: record keeping, time and energy saved on grading and providing feedback, and transparency and objective assessment, which are explained in detail below. Table 9.4 (see Appendix 6) illustrates these themes with a relevant quote from the interviews or the survey.

Record Keeping

Keeping a running record of students' writing assignments, filing past assignments in an organised way, and creating a system that would enable a professor to find specific student work when needed are usually perceived as challenging tasks for academic writing professors.

One of the most commonly stated advantages of using e-rubrics was the ease of record keeping in terms of accessing student work online without the boundaries of time and space. Online grading was found to reduce the possibility of losing or misplacing the assignments. For instance, William, one of the interviewees, commented that:

> *Papers are always turned in time, and everything is recorded on the computer, you can take these anywhere. Also the grades go directly to i-learn, and this is a very efficient form of record keeping than using traditional papers.*

This ease of record keeping described by William above was raised by all interviewees and also stated as one the most positive aspects of assessing student writing through e-rubrics by most of the anonymous survey participants. For instance, Laura explained the advantages of using e-rubrics in grading and providing feedback, comparing this process to the paper-based method she had used in the past:

> *My office is messy enough! I mean I can remember using paper-based methods because I have taught long enough! It was never easy carrying huge stacks of paper with me, and I have always been an environmentalist, so that was distasteful on a lot of levels.*

Ali explained how record keeping is easier for both the instructor and the student when e-rubrics are used:

> *Students sometimes tend to lose their hard copies. With e-rubrics, they can use their phones and computers to check their grades. It also allows the students to have flexibility while submitting and makes it easier for me to grade since everything is on my laptop. I can grade, and students can access those grades anywhere.*

All these benefits explained by the participants above are of paramount importance for academic writing professors who are usually overwhelmed with large numbers of student assignments that require timely grading and feedback.

Time and Energy Saved on Grading and Providing Feedback

Another major theme that emerged from both sets of data was the time and energy saved on grading and providing feedback. Seventy-two per cent of the respondents agreed or strongly agreed that e-rubrics saved time and energy. This perceived benefit was backed up with responses to open-ended questions in the survey and also raised in the follow-up interviews with the volunteers.

Comments such as *'typing is faster than handwriting'*, *'speed and accuracy of grading'*, and *'they save time and energy'* clearly show the instructors' views about the contribution of e-rubrics to their grading and providing feedback process.

Objective and Transparent Assessment

Another major theme emerging from the data was objective and transparent grading. This was highlighted in both data sources. For instance, one anonymous respondent in the survey commented:

> *Rubrics allow me to grade student work as objectively as possible. They also make it easier for students to understand what they have done well and what areas they still need to work on.*

Another comment by an anonymous respondent was:

> *Students know the criteria used to assess their assignment before submitting it. After submission, they have a clear justification for their grade, which in turn has reduced the number of students coming to ask about their grade.*

Similar thoughts were voiced in the interviews as well. For instance, Ali noted that:

Grading writing can be very subjective and students, a lot of times, get lost when rubrics are not used.

Objective and transparent grading is a significant aspect of accountability and effective assessment in academic writing. The comments above show the contribution of e-rubrics to students' learning in terms of clarifying the evaluation criteria and objectives of a writing assignment as well as the grades and feedback provided. In support of these comments, 72% of the respondents noted they agreed or strongly agreed that e-rubrics help them provide effective feedback.

Perceived Impact of E-rubrics on Students

This section addresses the second research question related to the impact of e-rubrics on students' advancement in the course. Data analysis revealed three salient themes: better understanding of the assignment objectives, ease of access to and a better understanding of grades and feedback, and finally reservations about e-rubric as a learning tool.

Table 9.5 (see Appendix 6) illustrates these themes with a relevant quote from the interviews or the survey.

Better Understanding of the Assignment Objectives

Most of the professors commented that students understand the objectives and requirements of assignments better when the e-rubrics are shared with them during the introduction of the assignment. In fact, 95% of the respondents noted that they explained the rubric to their students when introducing an assignment and 70% said using e-rubrics in writing assessment helped students understand the objectives of an assignment.

These findings were further supported by comments in response to the open-ended questions in the survey and the interviews. For instance, one anonymous respondent commented on the advantages of using e-rubrics as follows:

Good guidelines to follow, explaining the grading criteria to the students and the grade when they are finished.

A similar comment was that they provided *clear communication to students about expectations for the assignment.*

This was brought up and explained in the follow-up interviews with volunteers further. For instance, Ali noted that:

I always share the rubrics not just after the assignment but before the assignment...After grading, when they look at the rubric, it gives them a quick overview of their strengths and weaknesses...In that sense I think it is very useful and for the next assignment, they understand that there is something else that they need to focus on...Moreover, it makes it easier for me to explain what I expect from them and I think it makes it easier for them to understand, so it goes both ways.

Ease of Access to and Better Understanding of Grades and Feedback

Ease of access to and better understanding of grades and feedback had been frequently brought up as perceived advantages of e-rubrics from the student perspective. It was noted that students could access their grades and the feedback online as soon as the assignment had been graded, wherever they are, and that they could keep a record of their progress throughout the semester. One anonymous survey respondent noted that:

The students seem satisfied with a quantifiable assessment broken down into categories. Without it, they usually feel that the comments themselves are not enough to justify their grades.

Another anonymous comment was:

> It makes it easier for the students to identify their strengths and weaknesses.

Some faculty noted that typed feedback reduces the possibility of misunderstanding instructor comments, which could be a problem with handwritten comments. For instance, William noted:

> Students usually aren't able to understand my handwriting, and after getting into this system, a positive I see is that students can understand what I'm trying to say with the comments.

These comments show a significant contribution of e-rubrics to writing assessment: a clear, quicker, and more convenient method of conveying feedback to students, which emerge as a key advantage of e-rubrics as opposed to more traditional assessment tools.

Reservations About the Role of E-rubrics in Learning

At first glance, the views of the participants regarding e-rubric's role in learning were confusing: While 72% of the professors noted that using e-rubrics helped them provide effective feedback, 67% stated that e-rubrics helped students understand the objectives of an assignment; 50% stated that, overall, students' response to feedback provided through e-rubrics was positive while 44% were undecided. However, when it comes to the contribution of e-rubrics to enhancing students' writing skills, 33% disagreed or strongly disagreed, 33% were undecided, and only 33% agreed or strongly agreed. Analysing the interviews cleared this confusion.

Laura stated:

> I certainly think substituting a rubric for the kinds of comments that might be made is a bad idea. Students don't assimilate that very well. You can go through the rubric in class, but we know how things announced in class don't get assimilated to students…Students never ask about the rubric, but they will ask about comments made on their paper. There are always just questions on my responses.

She added:

> Maybe that's good news on some level, but I don't like it when rubrics become a tyranny. I would find that a problem.

Laura's comments above show her hesitance towards letting e-rubrics dominate her teaching and her concerns about e-rubrics as a restrictive tool in terms of limiting a teacher's role in assessment and standardising not only assessment but also, in a sense, limiting the definition of good writing.

Refusing to assign a major role to e-rubrics in students' overall experiences in learning academic writing, William noted:

> I don't think it's relevant what kind of method we use to let students know how they did and give feedback. What's relevant to their writing is the message they are getting from us and not how they get it.

William's comments suggest that he upholds the role of everyday teaching and learning practices in enhancing student writing, as opposed to that of a particular assessment tool or method.

These responses emphasise that e-rubrics alone are not enough to enhance students' writing skills. When responses from the survey and the interviews are considered, it seems that while the professors acknowledge many of the advantages of using e-rubrics, they only assign a complementary role to it in enhancing students' writing skills.

Challenges Faced by ELT Teachers While Using E-rubrics in Assessing Academic Writing

This section addresses the third research question regarding the challenges facing ELT faculty while using e-rubrics in an academic writing class. The analysis of the data regarding this research question revealed two salient themes: restrictions and technical difficulties. The following sections explain these themes in detail. Table 9.3 (see Appendix 6) illustrates these three themes with a relevant quote from the data.

Restrictions Faced in the Implementation of E-rubrics

One of the most commonly stated challenges voiced in both the survey and the follow-up interviews concerned the restrictions placed by the common e-rubrics required to be used in all courses and assignments, an issue summarised by one participant in the survey as *'the rigidity and lack of flexibility'*. This challenge is more about the requirement of using a common rubric than the particular medium of grading and providing feedback online; however, it emerged as a common issue raised in both sources of data.

One anonymous respondent explained this challenge as follows:

> *They [the e-rubrics] are too vague; I'd prefer using my rubrics that are more tailored to individual assignments and provide more feedback.*

Similarly, another anonymous respondent commented:

> *I wouldn't say it was a serious problem, but often a situation in the assignment isn't reflected adequately in the rubric and, while the prof. can clarify the issue in the comments, it is hard to know where to place the response in terms of generating a grade.*

The comments above show the limiting, standardising aspect of rubrics, which the participants voiced as part of their reservations about the role of e-rubrics in learning academic writing.

The extent to which the common e-rubrics could capture the complexity or the specific requirements of an assignment was also raised as an issue in the follow-up interviews. For instance, William, one of the interviewees, noted:

> *I'll also have something where I give a challenge to the student in class, and I'll want my students to relate these challenges to the essay students submit. I'd want to assess this in my rubric and give more emphasis to what I'm teaching in class. I'd want to be more transparent with the students. Common rubrics are fine as long as we can clarify what's being included, I don't have any issue with e-rubric. As long as it allows me to be clear with the students to what I'm looking for, I'd be happy.*

He added:

> *I don't see any disadvantage with rubrics unless they are common rubrics. Common rubrics often have to be negotiated with others, and this could lead to a conflict of opinion while creating these rubrics.*

Laura voiced her concerns about the same issue when she noted:

> *Rubrics seem like an imposition to me from on high and in some cases, it can preclude the grass roots level work that goes on in class. Every class is different. I have that agreement with this particular class. There are your experience and knowledge and the way you think things ought to be. The knowledge established within the class should also be included in the rubric ... I have always used them, but it wasn't until recently that I had to adhere to an agreed upon rubric. I think professors should be able to clarify and add on to the rubrics.*

These comments may explain why 53% of the participants stated that if they were given the freedom to choose their writing assessment method, they would use a revised version of the current e-rubrics, while 38% noted they would use completely different ones. Only 10% of the respondent said they would continue to use the existing e-rubrics.

Technical Difficulties

Another salient theme emerging from the data was technical difficulties faced while using e-rubrics as an assessment tool. While 61% of the participants noted that they received sufficient training in using e-rubrics and that the process had been hassle free, many expressed their dissatisfaction with some of the technical aspects of e-rubrics. These aspects ranged from the strain on their eyes due to spending hours in front of a computer monitor to the limited feedback functions provided by Blackboard, which were usually found difficult to use.

In response to an open-ended question in the survey regarding the most serious problems faced while using e-rubrics, one anonymous respondent noted that:

> Online rubrics are cumbersome. Unless one is using a huge screen computer, the endeavour is painful.

A similar comment written under the same open-ended question by an anonymous respondent was that:

> Blackboard is pretty awful—cumbersome, complex, not very user-friendly.

The issue of technical difficulties and limitations was also voiced in the interviews. For instance, Ali, who described himself as someone who loves integrating technology in his classes, described several technical issues that could be nettlesome for all faculty, particularly those who are not interested in, or who have limited experience in incorporating technology in teaching:

> I would say there are a lot of technical limitations... There are no track changes, which is more practical than highlighting. Not everybody is comfortable with using computers or i-learn the way I do so it could be a disadvantage for those type of people. Secondly, doing all these things on one computer for me is also not easy... Overall, if you want to do things more efficiently and effectively, you need two monitors. Thirdly, some people are not comfortable with looking at computer screens for extended periods. So far, I haven't had an issue with that, but I can understand that that is a concern for people.

The technical difficulties noted above could be demotivating and cause e-rubrics to be seen as counter-productive tools by some faculty, particularly those who have limited familiarity with e-rubrics.

Implications

Some implications can be drawn from the findings discussed above when they are reconsidered holistically.

The data analysis reveals two important challenges faced by the participants: restrictions and technical difficulties. The sense of being restricted was voiced by participants as a reaction to the imposition of a standard e-rubric, which they found not flexible enough to address the specific requirements or aspects of a writing assignment. The feeling of discomfort experienced by the participants can be explained by 'the law of distal diminishment', which says 'that any educational tool becomes less instructionally useful and more potentially damaging to educational integrity the farther away from the classroom it originates or travels' (Turley & Gallagher, 2008, p. 88). However, considering the pressure on colleges and universities to become more accountable for student learning as a result of a variety of factors such as 'decreasing graduation rates and increasing demand, cost, time-to-degree, economic return and public concern for higher education' (p. 287) as well as the increasing importance of student learning as one of the top priorities for college accrediting agencies, it seems the interest in accountability measures based on value-added constructs is likely to continue to have a significant impact on how writing is assessed in US colleges and universities (Pagano et al. 2008).

Another challenge was the technical difficulties experienced by the professors when transitioning from paper-based to electronic assessment process, which suggests the importance of assistance and training for faculty who are less familiar with technology. Some technical difficulties, on the other hand, were not experienced as a result of limited familiarity with technology, but due to the limitations of the feedback functions offered by ilearn e-rubrics, which many instructors found cumbersome. As online writing assessment and feedback tools become more widespread, solutions to these technical limitations are very likely to be sought by the various virtual course management systems that offer these tools.

Despite these challenges, the analysis of the data reveals that using e-rubrics in the assessment process of academic writing brings about important benefits that include the ease of record keeping, time and energy saved in grading and providing feedback, as well as transparency and objective assessment. The benefits concerning the time and energy saved along with transparent and objective assessment have been reported in other studies on the role of rubrics in writing assessment (Crusan, 2010; Czaplewski, 2009; Ferris & Hedgcock, 2014; Jonsson & Svingby, 2007; Weigle, 2002). Proponents of rubrics in writing assessment argue that rubrics offer objective and consistent evaluation (Crusan, 2010), clarify assignment criteria, and provide transparent evaluation (Ferris & Hedgcock, 2014; Weigle, 2002) as well as clear and easily accessible assessment materials, which help teachers establish credibility and accountability to their students (Crusan, 2015). Another advantage that has been particularly highlighted in this study is the ease of record keeping in terms of archiving and saving student work with feedback and grades as well as easy access to those saved work regardless of time and space thanks to using online e-rubrics during the assessment process.

Regarding the impact on student advancement in the course, the findings indicate that e-rubrics are helpful in clarifying objectives of a writing assignment as well as the grades and feedback provided. These findings are in line with past research studies that emphasise the role of rubrics in the formative assessment that support and enhance instruction and student learning (Black & Wiliam, 2009; Panadero & Jonsson, 2013; Wiliam, 2011). The contribution of e-rubrics to student learning in terms of clarifying the evaluation criteria of a writing assignment is particularly important as 'ensuring that all learners understand how they are to be assessed is an ethical imperative' for fair assessment; however, the significance of this issue is yet to be understood 'even in those countries where writing assessment is at its most advanced' (Hamp-Lyons, 2013, p. A2). Despite these advantages, the research on the impact of rubrics on learning has not been conclusive with some studies suggesting that rubrics can limit a teacher's assessment of writing or any other skills (Broad, 2003; Wilson, 2006), that they tend to standardise not only assessment but also prose (Kohn, 2006), that they promote a focus on error (Balester, 2012), and limit the definition of good writing (Weigle, 2007). The controversy surrounding the impact of rubrics on learning has also been reflected in the findings of this study as one of the themes that emerged from the data was *reservations about e-rubrics as a learning tool*. While the participants acknowledged some advantages of using e-rubrics, they were hesitant to assign a major role to them in enhancing student writing, mostly when they considered the role of e-rubrics as opposed to that of many other teaching and learning activities. These views suggest that the participants uphold the role of classroom practices in enhancing student writing, especially when they feel restricted with imposed rubrics that originate from outside of the classroom. These findings emphasise the importance of some level of flexibility, which would allow individual classroom practices and interactions to shape and contextualise the rubrics while still adhering to the common course assessment criteria.

The participants' responses also reveal a certain emphasis on the role of the professor as a mentor or master of the teaching and learning processes. Yet, the researchers in this paper still believe that e-rubrics could guide those mentors in providing clear, objective, fair, and continuous assessment of student writing.

In her editorial published in a special issue of *Assessing Writing* on the use of rubrics, Crusan (2015, p. 1) memorably notes:

> As a writing teacher first and a writing assessment researcher second, I view any discussion of rubrics from the perspective of a teacher struggling to provide a fair and equitable assessment of her students, and I am often troubled by questions that have been raised from my time in the trenches. I worry about allowing criteria in my head to shape my assessments; I worry about failing to inform students of assignment criteria; I worry about neglecting to provide students with some formalised scale to use as a guide.

The authors support Crusan's views and believe that when the challenges, advantages, and overall impact on student learning are considered holistically from the perspective of an academic writing instructor, the aforementioned benefits of e-rubrics overweigh their potential drawbacks and justify their use in academic writing classrooms.

Conclusion

This exploratory study was an attempt to examine the perspectives of ELT professors on the use of e-rubrics in a series of academic writing classes at the tertiary level. The data collection phase consisted of a mixed research method. Twenty-one faculty members were surveyed, and three of the 21 were interviewed. The results revealed that e-rubrics used as an assessment tool had great advantages in the course as they save time, energy, and space for the graders while being transparent and easy to access for the students. However, like any other technological tool, e-rubrics suffered from some technical issues, which can be easily addressed by the sponsors of the platform that developed them.

Another significant finding in the study was the emphasis of all participants on the role of the educators in the classroom. The instructor remains the mentor and the master of the teaching and assessing process even with the use of e-rubrics. However, it is the grading tool, in this case the e-rubrics, that allows the educator to follow a consistent, unified, efficient, and transparent method to assess and provide feedback on the writing assignments of their students. According to participants' responses, students are in general satisfied with the assessment outcomes. Learners better understand the objectives of the assignment and respond to instructor's feedback accordingly. Hence, this relatively fair process of electronic assessment promotes an effective teaching and learning environment while creating a positive climate in the classroom, provided that some level of flexibility is given to allow individual classroom practices and interactions to shape and contextualize the rubrics.

As this study is interpretive in nature, it does not have claims of generalizability. However, we hope the findings can be inspiring for academicians in similar teaching contexts. We investigated the advantages, challenges, and the impact of e-rubrics on learning from the professor's perspective; an interesting direction for future research would be to examine the same from the student's perspective. Comparing both perspectives would give a more holistic view of the role of e-rubrics in academic writing instruction.

Acknowledgment The authors thank The American University of Sharjah for providing the necessary resources to complete this study. Many thanks also go to the participants who contributed to the completion of this study and research assistant Vishnu Narayanan who helped with the data collection.

… R. Raddawi and N. Bilikozen

Appendix 1: A Sample Student Paper Graded and Provided Feedback with the Department's Common E-rubric

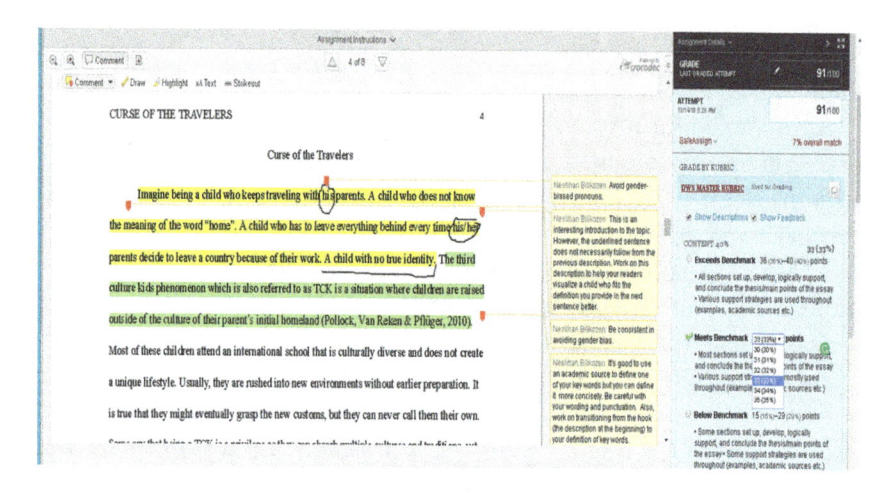

Image 1 Screenshot of a student essay being graded and commented on using the department's common e-rubric

Image 2 The department's common e-rubric

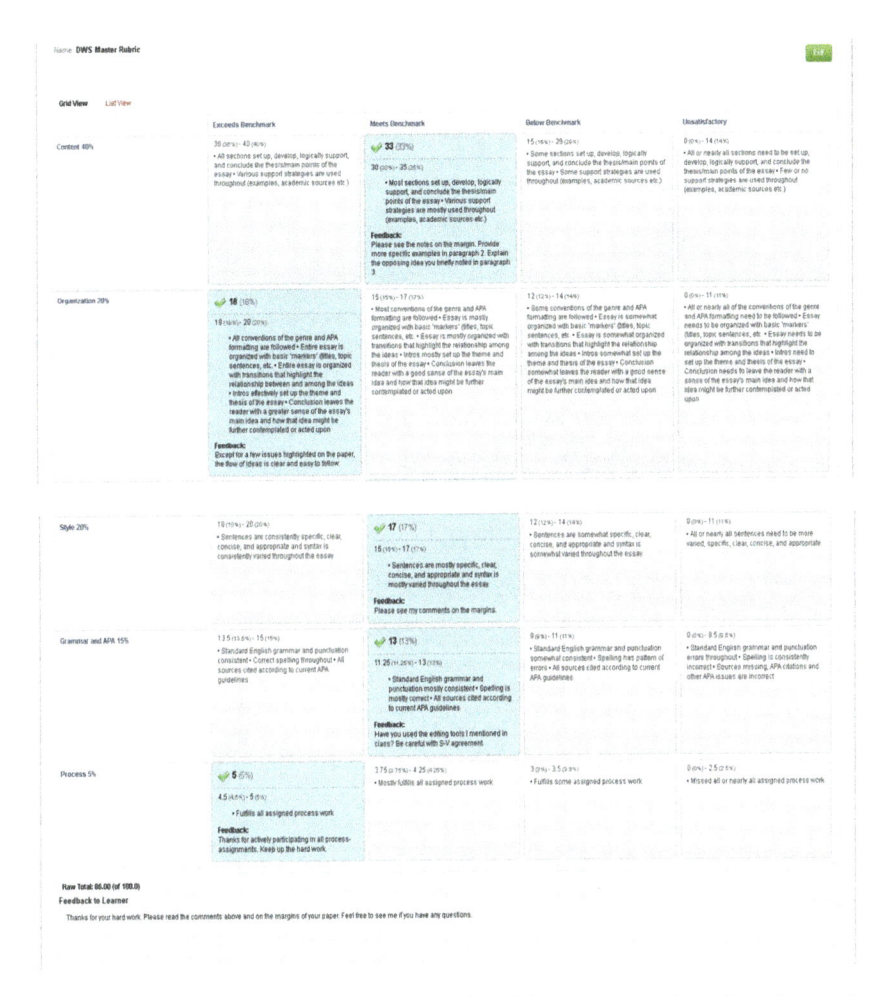

Image 3 The screenshots of the e-rubric with comments typed under each category

Appendix 2: Survey—E-rubrics in L2 Writing Assessment

Appendix B

Survey: E-Rubrics in L2 Writing Assessment

1. How long have you been teaching academic writing?
   - less than 5 years
   - 5-10 years
   - 11-15 years
   - 16-20 years
   - 20-25 years
   - more than 25 years
2. Please state your educational qualifications below.

---

3. Please indicate your preferred method of assessing student writing.
   - through holistic rubrics
   - through analytic rubrics
   - Other (please specify)

---

4. Please indicate your preferred medium of grading and giving feedback.
   - computer/web based
   - paper based

5. How long have you been using e-rubrics in writing assessment?
   - less than a year
   - 1-2 years
   - 3-4 years
   - 4-5 years
   - more than 5 years

6. Please indicate your level of agreement with the following statements.

	Strongly Disagree	Disagree	Undecided	Agree	Strongly Agree
The criteria used in our department's e-rubrics represent my views regarding how each assignment should be assessed.					
I have received sufficient assistance and training in using e-rubrics.					
Learning how to use e-rubrics has been hassle-free.					
I explain the rubric to my students when I introduce an assignment.					
Using e-rubrics in writing assessment helps students understand the objectives of an assignment.					
Using e-rubrics in writing assessment enhances their writing skills.					
Overall, my students' response to feedback provided through e-rubrics has been positive.					
Assessing student writing through e-rubrics saves time and energy.					
Using e-rubrics helps me provide effective feedback.					

7. Given the freedom to choose my own writing assessment method, I would use
    o the existing rubrics
    o revised versions of the existing rubrics
    o completely different rubrics
    o an alternative assessment method (please specify) _____

8. What has been the most positive aspect of assessing student writing through e-rubrics, if any? Please specify.
_____
_____

9. What has been the most serious problem you faced while using e-rubrics, if any? Please specify.
_____
_____

10. If you are willing to discuss certain issues further and clarify your view points, you may do so by typing your e-mail below.
_____

Appendix 3: Background of Participants and their General Preferences Regarding Assessment and Feedback on Student Writing

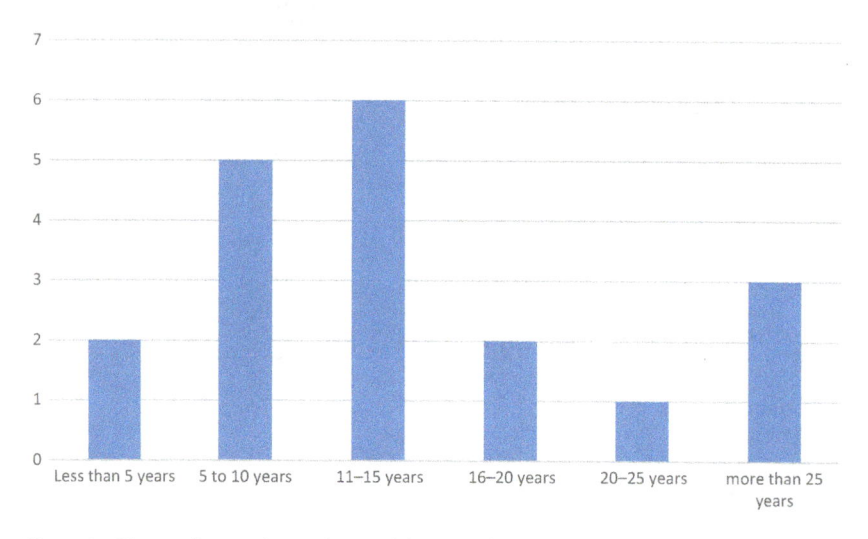

Chart 1 Years of experience in teaching academic writing

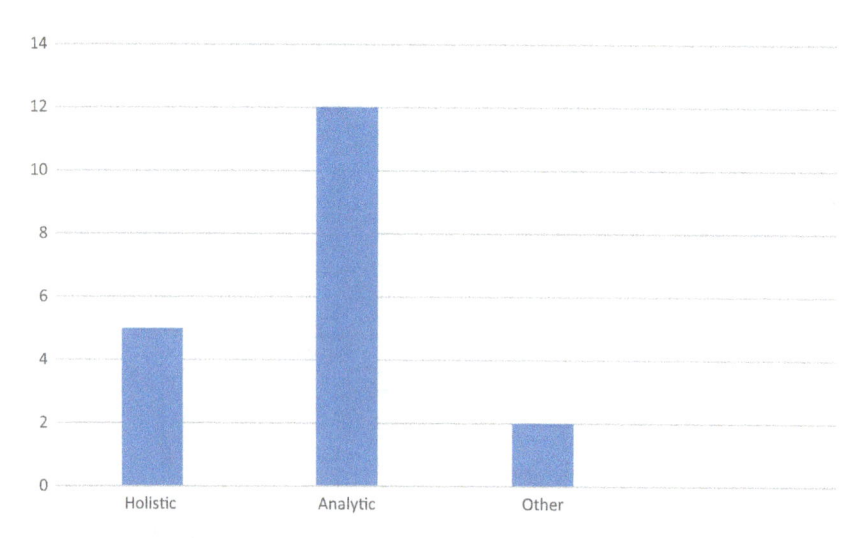

Chart 2 Preferred method of giving feedback

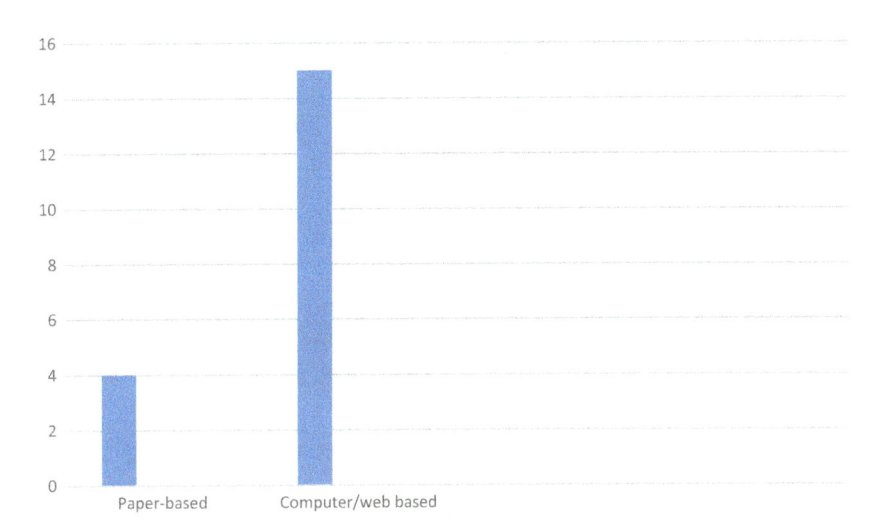

Chart 3 Preferred medium of giving feedback and grading

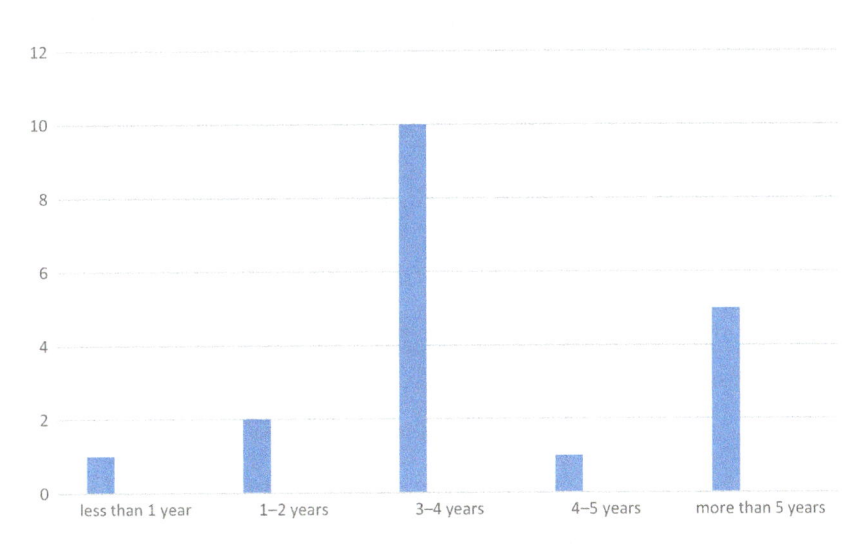

Chart 4 Years of experience in using e-rubrics for writing assessment

Appendix 4: Faculty Interview Questions

1. How long have you been using e-rubrics? What was your way of proving feedback and grading student writing before starting to use e-rubrics?
2. Has it been challenging to change your method (analytic, holistic, or any other method used by the interviewee) and/or medium (from paper-based to web-based) of providing feedback and grading student writing?
3. Having gone through this transition process, is there anything that could be done to make the transition process more hassle-free for professors?
4. What do you think about advantages, challenges, and drawbacks associated with using e-rubrics?
5. Given the freedom to choose your own writing assessment method, what would you do differently in assessing and proving feedback to student writing?
6. What do you think about the impact of using common e-rubrics on the development of students' writing skills?
7. Is there anything you would like to add?

Appendix 5: Topics, Codes, and Categories Identified in the Data

Topics, codes, and categories identified in the data		
Topic	Code	Categories
Challenges	C	1. Restrictions
		2. Technical difficulties
Benefits	B	1. Time and energy saved on grading
		2. Record keeping
		3. Objective and transparent assessment
Perceived impact of e-rubrics on students	PI	1. Ease of access to and better understanding of grades and feedback
		2. Better understanding of the assignment objectives
		3. Reservations about the role of e-rubrics in learning

Appendix 6: Themes

Table 9.3 Challenges

Theme	Quote
Restrictions	'They [the e-rubrics] are too vague; I'd prefer using my own rubrics that are more tailored to individual assignments and provide more feedback'
Technical difficulties	'Online rubrics are cumbersome. Unless one is using a huge screen computer the endeavour is painful'

Table 9.4 Benefits

Theme	Quote
Record keeping	'The grades go directly to i-learn and this is a very efficient form of record keeping than using traditional papers'
Time and energy saved on grading	'They save time and energy'
Objective and transparent assessment	'Rubrics allow me to grade student work as objectively as possible. They also make it easier for students to understand what they have done well and what areas they still need to work on'

Table 9.5 Perceived impact of e-rubrics on students

Theme	Quote
Better understanding of the assignment objectives	'Good guidelines to follow, explaining the grading criteria to the students and the grade when they are finished'
Ease of access to and better understanding of grades and feedback	'Students usually aren't able to understand my handwriting and after getting into this system a positive I see is that students can understand what I'm trying to say with the comments'
Reservations about the role of e-rubrics in learning	'I don't think it's relevant what kind of method we use to let students know how they did and give feedback. What's relevant to their writing is the message they are getting from us and not how they get it'

References

Angulo, J., & La Serna, M. C. (2011). Study of the impact on student learning using the E-rubric tool and peer assessment. In A. Méndez-Vilas (Ed.), *Education in a technological world: Communicating current and emerging research and technological efforts* (pp. 421–427). Badajoz, Spain: Formatex Research Center.

Balester, V. (2012). How writing rubrics fail: Toward a multicultural model. In M. Poe & A. Inoue (Eds.), *Race and writing assessment* (pp. 63–77). New York: Lang.

Black, P., & Wiliam, D. (2009). Developing the theory of formative assessment. *Educational Assessment Evaluation and Accountability, 21*, 5–31.

Broad, B. (2003). *What we really value: Beyond rubrics in teaching and assessing writing*. Logan: Utah State University Press.

Brown, J. (2001). *Using surveys in language programs*. Cambridge: Cambridge University Press.

Chapman, V., & Inman, M. (2009). A Conundrum: Rubrics or creativity/metacognitive development? *Educational Horizons, 87*(3), 198–202. Retrieved from http://www.jstor.org/stable/42923766

Cohen, L., Manion, L., & Morrison, K. (2011). *Research methods in education*. London: Routledge.

Connors, R. (1997). *Composition-rhetoric: Backgrounds, theory and pedagogy*. Pittsburgh: University of Pittsburgh Press.

Cooper, B., & Gargan, A. (2009). Rubrics in education: Old term, new meanings. *The Phi Delta Kappan, 91*(1), 54–55. Retrieved from http://www.jstor.org/stable/40344878

Creswell, J. W. (2007). *Qualitative inquiry and research design: Choosing among five approaches* (2nd ed.). London: Sage.

Crusan, D. (2010). *Assessment in the second language writing classroom*. Ann Arbor MI: University of Michigan Press.

Crusan, D. (2015). Dance, ten; looks, three: Why rubrics matter. *Assessing Writing, 26*, 1–4.

Czaplewski, A. (2009). Computer-assisted grading rubrics: Automating the process of providing comments and student feedback. *Marketing Education Review, 19*, 29–36. Retrieved from http://www.iddblog.org/wp-content/uploads/2016/02/autograding-with-excel.pdf

Davies, A. (2007). Assessing academic English testing English proficiency 1950–89: The IELTS solution. *Cambridge.org*. Retrieved from http://www.cambridge.org/download_file/591108/0/

DePaul University Teaching Commons. (n.d.). *Resources.depul.edu*. Retrieved from http://resources.depaul.edu/teaching-commons/teaching-guides/feedback grading/rubrics/Pages/types-of-rubrics.aspx

De Silva, R. (2014). Rubrics for assessment: Their effects on ESL students' authentic task performance. Retrieved from http://www.nus.edu.sg/celc/research/books/4th%20Symposium%20proceedings/19).%20Radhikda%20De%20Silva.pdf

El Ebyary, K. (2013). Profiling formative assessment culture in EFL teacher education programs in the Middle East. *Theory and Practice in Language Studies, 3*(12), 2169–2177. https://doi.org/10.4304/tpls.3.12.2169-2177

Fast Facts. (2017). Retrieved from https://www.aus.edu/info/200129/why_aus/434/fast_fact

Ferris, D. R., & Hedgcock, J. S. (2014). *Teaching L2 composition. Purpose, process, and practice.* New York: Routledge.

Gallagher, K. (2011). Bilingual education in the UAE: Factors, variables and critical questions. *Education, Business and Society: Contemporary Middle Eastern Issues, 4*(1), 62–79. https://doi.org/10.1108/17537981111111274

Hamp-Lyons, L. (2013). The challenge of classroom-based assessment. Retrieved from https://www.scribd.com/document/196526835/

Jonsson, A., & Svingby, G. (2007). The use of scoring rubrics: Reliability, validity and educational consequences. *Educational Research Review, 2*(2), 130–144. https://doi.org/10.1016/j.edurev.2007.05.002

Kohn, A. (2006). Speaking my mind: The trouble with rubrics. *The English Journal, 95*(4), 12–15. Retrieved from http://www.jstor.org/stable/30047080

Leggette, H. R., McKim, B. R., & Dunsford, D. (2013). A case study of using electronic self-assessment rubrics in a core curriculum writing course. *NACTA Journal, 57*(2), 2–10.

Li, J., & Lindsey, P. (2015). Understanding variations between student and teacher application of rubrics. *Assessing Writing, 26,* 67–79.

Mabry, L. (1999). Writing to the rubric: Lingering effects of traditional standardized testing on direct writing assessment. *The Phi Delta Kappan, 80*(9), 673–679. Retrieved from http://www.jstor.org/stable/20439535

Mertler, C. A. (2009). *Action research: Teachers as researchers in the classroom* (2nd ed.). Los Angles: Sage.

Nahyan: English to stay as medium of instruction in varsities. (2009, November 22). *Gulf News*. Retrieved from http://gulfnews.com/news/gulf/uae/education/nahyan-english-to-stay-as-medium-of-instruction-in-varsities-1.530758

Normand-Marconnet, N. (2012). Is self-assessment a pedagogical challenge in an Islamic context? A case study of Iranian students learning French. *International Journal of Pedagogies and Learning, 7*(3), 200–210. https://doi.org/10.5172/ijpl.2012.7.3.200

Pagano, N., Bernhardt, S., Reynolds, D., Williams, M., & McCurrie, M. (2008). An inter-institutional model for college writing assessment. *College Composition and Communication, 60*(2), 285–320.

Panadero, E., & Jonsson, A. (2013). The use of scoring rubrics for formative assessment purposes revisited: A review. *Educational Research Review, 9*, 129–144.

Phillips, E. (1658). *The new world of English words: Or, a general dictionary*. London: Taylor.

Punch, F. K. (2009). *Introduction to research methods in education*. London: Sage.

Purcell, K., Buchanan, J., & Friedrich, L. (2013). The impact of digital tools on student writing and how writing is taught in schools. *Pew Research Center: Internet, Science & Tech*. Retrieved from http://www.pewinternet.org/2013/07/16/the-impact-of-digital-tools-on-student-writing-and-how-writing-is-taught-in-schools/

Radnor, H. (2002). *Researching your professional practice: Doing interpretive research*. Buckingham: Open University Press.

Randall, M., & Samimi, M. (2010). The status of English in Dubai. *English Today, 26*, 43–50. https://doi.org/10.1017/S0266078409990617

Reddy, Y. M., & Andrade, H. (2010). A review of rubric use in higher education. *Assessment and Evaluation in Higher Education, 35*(4), 435.

Reynolds, D. (2010). Writing assessment across the curriculum. *Marifa.hct.ac.ae*. Retrieved from http://marifa.hct.ac.ae/2010/104

Richards, K. (2003). *Qualitative enquiry in TESOL*. Basingstoke: Palgrave Macmillan.

Schreiber, J., & Asner-Self, K. (2011). *Educational research: The interrelationship of questions, sampling, design, and analysis*. Hoboken, NJ: Wiley.

Silverman, D. (2000). *Doing qualitative research: A practical handbook*. London: Sage.

Troudi, S., Coombe, C., & Al-Hamliy, M. (2009). EFL teachers' views of English language assessment in higher education in the United Arab Emirates and Kuwait. *TESOL Quarterly: A Journal for Teachers of English to Speakers of Other Languages and of Standard English as a Second Dialect, 43*(3), 546–555. Retrieved from http://www.jstor.org/stable/27785037

Troudi, S., & Jendli, A. (2011). Emirati students' experiences of English as a medium of instruction. In A. Issa & L. Dahan (Eds.), *Global English and Arabic: Issues of language, culture, and identity* (pp. 23–48). Oxford: Peter Lang.

Turley, E. D., & Gallagher, C. W. (2008). On the uses of rubrics: Reframing the great rubric debate. *English Journal, 97*(4), 87–92.

U-M LSA English Language Institute. (n.d.). *Lsa.umich.edu*. Retrieved from http://lsa.umich.edu/eli/about-us

Weigle, S. C. (2002). *Assessing writing*. Cambridge, UK: Cambridge University Press.

Weigle, S. C. (2007). Teaching writing teachers about assessment. *Journal of Second Language Writing, 16*, 194–209.

Wiliam, D. (2011). What is assessment for learning? *Studies in Educational Evaluation, 37*, 2–14.

Wilson, M. (2006). *Rethinking rubrics in writing assessment*. Portsmouth, NH: Heinemann.

Wolf, K., & Stevens, E. (2007). The role of rubrics in advancing and assessing student learning. *The Journal of Effective Teaching, 7*(1), 3–14.

Writing@CSU. (n.d.). *Writing.colostate.edu*. Retrieved from http://writing.colostate.edu/guides/teaching/commenting/holistic.cfm

Yancey, K. (1999). Looking back as we look forward: Historicizing writing assessment. *College Composition and Communication, 50*(3), 483–503. Retrieved from http://www.jstor.org/stable/358862 doi:1

Rana Raddawi is Associate Professor, at the American University of Sharjah. She teaches in the Master TESOL Programme in the Department of English in addition to intercultural communication, English for Specific Purposes (ESP), curriculum development, and Advanced Academic Writing as undergraduate courses. She has supervised a number of Masters and Ph.D. theses. She masters five languages, English, Arabic, French, Portuguese, and Turkish. She has many publications and translations in her areas of expertise. She is the editor of the book *Intercultural Communication with Arabs (2015)*. Her research interests relate to Cross-Cultural Studies, TESOL, Critical Pedagogy, and Emotional Intelligence. She was a keynote speaker at several international conferences in the USA and the Middle East.

Neslihan Bilikozen is an assistant professor in the Department of Writing Studies at American University of Sharjah, UAE. She has received her doctorate from the University of Exeter, UK. Her current research interests include L2 writing assessment, acquisition of L2 academic literacy, language and identity, critical issues in L2 writing, and technology use in education.

10

EFL Writing Assessment and Evaluation Rubrics in Yemen

Thikra K. Ghalib

Introduction

'Good writing' is a growing pedagogic demand. In educational settings, such as in undergraduate contexts where I have learned and taught, writing is the basis upon which a candidate's achievement, learning, and intelligence are judged. Good writing skills are critical to academic and professional success—they can lead to good grades, admission into college, successful completion of college, and a good profession.

Consequently, and expectedly, testing for writing ability is becoming a very pressing demand. The writing ability is tested for such purposes as awarding grades, certifying proficiency, testing suitability for a particular profession, placing candidates in the appropriate component of a language programme, and allowing candidates to exit programmes. While the stakes are not high for some of these purposes, they are very high for others—they have important consequences that significantly impact the test taker's life.

T. K. Ghalib (✉)
Taiz University, Taiz, Yemen

Qassim University, Buraydah, Saudi Arabia

© The Author(s) 2018
A. Ahmed, H. Abouabdelkader (eds.), *Assessing EFL Writing in the 21st Century Arab World*, https://doi.org/10.1007/978-3-319-64104-1_10

The measurement of the writing ability is impacted by four factors, namely, the student, the scoring method, the test administration, and the test itself (Mousavi, 2002). While all of the other three factors are equally significant, the most relevant to the concerns of the present chapter is the scoring method—the method selected by the rater to pass judgements about the writing ability. The literature on language testing includes numerous attempts to introduce methods of scoring (e.g., Hamp-Lyons, 1991; Shohamy, 1995) and other attempts to improve the accuracy and consistency of these methods (Brown, 1996; McNamara, 1996; Wiseman, 2012). The decisions about writing competence that are derived from one scoring method do not always, and do not necessarily, comply with decisions from another scoring method. These scoring systems are very important because they are used to classify test-takers and, accordingly, make high-stakes decisions that define the course of their lives.

Moving down to our research context, the success of undergraduate students of English at Taiz University in Yemen is also largely dependent on their ability to write. The programme is eight semesters long, comprising 52 courses among which 45 are in English language and literature. Each of the 45 English courses involves a mid-term test and a final examination—a total of 90 achievement tests overall. Passing these achievement tests and exiting the programme rests mainly on the students' writing ability. The improvement of the ability to write in English is, therefore, one of the objectives of the programme of instruction.

Informal interviews with the teaching staff of the department and an examination of a random sample of mid-term and final examination answer sheets suggest that a general impression-marking scheme is the norm. The criteria for evaluation, according to the teacher-raters, are the relevance and coverage of content and grammatical correctness. Test takers who address all the points adequately are rewarded and those who do not are penalised. No clear descriptors exist for awarding marks to intermediate levels of writing proficiency, except a general impression. The descriptors are not explicitly stated; they are neither clear to the teacher-rater nor known to the test takers. The result is impressionistic judgements of writing proficiency that depend more upon the rater than upon text qualities and that fail to make valid distinctions between test takers across a continuum of writing proficiency.

In light of these considerations, it becomes of paramount importance to improve consistency across evaluator's judgements about writing proficiency and to improve the reliability and validity of these judgements to avoid bias and produce a greater agreement between raters about test taker's achievement. An important move towards achieving this objective is using scoring rubrics. Different kinds of rubrics have been in use since at least the 1960s and have received much scholarly attention. This chapter focuses on the major types of rubrics to measure writing proficiency, considers the uses of each scoring rubric, and outlines the theoretical and practical advantages and disadvantages of each.

Literature Review

A rubric is a tool for evaluating the quality of student work on a continuum of performances from excellent to poor (Schafer, 2004). It contains a set of well-established criteria corresponding to a scale of possible points to be assigned in scoring a piece of work, spoken or written (Campbell, Melenyzer, Nettles, & Wyman, 2000). The highest point goes to the best performance and the lowest to the worst one. A scoring rubric provides descriptors for the different levels of proficiency on the scale. These descriptors are detailed enough to enable fine judgements and rich to enable reliable, unbiased, and valid discrimination.

Herman, Aschbacher, and Winters (1992) posited four characteristic features of a rubric—criteria, standards, scale, and examples. An effective rubric has a well-defined list of criteria for the test-takers to know what is expected from them and for the raters to be able to properly evaluate the responses. Second, an effective rubric contains standards of excellence for the different levels of performance. Third, an effective rubric has gradations of quality, or a scale, based on the degree to which the standard has been met. The gradations are constituted by detailed descriptions that represent what should earn which point on the scale. Last, but not least, an effective rubric contains model exemplars of expected performance at the different levels on the scale.

Another important characteristic of a rubric—one that is well attested in the literature though not mentioned in the previous list, is reliability.

An effective rubric is one that is used by different raters on a given assessment task and generates similar judgements/scores. Consistency across raters' judgement about the relative standing of performance ratings is referred to as 'inter-rater reliability', and the frequency of two or more raters assigning the same rating to a particular performance is known as 'inter-rater agreement'. While these two forms of reliability estimators are frequently employed in research contexts, the inter-rater agreement is more relevant to the present research context where decisions about passing examinations, exit programmes, and even about tenure are made based on a score threshold. In Yemen, for example, a student receiving 47 marks fails the test whereas a student receiving 48 is pushed to the cut-off score and passes the test.

Weigle (2002) argued that three types of rubrics are used in the evaluation of written proficiency: primary trait, holistic and analytic scoring rubrics. These three types differ in their impact, discriminatory power, inter-rater reliability, the degree of bias, and the cost-effectiveness—in terms of time, effort, and money (Kuo, 2007). The choice of one scoring rubric or the other is significant because it 'represents, implicitly or explicitly, the theoretical basis upon which [a] test is founded' (Weigle, 2002, p. 109). Some studies that have used holistic scoring rubrics, analytic scoring rubrics, and studies that have compared both types of rubrics are reviewed below.

Holistic scoring is 'a global approach' to scoring that is underscored by the idea that 'writing is a single entity which is best captured by a single scale that integrates the inherent qualities of the writing' (Wiseman, 2012, p. 59). As such, holistic scoring considers the entire written response and assigns an overall score to the performance (Hyland, 2002; Weigle, 2002; White, 1985). This cost-effectiveness of holistic scoring makes it a suitable approach for large-scale assessment of written performance, especially for decisions concerning placement (Cumming, 1990; Hamp-Lyons, 1990; Reid, 1993).

Holistic scoring criteria consist of general guidelines that define good performance at each score point. This has prompted some researchers (e.g., Cohen, 1994; White, 1985) to argue that holistic scoring focuses on the strengths of the writing rather than on the deficiencies. The holistic rubric generates a composite score that 'does not provide specific evidence of where and how much additional writing instruction is needed' (Becker, 2011, 116). Despite this shortcoming, if indeed it is, Weigle (2002) argues that holistic scoring rubrics are very practical. They are short, lacking detailed criteria of evaluation, and make the evaluation of an essay possible by assigning one score to it after only one reading—thus serving the economic interests of university departments and employers. Holistic rubrics are therefore typical for evaluating written performance in large-scale assessment contexts. This has made holistic scoring the method of assessing written performance in the computer-based Test of English as a Foreign Language (TOEFL), Graduate Record Examination (GRE), and Graduate Management Admission Test (GMAT).

Diederich (1964) was one of the earliest studies to make use of holistic scoring rubrics in such large-scale testing situations. Three hundred written performances were evaluated by 53 raters, and the study concluded that the variation in the ratings is mostly attributable to three criteria—ideas, language, and organisation. Twenty years later, Breland and Jones (1984) analysed 800 written samples and also attributed the variations of raters to ideas, organisation, and use of supporting materials. Other studies have examined the issues of the validity of holistic scoring (Charney, 1984), inter-rater reliability (Erickson, 2001), the consistency of agreement among raters (Huot, 1990; Legg, 1998), the importance of rater training for achieving internal consistency and normative rating behaviour (Kim, 2010; Kondo-Brown, 2002), the difference in the ratings of native and non-native English speaking raters in China (Shi, 2001), and alternative methods of evaluating writing performance (Reid, 1993).

As an alternative, analytic scoring, which involves 'the separation of the various features of a composition into components for scoring purposes', has also received considerable scholarly attention (Wiseman, 2012, p. 60). An analytic scoring rubric typically includes writing components relating to the test-taker's lexical, syntactic, discourse, and rhetorical competence. As such, an analytic scoring rubric offers more detailed information about a test taker's writing performance than does the single score of a holistic scoring rubric. An analytic rubric provides orderly and comprehensive feedback to teachers and assists them to distinguish between the weak and strong aspects in students' writing performance (Crehan, 1997; Hamp-Lyons, 1995). In other words, an analytic rubric has higher discriminating power (Mendelsohn & Cumming, 1987).

The first analytic scoring rubric was the ESL Composition Profile (Jacobs, Zingraf, Wormuth, Hartfiel, & Hughey, 1981). It was used to measure the writing performance of ESL students at North American universities and consisted of five different rating dimensions of writing quality, each having a different weight: content (30 points), organisation (20 points), vocabulary (20 points), language use (25 points), and mechanics (5 points). Other well-known examples of analytic scales are the Test in English for Educational Purposes (TEEP; Weir, 1990) and the Michigan Writing Assessment Scoring Guide (Hamp-Lyons, 1991). But of all the existing rating scales for examining written performance (see Shohamy, 1995), the present study indeed adapts Bachman and Palmer's (1996) model of communicative language ability.

A distinguishing feature of the Bachman and Palmer (1996) model is that it extends the factors that influence performance on a test to non-linguistic elements such as 'affective schema, metacognitive strategies in approaching the test task, and topical knowledge beyond the level of language'. Brindley (2001) comments on Bachman and Palmer's (1996) inclusion of personality and background knowledge as parts of communicative ability as 'an important development since it recognises the key role that personal characteristics may play in language performance and opens the way for the development of assessment procedures which attempts to build such factors into the assessment situation' (p. 142). Other important features of the model include the framework of test task characteristics, which 'provides a means for systematically describing various characteristics of tests and testing procedures. It is primarily intended as a tool for designing and constructing language tests' (p. 269). The model also introduces the concept of 'test usefulness'. In Bachman and Palmer's words, the 'most important consideration in designing and developing a language test is the use for which it is intended so that the most important quality of a test is its usefulness' (p. 17). To achieve test usefulness, Bachman and Palmer propose six qualities, namely, construct validity, reliability, authenticity, interactiveness, impact, and practicality.

Bachman and Palmer also argue that test developers need to find an appropriate balance among these qualities. This balance will vary from one testing situation to another because what constitutes an appropriate balance can be determined only by considering the different qualities in combination as they affect the overall usefulness of a particular test.

The ability to write an essay requires knowledge schemata (knowledge of the topic), strategic competence (strategies for content development), rhetorical knowledge (strategies for producing cohesive supporting arguments), grammatical competence, and knowledge of vocabulary and register. This is the knowledge that defines L2 writing ability in Bachman and Palmer's approach and the knowledge that informs their analytic scoring rubric.

But which scoring rubric, holistic or analytic, do practitioners prefer? Some studies have compared the behaviour of holistic and analytic rubrics resulting in interesting findings. Chi (2001) compares holistic and analytic scoring rubrics, using many-faceted Rasch measurement, in terms of the appropriateness of the scoring rubrics, the agreement of the student scores, and the consistency of rater's severity. The study reports significant differences between raters using holistic scoring rubrics, but not analytic scoring rubrics. Other studies confirm this advantage of analytic scoring in terms of inter-rater and intra-rater reliability (Al-Fallay, 2000; East & Young, 2007; Knoch, 2009; Nakamura, 2004). Analytic scoring also provides an individualised profile of the test-taker's written performance (Weigle, 2002) and direct, useful feedback to students and teachers (Brown & Hudson, 2002). For this reason, analytic scoring rubrics are often chosen for placement and diagnostic purposes (Hamp-Lyons, 1991; Jacobs et al., 1981; Perkins, 1983).

By contrast, holistic scoring rubrics offer the advantage of reduced time and money costs (Wiseman, 2012). Bauer (1981) compared the cost-effectiveness of analytic and holistic scoring rubrics in scoring secondary school students' essays. The study reports that the time needed to train the raters to use the analytic rubrics was double the time needed to train raters to use the holistic rubrics, and the time needed to grade the essays using the analytic rubrics was four times longer than the time needed to grade the essays using the holistic rubrics. Other studies in different contexts reported similar findings (Arter, 1993; Bainer & Porter, 1992; Klein et al., 1998). For this reason, holistic scoring is the preferred method of scoring in large-scale testing contexts that involve a large concentration of test-takers taking the test at the same time (Becker, 2011).

The choice of one type or rubric or the other, therefore, depends mainly on the purpose of using the rubric and is driven by context-specific considerations. The present study is an extension of this tradition of examining the performance of holistic and analytic scoring rubrics. The study used different psychometric statistics (inter-rater agreement, intra-class correlation, t-test and ANOVA) to compare the holistic and analytic scoring rubrics as reliable instruments for evaluating EFL writing for achievement purposes. The authors of this study tried to find answers to the following questions:

1. Is there a significant difference between holistic and analytical rubrics in enhancing the reliability of scoring?
2. Is there a correlation between each rater's assessment of the same essay using holistic and analytic rubrics?
3. Is there a correlation between different raters' assessment of the same essay using holistic rubrics?
4. Does the use of rubrics enhance the consistency of scoring?

Methods

Participants

The participants of the study consisted of 30 (15 male and 15 female) Yemeni undergraduate students of English at the Faculty of Arts, Taiz University. They were aged between 21 and 25 and were all non-native speakers of English attending the three-credit, 14-week senior-level course Advanced Writing Skills. The course is offered in the penultimate semester of the eight-semester Bachelor Programme in English Language and Literature. The researcher chose the participants by their overall GPA in the first three years of college. The participants in this study were the top 30 students in the six semesters leading to the year 2014-2015. They were senior students at the English department. They took a class on advanced writing skills and have reached a level of competence that should enable them to write an essay.

Raters

The raters of the writing task consisted of three experienced teaching staff of the same department. They were selected based on their similarity in terms of qualifications, years of experience in teaching, and years of experience in scoring high-stakes tests. The three raters all had a doctoral degree in English with at least five years of teaching experience in the same department. They also had taught different writing courses at the department and had marked at least three rounds of the annual large-scale English admission tests administered by the department.

The raters were invited to a two-hour training session conducted by the researchers. The training, which eventually aimed at improving rating accuracy and rater agreement, involved an explanation of the rating system, a discussion of common rating problems, and advice on avoiding bias.

Scripts and the Writing Task

The scripts consisted of essays written by the 30 participants in response to an independent, timed writing task. The students were given 25 minutes to write the task and 5 minutes to proofread and revise it, a total of 30 minutes. This is the average time students in the programme take to write essays on final examinations. The task prompt to the essay was as follows:

> Reflecting on your own first day in college, write a descriptive essay of about 250 words in response to the following question: *What was your first day in college like? How did you feel like a newcomer? What did you do?*

Rating Rubrics

The study employed two rubrics—a holistic rubric and an analytic rubric. The holistic rubric is a six-point scale that offers a general description at each point for typical writing performance at that point (see Appendix 1). It emulates the rubric used by teachers of the department for assessing students' performance on written tasks. In fact, it was constructed by the researchers after informal interviews with the teachers about the criteria they use for evaluating written work. The suggested rubric, therefore, comprises two performance criteria—understanding of the topic and correctness of language.

The analytic rubric, on the other hand, is an adapted version of Bachman and Palmer (1996). The researchers contributed a fifth sub-domain to Bachman and Palmer's criterion-referenced rating scale for the assessment of writing ability. This addition was driven by context-specific considerations. The end product is a five-point scale with five sub-domains of writing ability: content, cohesion, syntactic structures, vocabulary, and mechanics of writing. Within each domain, there are several well-defined standards of performance points that each rater understands (see Appendix 2).

Rating Procedures

Each rater worked independently and in two separate sessions. In the first session, the raters were given the 30 (anonymous) writing samples and a copy of the holistic rubric. The raters were instructed to assign a single 'holistic' score to each essay from 0 to 5. The scores were then converted into 20 and the total score written next to the number assigned to each participant. The scored writing samples and the rubrics were returned to the researchers in three days. The second session took place a month later to allow a gap long enough to ensure a more independent judgement. In this session, the raters were given the same 30 (also anonymous) writing samples and a copy of the analytic rubric. They were instructed to assign a score from 0 (zero knowledge) to 4 (complete knowledge) for each sub-domain of writing proficiency and then add the scores and convert them into a total of 20. The scored writing samples and the rating rubrics were returned to the researchers in a week.

Results

Some statistical procedures were employed to answer the study research questions. First, the descriptive statistics of the students' scores using the holistic and analytic rubrics were calculated. This was followed by the descriptive statistics of each rater's assessment of the writing sample using both rubrics. A *t*-test was used to measure the significant difference (if any) between the means of the two scoring rubrics, and analysis of variance was conducted to measure the significant differences (if any) among the three raters' scoring decisions for each of the two scoring rubrics. In addition, to investigate the agreement among the three raters and measure the inter-rater reliability, an intra-class correlation coefficient test was implemented. The findings of this study are discussed below.

The results showed that the mean score using the holistic rubric was 14.67 with a standard deviation of 3.12. Using the analytical rubric to assess students' performance yielded a mean of 13.72 and a standard deviation of 2.82.

Descriptive statistics for each of the three raters within each of the two rubrics are presented below.

A *t*-test was performed to examine the significant difference (if any) between the means of the two scoring rubrics, holistic and analytic. The results showed that the difference was significant between the two rubrics, $t_{(178)} = 2.132$, $p < 0.05$. Using the analytical rubric proved to be more rigorous (M = 13.72, SD = 2.821) than using the holistic approach of scoring (M = 14.67, SD = 3.116).

Assessment should be independent of who does the scoring and the results are supposed to be similar. The more consistent the scores are over different raters, the more reliable the assessment is. Analysis of variance was used to investigate significant differences (if any) among the three raters for each of the rubric method. The findings showed no significant difference, $F_{(2, 87)} = 0.373$, $p = 0.690$, among the three raters when they used an analytical rubric to grade students' performance. However, the raters' scorings did significantly differ, $F_{(2, 87)} = 4.833$, $p < 0.05$ when they used a holistic rubric. Post hoc analysis was run to find where the differences lay. The results showed that the difference was between rater 2 and rater 3 at $p < 0.05$.

Checking the correlation between the two scoring methods is worth investigating. If the correlation is high, this means that the two scoring methods may produce similar results. The results here indicated that there was a highly significant correlation, $r = 0.80$. Nevertheless, a correlation in this context should be more than 0.90.

Studies in the literature indicated that rubrics seem to aid raters in achieving high internal consistency when scoring performance tasks. The intra-class correlation coefficient was used to measure intra-rater reliability; the average measures equal the reliability across the raters. For the holistic rubric, the average measure of the ICC was 0.797 with a 95% confidence interval from 0.567 to 0.904 ($F_{(29, 58)} = 6.627$, $p < 0.001$). Whereas for the analytical rubric, the average measure of the ICC was 0.958 with a 95% confidence interval from 0.921 to 0.979 ($F_{(29, 58)} = 25.364$, $p < 0.001$). Overall, a high degree of reliability was found for the internal consistency. The average measure of the ICC was 0.879 with a 95% confidence interval from 0.788 to 0.930 ($F_{(59, 118)} = 10.104$, $p < 0.001$).

Cohen's kappa was also used to estimate the degree of agreement among the raters. The results for each pair of the three raters and overall across the two scoring rubrics are presented in Tables 10.1, 10.2, and 10.3.

Table 10.1 Descriptive statistics for each of the scoring rubrics ($N = 90$)

Rubrics	Minimum	Maximum	Mean	Std. deviation
Holistic	8	20	14.67	3.116
Analytical	6	19	13.72	2.821

Table 10.2 Descriptive statistics for each of the three raters within each of the two rubrics ($N = 30$)

Rubrics	Raters	Minimum	Maximum	Mean	Std. deviation
Holistic	Rater #1	8	20	14.67	3.536
	Rater #2	12	20	15.87	2.675
	Rater #3	8	16	13.47	2.675
Analytical	Rater #1	6	18	13.73	3.162
	Rater #2	9	19	14.03	2.606
	Rater #3	6	18	13.40	2.724

Table 10.3 Descriptive statistics for each pair of the three raters and the overall across the two scoring rubrics ($N = 30$)

	Pair 1 and 2	Pair 1 and 3	Pair 2 and 3	Total reliability
Overall	0.51	0.25	0.09	0.28
Holistic	0.49	0.14	−0.05	0.23
Analytic	0.42	0.18	0.04	0.21

Discussion

Assessment of students' performance needs to be as accurate as possible because it may have consequences for the candidates (Black, 1998). Some sources of variability exist in any assessment, one of which is raters' judgements of students' performance (Black, 1998). This was the focus of this study.

The difference between holistic and analytical rubrics in enhancing the reliability of scoring was investigated, and the results of this study showed a significant difference between the means of the two scoring rubrics, holistic and analytic. It was found that when raters use an analytical scoring rubric, they give lower scores than when using a holistic scoring rubric. Such findings make sense because analytical rubrics have many details and scoring them is more rigorous. Studies in the literature indicated that analytical scoring rubrics are often used for diagnostic purposes because of their rigour (Hamp-Lyons, 1991; Jacobs et al., 1981; Perkins, 1983).

The correlation between the two scoring methods was also computed using the intra-class correlation coefficient. The results indicated a highly significant correlation. However, this does not necessarily suggest an agreement among the raters; another analysis was conducted below. The correlation between the two scoring methods was 0.80, which is deemed acceptable (Stemler, 2004).

The students' scores are supposed to be similar regardless of who does the scoring. The more consistent the scores are over different raters, the more reliable the assessment (Moskal & Leydens, 2000). The analysis of variance (ANOVA) showed no significant differences among the three raters when they used an analytical rubric to grade students' performance. However, the raters' scorings did significantly differ when they used a holistic rubric. These findings are consistent with Chi's (2001) findings of the significant differences between raters using holistic and analytical scoring rubrics. The findings in this study suggest that using analytical rubrics produces more consistent and reliable results.

Variations in raters' judgements can occur either across raters, known as inter-rater reliability, or in the consistency of one single rater, called intra-rater reliability. Intra-class correlation was performed to measure inter-rater reliability and the consistency of the raters in measuring the students' performance. The intra-class correlation coefficient was above 0.80 indicating that the results are consistent. The majority of studies investigating intra-rater reliability reported alpha values above 0.70, which, according to Brown, Glasswell, and Harland (2004), is considered sufficient.

An inter-rater agreement refers to the extent to which independent raters provide the same rating of a particular person. Cohen's kappa was used to estimate the degree to which consensus agreement ratings vary from the rate expected by chance. The results of the study showed that the correlation between two raters appeared to be high, and the correlation between two other raters appeared to be low. Kappa values between 0.40 and 0.75 represent fair agreement beyond chance (Stoddart, Abrams, Gasper, & Canaday, 2000).

Conclusion

Teachers use rubrics to evaluate students' performance on specific tasks. A rubric is a scoring scale used to assess students' performance along with a task-specific set of well-defined criteria. Some benefits were discussed for using rubrics as a tool to evaluate students on performance tasks. The use of rubrics can (1) increase the consistency of judgement when assessing performance tasks, (2) provide a valid judgement of performance assessment that cannot be achieved by not using the rubric, (3) give positive educational consequences, such as promoting learning and/or improve instruction, and (4) provide students with quality feedback (Archbald & Newmann, 1988; Jonsson & Svingby, 2007).

Having explored the differences between the widely used scoring systems for wiring ability, and having underscored the importance of implementing rubrics for better diagnosis of writing problems and for more reliable scoring, the present study focuses on two kinds of rubrics, holistic and analytic rubrics, and examines the performance of these two rubrics in assessing writing ability. Specifically, the study compares Yemeni EFL students' scores on a writing task using holistic and analytic scoring rubrics.

This study analysed different psychometric statistics to compare the holistic and analytic scoring rubrics as reliable instruments for evaluating EFL writing for achievement purposes. The results showed that using rubrics yields more accurate scores than not using them; this was also clearly stated in the literature. However, it was concluded that analytical scoring provides even more consistent scores than using holistic scoring methods. Analytical scoring seems to be very useful in the classroom because the results can help both the teachers and learners identify students' strengths and weaknesses as well as their learning needs. Educators need to accept that the use of rubrics adds to the quality of the assessment.

In summary, scoring with rubrics seems to be more reliable. Rubrics ought to be encouraged as a regulatory device for scoring. The results of this study showed that using a holistic rubric can give reliable scores and using an analytic rubric gives even more reliable scores. The consistency of scoring can be enhanced by being analytic and topic-specific and providing rater training.

Limitations

The main aim of this chapter was to measure the consistency of scoring across raters' judgement using different correlation coefficients using the Many-Facets Rasch Model (MFRM). However, due to the small sample size, MFRM was not used in this study. MFRM is a multivariate extension of Rasch measurement models that can be used to provide a framework for calibrating both raters and writing tasks within the context of writing assessment. Another limitation is that the study was conducted in one institution and used a convenience sample. Therefore, the researcher recommends using a larger random sample of students from multiple institutions for future research.

Appendix 1: Holistic Rubric

5. Provides a complete response to the prompt; demonstrates complete understanding of the topic; exhibits a strong command of essay writing skills; presents the argument in flawless English
4. Provides a fairly complete response to the prompt; demonstrates considerable understanding of the topic; exhibits good knowledge of essay writing skills; presents the argument in very good English with a few errors
3. Provides a satisfactory response to the prompt; demonstrates partial understanding of the topic; exhibits a limited command of essay writing skills; presents the argument in good English with many errors
2. Provides a poor response to the prompt; demonstrates little understanding of the topic; exhibits little command of essay writing skills; presents the argument in poor English with too many errors
1. Provides no poor response to the prompt; demonstrates no understanding of the topic; exhibits no command of essay writing skills; presents the argument in barely comprehensible English
0. No response

Appendix 2: Analytical Rubric

Rating	CONTENT	Rating	COHESION	Rating	SYNTACTIC STRUCTURES	Rating	VOCABULARY	Rating	MECHANICS OF WRITING
0 Zero Knowledge	Range: inadequate to produce even the simplest organized text Accuracy: not relevant	0 Zero Knowledge	Range: no evidence of knowledge of cohesive relationships Accuracy: not relevant	0 Zero Knowledge	Range: no evidence of knowledge of syntactic structures – inadequate to use even the simplest structures Accuracy: not relevant	0 Zero Knowledge	Range: no evidence of knowledge of vocabulary – inadequate even of simplest formal vocabulary Accuracy: not relevant	0 Zero Knowledge	Range: no evidence of knowledge of the mechanics of writing Accuracy: not relevant
1 Limited Knowledge	Range: little evidence of deliberate, correct and relevant text Accuracy: organization generally unclear or irrelevant to topic	1 Limited Knowledge	Range: a few markers of cohesion Accuracy: relationships between sentences frequently confusing; composition barely intelligible	1 Limited Knowledge	Range: small range including a few basic structures Accuracy: poor to moderate accuracy within range; if structures outside of the controlled range are attempted, accuracy may be poor	1 Limited Knowledge	Range: small range lacking the formal and appropriate vocabulary required to produce good piece of writing. Accuracy: vocabulary items frequently used imprecisely (limited success in conveying meaning)	1 Limited Knowledge	Range: little evidence of deliberate use of correct spelling, punctuation, capitalization and paragraphing techniques Accuracy: poor or moderate accuracy

(continued)

continued

Score	Organization	Textual devices	Structures	Vocabulary	Mechanics
2 Moderate Knowledge	Range: moderate range of explicit text organization al devices. Accuracy: organization generally clear but could often be more explicitly marked	Range: moderate range of explicit textual devices. Accuracy: relationships between sentences generally clear but could often be more explicitly marked and the composition could be more fluid and intelligible	Range: medium range – uses basic structures and avoids complex structures. Accuracy: moderate to good accuracy within range; if structures outside of the controlled range are attempted, accuracy may be poor	Range: moderate range – sufficient to produce a fairly comprehensible piece of writing. Accuracy: vocabulary items sometimes used imprecisely (some paraphrasing is used)	Range: moderate range of proper spelling, punctuation, capitalization and paragraphing techniques. Accuracy: moderate to good accuracy but could be more explicitly marked
3 Extensive Knowledge	Range: wide range of explicit text organization al devices on essay and paragraph levels. Accuracy: highly organized text	Range: wide range of explicit cohesive devices including complex subordination. Accuracy: highly accurate with only occasional errors in cohesion; composition easily intelligible	Range: wide range basic structures with some uses of complex structures. Accuracy: good accuracy, few errors but these errors do not affect the meaning that is conveyed accurately	Range: wide range of general and specific vocabulary. Accuracy: vocabulary items adequately cover the assigned task and are seldom used imprecisely	Range: wide range of proper spelling, punctuation, capitalization and paragraphing techniques. Accuracy: good accuracy, few errors but these errors do not affect the meaning that is conveyed accurately

	4 Complete Knowledge		4 Complete Knowledge		4 Complete Knowledge		4 Complete Knowledge		4 Complete Knowledge
	Range: evidence of complete range of explicit textual organizational devices Accuracy: evidence of complete accuracy of use		Range: evidence of complete range of cohesive devices Accuracy: evidence of complete accuracy of use; composition perfectly intelligible		Range: evidence of unlimited range; using syntactic structures ranging from simple to complex Accuracy: evidence of complete control or accuracy		Range: evidence of complete range of vocabulary Accuracy: evidence of complete accuracy of usage		Range: evidence of unlimited range of proper spelling, punctuation, capitalization and paragraphing techniques; Accuracy: evidence of complete accuracy of use
Score									

References

Al-Fallay, I. (2000). Examining the analytic marking method: Developing and using an analytic scoring schema. *Language & Translation, 12*, 1–22.

Archbald, D. A., & Newmann, F. M. (1988). *Beyond standardized tests*. Reston, VA: National Association of Secondary School Principals.

Arter, J. (1993, April). *Designing scoring rubrics for performance assessments: The heart of the matter*. Paper presented at the Annual Meeting of the American Educational Research Association, Atlanta, GA.

Bachman, L., & Palmer, A. (1996). *Language testing in practice: Designing and developing useful language tests*. Oxford: Oxford University Press.

Bainer, D., & Porter, F. (1992, October). *Teacher concerns with the implementation of holistic Scoring*. Paper presented at the annual meeting of the Midwestern Educational Research Association, Chicago.

Bauer, B. A. (1981). *A study of the reliabilities and the cost-efficiencies of three methods of assessment for writing ability*. Champaign: University of Illinois.

Becker, A. (2011). Examining rubrics used to measure writing performance in US intensive English programs. *The CATESOL Journal, 22*(1), 113–130.

Black, P. (1998). *Testing: Friend or foe?* London: Falmer Press.

Breland, H. M., & Jones, R. J. (1984). Perceptions of writing skills. *Written Communication, 1*, 101–109.

Brindley, G. (2001). Language assessment and professional development. In C. Elder, A. Brown, E. Grove, K. Hall, N. Iwashita, T. Lumley, T. McNamara, & K. O'Loughlin (Eds.), *Experimenting with uncertainty. Essays in honour of Alan Davies* (pp. 126–136). Cambridge: Cambridge University Press.

Brown, G. T. L., Glasswell, K., & Harland, D. (2004). Accuracy in the scoring of writing: Studies of reliability and validity using a New Zealand writing assessment system. *Assessing Writing, 9*, 105–121.

Brown, J. D. (1996). *Testing in language programs.* Upper Saddle River, NJ: Prentice Hall Regents.

Brown, J. D., & Hudson, T. (2002). *Criterion-referenced language testing.* Cambridge: Cambridge University Press.

Campbell, D. M., Melenyzer, B. J., Nettles, D. H., & Wyman, R. M., Jr. (2000). *Portfolio and performance assessment in teacher education.* Boston: Allyn and Bacon.

Charney, D. (1984). The validity of using holistic scoring to evaluate writing. *Research in the Teaching of English, 18*, 65–81.

Chi, E. (2001). Comparing holistic and analytic scoring for performance assessment with many-facet Rasch model. *Journal of Applied Measurement, 2*(4), 379–388.

Cohen, A. D. (1994). *Assessing language ability in the classroom.* Boston, MA: Heinle & Heinle.

Crehan, K. (1997, October). *A discussion of analytic scoring for writing performance assessments.* Paper presented at the Arizona Education Research Association, Phoenix, AZ.

Cumming, A. (1990). Expertise in evaluating second language compositions. *Language Testing, 7*(1), 31–51.

Diederich, P. B. (1964). Problems and possibilities of research in the teaching of written composition. In D. H. Russell, M. J. Early, & E. J. Farrell (Eds.), *Research design and the teaching of English: Proceedings of the San Francisco Conference 1963* (pp. 52–73). Champaign, IL: National Council of Teachers of English.

East, M., & Young, D. (2007). Scoring L2 writing samples: Exploring the relative effectiveness of two different diagnostic methods. *New Zealand Studies in Applied Linguistics, 13*, 1–21.

Hamp-Lyons, L. (1990). Second language writing: Assessment issues. In B. Kroll (Ed.), *Second language writing: Research insights for the classroom* (pp. 69–87). New York: Cambridge University Press.

Hamp-Lyons, L. (1991). Scoring procedures for ESL context. In L. Hamp-Lyons (Ed.), *Assessing second language writing* (pp. 241–277). Norwood, NJ: Ablex.

Hamp-Lyons, L. (1995). Rating non-native writing: The trouble with holistic scoring. *TESOL Quarterly, 29*, 759–762.

Herman, J. L., Aschbacher, P. R., & Winters, L. (1992). *A practical guide to alternative assessment.* Alexandria, VA: Association for Supervision and Curriculum Development.

Huot, B. A. (1990). Reliability, validity, and holistic scoring: What we know and what we need to know. *College Composition and Communication, 41*(2), 201–211.

Hyland, K. (2002). *Teaching and research Writing.* Harlow: Pearson Education Limited.

Jacobs, H. L., Zingraf, S. A., Wormuth, D. R., Hartfiel, V. F., & Hughey, J. B. (1981). *Testing ESL composition: A practical approach.* Rowley, MA: Newbury House.

Jonsson, A., & Svingby, G. (2007). The use of scoring rubrics: Reliability, validity and educational consequences. *Educational Research Review, 2*, 130–144.

Kim, H. J. (2010). *Investigating raters' development of rating ability on a second language speaking assessment.* Unpublished doctoral dissertation, Teachers College, Columbia University.

Klein, S. P., Stecher, B. M., Shavelson, R. J., McCaffrey, D., Ormseth, T., Bell, R. M., et al. (1998). Analytic versus holistic scoring of science performance tasks. *Applied Measurement in Education, 11*, 121–137.

Knoch, U. (2009). Diagnostic assessment of writing: A comparison of two rating scales. *Language Testing, 26*(2), 275–304.

Kondo-Brown, K. (2002). A FACETS analysis of rater bias in measuring Japanese second language writing performance. *Language Testing, 19*(1), 3–31.

Kuo, S. (2007). Which rubric is more suitable for NSS liberal studies? Analytic or holistic? *Educational Research Journal, 22*(2), 179–199.

Legg, S. M. (1998). Reliability and validity. In W. Wolcott & S. M. Legg (Eds.), *An overview of writing assessment: Theory, research, and practice* (pp. 124–142). Urbana, IL: National Council of Teachers of English.

McNamara, T. (1996). *Measuring second language performance.* New York: Addison Wesley Longman.

Mendelsohn, D., & Cumming, A. (1987). Professors' ratings of language use and rhetorical organisation in ESL compositions. *TESL Canada Journal, 5*(1), 9–26.

Moskal, B. M., & Leydens, J. A. (2000). Scoring rubric development: Validity and reliability. *Practical Assessment, Research & Evaluation, 7,* 71–81.

Mousavi, S. A. (2002). *An encyclopaedic dictionary of language testing* (3rd ed.). Taipei: Tung Hua Publications.

Nakamura, Y. (2004). *A comparison of holistic and analytic scoring methods in the assessment of writing.* Retrieved April 9, 2015, from https://jalt.org/pansig/2004/HTML/Nakamura.htm

Panou, D. (2013). L2 writing assessment in the Greek school of foreign languages. *Journal of Language Teaching and Research, 4*(4), 649–654. https://doi.org/10.4304/jltr.4.4.649-654

Perkins, K. (1983). On the use of composition scoring techniques, objective measure, and objective tests to evaluate ESL writing ability. *TESOL Quarterly, 17*(4), 651–671.

Reid, J. (1993). *Teaching ESL writing.* Englewood Cliffs, NJ: Regents Prentice Hall.

Rezaei, A. R., & Lovorn, M. (2010). Reliability and validity of rubrics for assessment through writing. *Assessing Writing, 15*(1), 18–39.

Schafer, L. (2004). Rubric. Retrieved February 9, 2015, from http://www.etc.edu.cn/eet/articles/rubrics/index.htm

Shi, L. (2001). Native- and non-native-speaking EFL teachers' evaluation of Chinese students' English writing. *Language Testing, 18,* 303–325.

Shohamy, E. (1995). Performance assessment in language testing. *Annual Review of Applied Linguistics, 15,* 188–211.

Stemler, S. E. (2004). A comparison of consensus, consistency, and measurement approaches to estimating interrater reliability. *Practical Assessment, Research & Evaluation, 9*(4), 1–19.

Stoddart, T., Abrams, R., Gasper, E., & Canaday, D. (2000). Concept maps as assessment in science inquiry learning—A report of methodology. *International Journal of Science Education, 22,* 1221–1246.

Weigle, S. C. (2002). *Assessing writing.* Cambridge: Cambridge University Press.

Weir, C. J. (1990). *Communicative language testing.* Englewood Cliffs, NJ: Prentice Hall Regents.

White, E. M. (1985). *Teaching and assessing writing.* San Francisco, CA: Jossey-Bass.

Wiseman, S. (2012). A comparison of the performance of analytic vs. holistic scoring rubrics to assess L2 writing. *Iranian Journal of Language Testing, 2*(1), 59–92.

Thikra K. Ghalib, an assistant professor of English at Taiz University, is currently working for Qassim University, KSA. Her research covers criterion-referenced testing, diagnostic assessment, test construction and evaluation, and item banking. She is the author of 'Content Analysis of an English Admission Test', a book chapter published by Orient Black Swan, India.

11

Conclusion and Discussion

Hassan Abouabdelkader

The growing interest in language assessment reported in this edited collection provides a succinct description of the changes that have taken place in the structure of several universities in the Arab World. The ten chapters of this volume offer a wide range of perspectives on EFL writing assessment in Arab universities from varied and compelling perspectives. Altogether, the studies offer abundant information concerning the educational programmes provided by many universities in the Arab world.

Most of the studies reported in this volume seem to be critical of the state of EFL writing assessment in their respective countries, a state of affairs that is equally shared by many other universities worldwide. Besides, the problems raised in the different chapters seem to be shared by most of the co-authors of the book despite not knowing each other. The chapters reported in this book share several features. Examination of the findings of the book chapters reveals that a number of concepts, like validity and reliability, are reiterated, analysed, and debated in most

H. Abouabdelkader (✉)
Ecole Nationales Supérieure des Arts et Métiers, Moulay Ismail Univerity, Meknes, Morocco

© The Author(s) 2018
A. Ahmed, H. Abouabdelkader (eds.), *Assessing EFL Writing in the 21st Century Arab World*, https://doi.org/10.1007/978-3-319-64104-1_11

studies, with the concept of validity referring to the features of tests and reliability to the accountability of the test scores. Below is an extended analysis of the findings of each chapter.

The first chapter of the book is a review of the state of EFL writing assessment in the Arab world. It provides a global view of the problems associated with EFL writing assessment in the twenty-first century Arab world contexts (Algeria, Egypt, Morocco, Oman, Palestine, Saudi Arabia, Sudan, Tunisia, UAE, and Yemen). In this chapter, Abdelhamid Ahmed succinctly depicts the various facets of writing assessment and offers directions for further research. The insights and conclusions provided by the author can serve as a guide to curriculum designers and educational policy makers to reconsider the assessment of their respective EFL syllabi and curricula.

By probing the existing literature on assessment-related issues, the author of Chap. 1 seeks to identify the common features of EFL writing assessment in the regions under investigation. In trying to identify whether there is an assessment culture that affects the teaching and learning of English as a foreign language, Ahmed says that, based on the various deficiencies reported in the literature and gleaned from analysis of the art of writing assessment, the prevailing 'assessment culture' in these countries is still in its embryonic stages. He argues that a large number of problems are still hindering the educational systems of some Arab countries from being recognised as fully accredited higher education institutions. Finally, the author reports the factors contributing to this state of affairs as elicited in the reviewed literature.

Chapter 2 reports the findings of a study that focused on the effectiveness of criteria-based self-assessment as a revision technique. The analyses made by Nehal Sadek are potentially important and fully constructed. They are entrenched in EFL learners' attitudes towards self-assessment and explicit grammar instruction. The key finding reveals that the use of criteria-based self-assessment leads to significant improvement of EFL learners' expository essay writing. This finding is consonant with the claims made by Weber (this volume) and many other researchers, to mention but a few, who stressed the importance of providing EFL learners with a set of criteria to revise their essays (Flower & Hayes, 1983; Topping, 2003).

Like the work of Weber, Sadek's findings support the view that the teaching and assessing of written communication are two sides of the same coin, and the implementation of a set of criteria to revise writing, as a self-evaluation strategy, leads to the improvement of the language features of writing. In other words, this strategy can be employed in the EFL writing class to guide learners through the revision stage of the writing process. Moreover, self-assessment can provide learners with a chance to participate in their learning process through assessing their writing performance and developing autonomous control of their writing skills.

Chapter 3 highlights the benefits of assessing internal coherence of EFL writing. The findings reported by Shabana reveal that analytical tools that gauge the coherence of texts written by Egyptians students need to be oriented towards tracking the progression of themes and their development in each sentence throughout students' written discourse. The importance of this study lies in its focus on the essay progression structure used by some Egyptian university students and its delineation of students' topical strategies while constructing their argumentative texts. The issue at stake is important in the Arab world EFL writing context (Abouabdelkader and Bouziane, 2016) as it touches upon the threads of thinking displayed in the writing process. It is also an integral part of the current concerns of research in second language acquisition (Liangprayoon, 2013).

This feature of producing coherent texts by students in the Arab world—a real issue for language learners who come from a different cultural background —is concerned with higher-order processes of discourse that impact the coherence of written communication. The work produced by Shabana explicitly demonstrates how students' sequential progressions in their essays complicate the discourse and make it hard for the reader to follow. Interestingly, the findings reported in this chapter suggest that, for such discourse deviations to be remedied, teaching English as a foreign language needs to enhance students' ability to produce coherent texts through the provision of vocabulary and the development of organisation strategies. She also confirms that assessment of students' writing abilities is not simply a matter of looking at the form, but also at the content level of students' productions. The implications of Shabana's work are more valuable for EFL writing researchers and teachers who are interested in the types of progressions to be implemented in the EFL writing classroom. Like most authors of this volume, Shabana evokes the development of teaching materials that facilitate the assessment of coherence in students' writing and calls for the provision of academics and researchers with information about the thematic development that characterises the argumentative essays.

The findings of Chap. 4 support the claims that EFL writing assessment in some Moroccan universities could be characterised as unstructured and unsystematic (Bouziane, 2017) and that its negative backwash affects the accountability of composition assessment. The features investigated in this chapter relate to teachers' conceptions of EFL composition assessment principles and the way these conceptions are put into practice in higher education in some public Moroccan universities. The deficiencies observed in some teachers' designed tests are indicative of teachers' lack of the appropriate knowledge of skills and expertise to design their own tests. Investigation of these teachers' claims also indicates that the design of the composition tests administered to second-year students was done based on teachers' experience, without any collaboration between teachers.

In the same vein, teachers' knowledge of assessment techniques and principles has been found to be deficient, and most of the composition tests have not been scored on the basis of adequate rubrics. Whether at the level of test design or the scoring procedures, the discrepancies reported between the two tests have largely contributed to the difference of performance between the two groups. In addition, these findings also reveal that teachers' procedure of scoring students' compositions is holistic, but lacks systematic criteria. No rubrics have been implemented so far for their assessment, and most scoring is impressionistic. Neither the guidelines provided by the educational reform nor the ones designed by the English departments provide any rubrics that would help the raters provide reliable results of students' composing skills. To remedy this gap, the study puts emphasis on the teachers' preparation through professional development and establishing professional standards for assessment skills of teachers.

The study also reveals that composing is a real problem for EFL students and that first and third semester students seem to grapple with the linguistic, communicative, and cognitive aspects of composing in English as a foreign language. These deficiencies are attributed to the lack of clear bonds between learning and assessment practices. According to Abouabdelkader Soufiane, the first step to overcome these barriers is to set up clear criteria of learning that address students' needs, on one hand, and that can be tested for each level of instruction through an effective assessment system, on the other. To conclude, the advances made in Chap. 4 confirm that the problems associated with EFL composition assessment in some Moroccan universities need urgent treatment to secure quality education and the establishment of an assessment framework that secures the implementation of valid and reliable composition tests in universities.

In Chap. 5, Bouziane and Zyad examined the effects of a blended writing course based on peer and self-assessment on semester-two students' writing ability. The authors examined the nature of the feedback they collaboratively exchanged with one another and concluded that instruction into self-assessing writing helps students produce more helpful comments and shifts their attention towards meaning-level aspects of writing. Interestingly, the authors indicate that students' improvement of peer-feedback and self-assessment has been found to contribute significantly to EFL students' learning. Such findings have several implications for the teaching of writing in college-level, EFL contexts. Teachers' roles are determinant of learning outcome; they should make sure that that their courses are well focused and that their students are active participants in peer review activities.

Students' awareness of how assessment proceeds is likely to contribute to better understanding of how their work can be assessed by teachers and, therefore, lead to better composing skills. When a student knows how to assess a product, they become more skilful at improving their own writing by attending to its requirements. Surely, the results of the study have insightful implications for the development of learning how to write. One of these implications is the involvement of students in the process of peer review through hands-on rubric-based training sessions. A second implication is that Information Technologies (ITs), such as Moodle, could serve as a facilitator for students to extend their contact with one another and their instructor on a continuous basis. Third, the instructor has an important role to play in monitoring students' feedback through the provision of guidance on how to suggest a balanced assessment that cares for the most pertinent aspects of writing. Finally, these findings indicate that further research is needed on how the new technologies can be used to serve assessment practices that can apply to large populations of students without having biased and unfair judgments of students' composing skills. Another important implication of the findings is that further research is needed to establish the bond between peer assessment and self-assessment in the writing classroom.

The work reported by Alan C. Weber in Chap. 6 is very informative about the developments in language assessment in Qatar, an area that in the last few years has witnessed the proliferation of American universities that have affected the status of education and upgraded it to international norms. In this study, Weber amply demonstrates the impact of the 'American-style educational paradigm' of education on the evolution of L2 English writing assessment at WCM-Q programme at the instruction and assessment levels.

The analyses reported substantially depict the various features characterising instruction in these universities and their impact on the assessment of students' writing. As reported by the authors, the students in the First-Year Writing Seminars learn the linguistic, rhetorical, and stylistic features of the English language in various genres, while at the same time learn the fundamental academic and social functions of writing. These findings show the advantages of introducing both Writing Across the Curriculum (WAC) and Writing in the Disciplines (WD) models and new assessment models consisting of holistic grading with 'periodic calibration with anchor texts' that have been adjusted to a new cultural context with specific characteristics.

The value of Weber's work is clearly noticeable in the succinct descriptions of the writing curriculum in terms of learning outcomes and how these outcomes are assessed and introduced to students. For the purpose of illustration, a sample generic rubric is provided. According to Weber, this type of holistic grading can achieve high levels of reliability since there is no quantitative analytical method that objectively identifies these sub-skills (Swain & Mahieu, 2012, cited in Ahmed and Abouabdelkader, 2016). Details of these sub-skills and supportive evidence from current research are provided by the author to demonstrate the value of the suggested assessment scheme. Finally, Weber concludes that writing assessment improvement is tantamount to effective and systematic teaching and conducive to autonomous and creative writing. Such improvement can be achieved if students are provided with tools and methods that can help them develop successful writing habits.

Chapter 7 portrays some of the assets as well as the deficiencies of EFL writing assessment, as observed in some Tunisian universities. These observations are not specific to the Arab world; they are the concern of several countries around the world. One of the points raised by Athimni deals with the extent to which teachers are assessment literate. The findings of the study reveal that teachers' knowledge of the principles and practices required for the design of valid and reliable tests is far below the standards required. Teachers' knowledge is also limited to theoretical issues, which are not clearly converted into practice through designing adequate writing tests. This finding that is also reported Soufiane Abouabdelkader, this volume and Ahmed (2017) is a determinant factor affecting the state of EFL writing assessment in the Tunisian context. During the last few years, a bulk of research has been carried out on assessment measures used for educational purposes (McMillan, 2000). One of the focal interests of these studies is the examination of EFL writing assessment practices used by university teachers to gauge learners' outcomes. In fact the studies reported in the current work acknowledge that teachers are a force to be reckoned with in this enterprise and a key factor of its implementation.

In fact, Chap. 7 assesses teachers' knowledge of writing assessment principles and practices. The results of the study show that teachers' assessment literacy is quite good, but teachers' execution of this literacy into effective tests is below the standards recommended for effective and accountable practices in the testing literature (Volante & Fazio, 2007; Athimni, this volume).

This chapter also debates the question of aligning leaner outcome assessment with globally accepted norms of assessment as an alternative to the existing unfair and unethical approaches to assessing students' performance, for learning, graduation or any other purposes. Like most of the studies reported in this volume (e.g., Soufiane Abouabdelkader, this volume; Weber, this volume), Athimni's study puts a lot of emphasis on teachers' knowledge of the different approaches to assessment, their underlying theories and their actual realisation in valid and reliable tests. Like many other studies in this volume, Athimni's study amply supports the view that the teachers' conceptions of assessment impact teacher-designed writing tests enormously. In fact, being 'assessment literate' is meaningless in so far as this literacy is not defined in terms of its constituents. It is interesting to note that the type of knowledge required for assessment literacy includes procedural knowledge that enables teachers to construct valid and reliable tests rather than the theoretical constructs and their superficial meanings. Faculty collaboration on assessment issues through oral and informal communication has been reported by Athimni to be a common unproductive practice among teachers. According to the study, the absence of continuous access to knowledge on EFL writing assessment strategies and fruitful collaboration between teachers urges them to use writing prompts from certified testing centres and documents. Such practice is legitimate for teachers who strive to substantiate the criteria of validity and reliability through ready-made certified tests.

Some authors (e.g., Soufiane Abouabdelkader, this volume), however, are not advocates of teachers' use of 'pre-fabricated' tests for EFL writing assessment. They believe that adjusting university tests with international standardised tests, as an indicator of quality of education, is improper in contexts where both the culture and the objectives of instruction differ from those in the standardised tests. Abouabdelkader (2017) question the value of modelling assessment practices on the ground of contextual and instructional specificity goals and objectives. They consider this type of aligning 'local or indigenous assessment frameworks with internationally-accepted standards or recognized benchmarks' (Taylor, 2009) detrimental to the local standards and educational objectives. To conclude, the findings of Athimni stipulate the need for a series of decisions related to teacher training to promote assessment standards as a crucial part of education quality assurance for tertiary education. They also confirm the need for improving the tests of language proficiency and tests of language skills for situations that match the components of composition course at different semesters of instruction. Future research needs to explore issues of awareness and knowledge of assessment theories and practices into valid and reliable rubrics for the different types of writing at university.

Chapter 8 reflects the reality of privileged universities in the Arab world. These institutions enjoy better conditions for learning and doing research. As is the case in universities in Qatar (see Chap. 3), the aspect of writing assessment handled in this chapter shows the theoretical foundations underlying the teaching and the assessment principles and practices in these universities. In short, Chap. 8 describes the assessment practices of writing teachers as perceived by freshmen university students in the United Arab Emirates (UAE). The three themes revealed in the data analysis suggest that university-level educators in the Gulf should engage in specific pedagogical and assessment practices to assist EFL students develop their writing skills. The study ends by suggesting that instructors must deconstruct the conventions of their own assessment practices so that students can better understand to build up appropriate academic discourse.

Chapter 9 extends the debate brought about by several researchers in this volume on the use of scoring rubrics for writing assessment in higher education. One of the features of this chapter is that it tackles the issue of scoring rubrics using information technology. This orientation to the new technology-bound practice is used to match the expectations of the instructors involved in the study. This view, however, may not be shared in contexts where these technologies are not available. Raddawi and Bilikozen found that, although e-rubrics had positive effects, as they helped teachers provide effective feedback to students' writing and save time and energy, they also reported instructors' mixed feelings about the effects of these e-rubrics in enhancing students' writing skills. In fact, the major asset reported by the authors is that e-rubrics allow for consistent, unified, efficient, and transparent results, but that they are not liable to promote effective teaching and learning environments. The implication of these results is that further involvement of students and teachers on the issue is needed and that there are several aspects of e-rubrics that need to be researched.

The central focus of Chap. 8 is the reliability and validity of holistic and analytic scoring rubrics in the EFL writing assessment in Yemen. Ghalib's research contributed to stimulating the interest of educational policy makers in Yemen and other Arab countries in finding solutions to the language assessment problems inherent in their respective universities. In this chapter, Ghalib analyses the efficacy and reliability of scoring rubrics in assessment, which will surely have an impact on the teaching and assessment of EFL writing in Yemen as well as many other countries in the world. The chapter is well documented and offers new insights into the field of writing assessment to EFL researchers and teachers of writing in higher education. By highlighting the importance of the use of scoring rubrics, Ghalib confirms the claims in vogue in the writing assessment literature that rubrics are becoming useful and promising for language instruction and evaluation (Andrade, 2005; Crusan, 2015; Knoch, 2009). In fact, evidence supporting the use of rubrics as an assessment tool in library instruction (Rubric Assessment for Information Literacy Skills) (http://railsontrack.info/) offers new directions to writing assessment issues.

In the case of Yemen, the findings reported by Ghalib sustain the validity and reliability of these two measures of EFL writing assessment. She particularly underscores the value of analytical scoring rubrics on the ground that they tap different composing skills. The findings of this study raise a number of useful questions for the writing teachers, especially in the design of their own tests. According to the existing literature, making the proper choice of rubrics for effective writing assessment should be done in light of the assessment demands and based on contemporary theories of learning. The value of rubrics, as demonstrated in Ghalib's work, is significant (Weigle, 2002) because they constitute a workable path towards freedom for the scoring logistics and quality assurance in writing assessment. In other words, using rubrics implies that assessment of EFL writing in the Arab world countries, reported in this volume, is likely to be accountable and reliable. Overall, Ghalib's work recommends the use of scoring rubrics in writing assessment as a tool that allows high degrees of validity and reliability, with more bias for analytic rubrics for the delineation of the students' weaknesses and strengths in EFL writing.

To conclude, the chapters of this volume on EFL writing assessment in some Arab world university contexts express a wave of contests similar to the social unrest portrayed in the Arab social media and echoed globally. These contests express certain dissatisfactions with what occurs in their respective social contexts in an attempt to draw the attention of educational policy makers so that they will take action and remedy the shortcomings occurring in education. This 'red flag' is also raised in other western contexts and reveals the critical state of EFL writing assessment all over the world. The work combines different types of views and perspectives and provides useful insights into the problems at stake. It is hoped that researchers, academics, and educationalists will benefit from the findings of the studies reported in this volume and strive towards bridging the gap between researchers' claims and the reality of writing assessment in the modern classroom.

References

Abouabdelkader, H., & Bouziane, A. (2016). The teaching of EFL writing in Morocco: Challenges and realities. In A. Abdelhamid & H. Abouabdelkader (Eds.), *Teaching EFL writing in the 21st century Arab world*. Basingstoke: Palgrave Macmillan.

Ahmed, A. (2017). Assessment of EFL writing in some Arab world university contexts: Issues and challenges. In A. Ahmed & H. Abouabdelkader (Eds.), *Assessing EFL writing in the Arab world universities in 21st century Arab world: Revealing the unknown*. Basingstoke: Palgrave Macmillan.

Ahmed, A., & Abouabdelkader, H. (2016). *Teaching EFL writing in the 21st century Arab world: Realities & challenges*. Palgrave Macmillan, UK.

Andrade, H. G. (2005). Teaching with rubrics: The good, the bad, and the ugly. *College Teaching, 53*(1), 27–31.

Crusan, D. (2015). Dance, ten; looks, three: Why rubrics matter. *Assessing Writing, 26*, 1–4.

Flower, L., & Hayes, J. (1983). Uncovering cognitive processes in writing: An introduction to protocol analysis. In P. Mosethal, L. Tamor, & S. Walmsley (Eds.), *Research in writing: Principals and methods* (pp. 269–274). New York: Longman.

Knoch, U. (2009). Diagnostic assessment of writing: A comparison of two rating scales. *Language Testing, 26*(2), 275–304.

Liangprayoon, S. (2013). The effect of topical structure analysis instruction on university students' writing quality. *English Language Teaching, 6*(7), 60–71.

McMillan, J. (2000). *Fundamental assessment principles for teachers and school administrators*. Paper presented at the Annual Meeting of the American

Educational Research Association, New Orleans, April 24. Retrieved May 24, 2017, from http://pareonline.net/htm/v7n8.htm

Swain, S., & Mahieu, P. L. (2012). Assessment in a culture of inquiry: The story of the national writing projects analytical writing continuum. In N. Elliot & L. Perelman (Eds.), *Writing assessment in the 21st century: Essays in honor of Edward M. White* (pp. 45–68). New York: Hampton Press.

Taylor, L. (2009). Developing assessment literacy. *Annual Review of Applied Linguistics, 29,* 21–36.

Topping, K. (2003). Self and peer assessment in school and university: Reliability, validity and utility. In M. Segers, F. Dochy, & E. Cascallar (Eds.), *Optimising new modes of assessment: In search of qualities and standards* (pp. 55–87). Dordrecht: Springer.

Tzipora, R., & Baram-Tsabari, A. (2017). To make a long story short: "A rubric for assessing graduate students' academic and popular science writing skills". *Assessing Writing, 32,* 28–42.

Volante, L., & Fazio, X. (2007). Exploring teacher candidates' assessment literacy: Implications for teacher education reform and professional development. *Canadian Journal of Education, 30*(3), 749.

Weigle, S. C. (2002). *Assessing writing.* Cambridge: Cambridge University Press.

Hassan Abouabdelkader is currently a freelance writer and researcher. He was formerly the chair of the English Department at the École Nationale d'Arts et Métiers, at Molay Ismail University, Meknes, Morocco. He graduated from the Faculty of Education, Mohamed V University, and the Institute of Education, London, where he was awarded the degree of PhD in Science Education. Dr. Hassan Abouabdelkader has had a rich experience as a librarian at the British Council, Rabat, Morocco, and as an active academic with several publications. As a professional in the TEFL enterprise, Dr. Abouabdelkader participated in several conferences locally, regionally, and internationally. Due to his commitments, he has been awarded an honorary member of ICC, the International Language Association, and has also acted as President of the Moroccan Association of Teachers of English (MATE) branch of Meknes for several years. He is the co-editor of and a chapter author in *Teaching EFL Writing in the 21st Century Arab World: Realities & Challenges.*

Index[1]

A

Abbreviation, 230
Abouabdelkader, H., 5
Abouabdelkader, S., 5
Academia, 82, 196, 199, 224
Academic divisions, 209, 227
Academic essays, 61, 177, 193
Academic language, 228
Academic performances, 223
Academic writing, 10, 58, 63, 74–76, 149, 192–196, 198, 201, 207, 212, 221
Academic writing courses, 192, 193, 202, 204, 228
Access, 230, 235, 238, 239, 245, 247, 292
Accountability, 3, 14, 83, 88, 91, 92, 96, 97, 100, 101, 163, 237, 244, 245, 286, 288
Accountable, 83, 87, 88, 95, 244, 291, 294
Accrediting, 84, 91, 244, 286
Accuracy, 2, 13, 26, 113, 118, 123–126, 129, 130, 132, 139, 181, 204, 262, 269
Achievement, 22, 36, 83, 85, 99, 102, 114, 119, 153, 176, 194, 204, 261–263, 268, 275
Achievement Academy Bridge Program (AABP), 227
Achieving coherence, 53, 54, 56, 67, 73
Acknowledge, 6, 152, 211, 240, 245, 291
Action, 123, 151, 183, 204, 228, 295
Activity theory, 113–116, 130
Adapting, 199, 208, 226, 266, 270

---

[1] Note: Page numbers followed by 'n' refer to notes.

Index

Add on, 242
Adding, 144
Adhere, 242
Adhering, 246
Admission standards, 227
Advanced placement, 225
Advancement course, 229, 245
Advancements, 225
Advantages, 22, 25, 71, 92, 97, 202, 229, 232, 234, 235, 238–240, 245–247, 254, 263, 267, 290
Agencies, 199, 211, 244
Agreed, 64, 236, 237, 239, 242
Agreement, 2, 10, 62, 64, 75, 92, 157, 158, 242, 263, 265, 267, 269, 271–274
Algeria, 2, 3, 12, 286
Alternative assessment, 117, 228
American university, 143, 191–193, 222, 266, 290
Analysis, 5, 8, 11, 80, 81, 84–86, 88, 90, 91, 94, 97, 101, 102, 119, 122–124, 132, 150, 152, 159, 166, 174–176, 178–180, 182, 197, 202, 203, 229–232, 237, 239, 243, 265, 271–273, 275, 285, 286, 290, 293, 294
Analysis of the data, 122, 231, 234, 240, 244
Analysis of variance (ANOVA), 124, 127, 268, 274
Analytic, 6, 12, 14, 55, 104, 106, 137, 140, 145, 146, 155, 157, 254, 264–268, 271–273, 275, 287, 290
Analytical scoring rubrics, 112, 273, 274, 294
Analytic assessment, 6, 123, 268, 271, 293
Analytic rubrics, 234, 265–268, 270, 271, 275, 294
Anonymity, 41, 172, 202, 232, 233, 235, 238, 239, 270
Anonymous respondent, 236, 238, 241, 242
AP, 157, 223
Appendix, 26, 40, 48–50, 102–107, 171, 185–187, 228, 230, 234, 237, 240, 248–255, 270, 276–279
Approach, 9, 11, 14, 21, 22, 58, 97, 99, 100, 118, 146–149, 151, 155, 197, 201–203, 208, 212, 231, 264, 266, 267, 271, 291, 292
Arab bureau of education for the gulf states (ABEGS), 144
Arabic, 12, 137, 192, 227
Arabic literacy, 141
Arab world, 2, 12–14, 47, 285–287, 291, 293, 294
Arab world university contexts, 1–14, 294
Archiving, 245
Argue, 55, 58, 74, 100, 113, 115, 165, 167, 195, 197, 201, 208, 244, 264, 265, 286
Argumentative essays, 59–62, 65, 72, 74–76, 107, 175, 288
Argumentative writing, 9, 60, 104
Argument development, 54
Assessment, 9, 25, 137, 163–171, 174, 175, 181, 184, 191, 212, 244, 245, 285

Assessment competencies, 169, 174–183
Assessment literacy, 291, 292
Assessment literate, 14, 166, 168, 169, 183, 184, 291, 292
Assessment materials, 245
Assessment methods, 26, 145, 155, 166, 169, 170, 175–178, 183, 222, 228, 231, 239, 242, 254
Assessment of EFL writing, 83, 294
Assessment platforms, 229
Assessment practices, 3–5, 9, 13, 14, 79, 80, 84–86, 98, 138, 145, 157, 167, 168, 171, 172, 182–184, 192, 211, 213, 289, 290, 292, 293
Assessment process, 93
Assessment techniques, 147, 156, 225, 288
Assessment tools, 111, 228, 240, 294
Assignment criteria, 119, 245, 246
Assignments, 5, 8, 13, 21, 22, 24, 42, 88, 90, 91, 117–119, 121, 122, 127, 128, 131, 147, 153, 155, 159, 177, 193, 204, 210, 223–225, 228, 235–239, 241, 244, 245, 247, 254, 255
Assimilate, 95, 168, 239
Assistance, 93, 114, 152, 244
Attempts, 2, 3, 9, 24, 42, 55, 57, 59, 60, 79, 124, 132, 140, 210, 211, 222, 246, 262, 266, 295
Attitudes, 3, 27, 40, 42–45, 82, 118, 143, 144, 168, 229, 286
Audio-recorded, 202, 232, 233
Authors, 153, 155–158, 194, 246, 268, 286, 288–293

B
Background, 54, 63, 91, 141, 166, 172–174, 184, 185, 192–194, 198, 233, 252–254, 266
Benefits, 25, 60, 112, 115, 117, 130, 132, 193, 196, 212, 226, 231, 234, 236, 244, 246, 254, 255, 274, 287, 295
Bilingual education, 226
Bilingualism (arabic/english), 144
Blackboard, 242, 243
Body language, 232
Boundaries, 92, 235
British universities, 233

C
Calibration in assessment, 290
Capabilities, 224, 225
Capture, 113, 191, 201, 241, 264
Case study, 200, 224, 229
Category, 46, 74, 93, 98, 123, 127, 175, 204, 209, 223, 230, 238, 249, 254, 255
Centre, 140, 147, 157, 163, 292
Challenges, 53, 92, 97, 212, 225, 229, 231, 241, 243, 244, 246, 254, 255
Clarification, 121, 232
Clarify, 95, 149, 157, 160, 212, 223, 237, 241, 242, 245
Class, 7, 26, 58, 60, 61, 96, 103, 116, 119, 120, 139, 141, 147, 150, 151, 153, 155, 158, 168, 171, 175, 177–179, 181–183, 204, 209, 210, 221, 224, 227, 243, 269, 287

Classroom, 4, 5, 12, 21, 25, 46, 115, 145, 148, 150, 155, 159, 165, 167, 168, 182, 192, 200, 201, 203, 204, 206, 208–213, 223, 244–247, 275, 288, 295
Clauses, 54, 57, 61–67, 69–71, 75, 76, 124, 129
Clear, 9, 11, 53, 73, 76, 80–82, 89, 91, 92, 94, 96, 99, 100, 102, 103, 129, 137, 148, 153, 156, 169, 175, 176, 179, 183, 223, 225, 226, 236, 239, 241, 245, 246, 262, 275, 289–291
Climate, 247
Code, 62, 164, 174, 230, 254, 255
Co-educational, 227
Cognitive skills, 90
Coherence, 2, 3, 7, 13, 82, 103, 131, 150, 181, 201, 287, 288
Coherence problems, 54, 59
Coherent texts, 53, 287
Cohesion, 2, 3, 7, 13, 58, 82, 122, 131, 270
Coincides, 93, 234
Collaboration, 93, 101, 113–115, 121, 130–132, 145, 152, 288, 289, 292
Collection, 172, 246, 285
College, 5, 53, 79, 93, 95, 96, 103, 119, 143, 155, 157, 164, 244, 261, 268, 269
Comfortable, 224, 243
Comments, 55, 62, 65, 70, 113, 116, 117, 122, 123, 126–128, 131, 132, 150, 172, 181, 200, 206, 207, 211, 212, 235–243, 248, 249, 255, 266, 289
Common assessment tool, 234
Common assignments, 228
Common courses set, 228
Common grading strategies, 228
Common rubrics, 228, 241, 242
Communicating, 106, 140, 143, 152, 169, 171, 174, 181–184, 207, 212
Communication, 94, 99, 104, 137, 167, 184, 196, 212, 226, 238, 287, 292
Communication of results, 182, 184
Communities, 83, 85, 98, 115, 130, 146, 148, 151, 152, 160, 164, 194, 196, 198–201, 206, 210
Competency, 12, 88, 95, 99, 100, 120, 166, 169, 174–176, 178–183, 195, 196, 227, 262, 265, 267, 269
Complementary, 96, 240
Complex, 62, 76, 90, 93, 106, 172, 200, 209, 243
Components of assessment, 166–167
Composing ability, 83, 85, 97
Composition, 7, 24, 58, 59, 74, 80–83, 85–90, 92, 93, 95, 96, 111, 113, 118, 127, 130, 131, 146, 147, 149, 193, 201, 232, 265, 288, 289, 292
Composition assessment, 79–81, 84, 96, 99, 101, 102, 288, 289
Compositions, 91
Computer, 12, 114, 142, 235, 242, 243
Computer-assisted system, 225
Computer/web based medium, 234
Computes, 124

Concern, 4, 11, 12, 14, 22, 29, 30, 33, 36, 39, 43, 63, 72, 80, 82, 94, 97, 98, 100, 117, 121, 127, 152, 155, 163, 165, 178, 191, 194, 196, 224, 225, 233, 241–244, 262, 264, 285, 287, 291
Conclusions, 34, 150, 184, 211, 229
Conclusive, 245
Condensing, 230
Confidentiality, 172, 185, 202, 232, 233
Conflicts, 197, 208, 209, 229, 233, 242
Confusion, 88, 122, 212, 239
Consistency, 158, 262–265, 267, 268, 272, 274–276
Consistent, 4, 80, 92, 130, 148, 193, 244, 247, 271, 274, 275, 293
Constructivism, 99, 151, 155
Context, 81, 84, 90, 95, 104, 111, 112, 119, 133, 139, 140, 146, 151, 159, 164, 166, 192–201, 203, 207, 209, 210, 213, 225–227, 229, 261, 264, 265, 268, 272, 276, 286, 287, 289, 290, 292, 293, 295
Contextualise, 138, 246
Continuous assessment, 4, 246
Contributions, 81, 236, 237, 239, 245
Controversy, 245
Convenient, 26, 239
Conventional rubric, 223
Conversations, 202, 233
Co-requisite, 228
Cost, 244, 267
Counter-productive, 98, 243

Countries, 2, 10, 12–14, 89, 139, 142, 163, 164, 192, 226, 227, 245, 285, 286, 291, 294
Course assessment criteria, 246
Course objectives, 82, 99, 175
Creativity, 88, 94, 96, 151, 224, 225
Credibility, 97, 203, 245
Criteria, 5, 9, 13, 22, 25, 26, 42, 45, 80, 81, 90, 91, 100, 102, 118–120, 122, 131, 147, 168, 170, 172, 177–181, 183, 184, 196, 223, 228, 229, 236, 238, 246, 255, 262–265, 270, 274, 286–288, 292
Criteria-based rubric, 116, 130, 131
Criteria of evaluation, 237, 245, 265
Criterion-referenced rating scale, 270
Critical thinking, 3, 4, 10, 13, 106, 151, 193, 228
Criticism, 167, 209, 210, 224
Cultural, 10, 12, 13, 144, 152, 159, 194, 197, 198, 290
Cultural background, 53, 233, 287
Culture, 4, 13, 14, 54, 57, 81, 139–141, 144, 195, 201, 208, 286, 292
Cumbersome, 243, 244, 255
Curriculum, 24, 39, 97, 137, 149, 168, 193, 224, 286, 290

D

Damaging, 209, 244
Data, 4, 7, 59, 62–65, 80, 81, 85–88, 118, 119, 122–124, 127, 131, 152, 171, 172, 192, 201–203, 229–231, 236, 237, 240–243, 245, 246, 254, 255, 293

Data collection, 203, 229–233
Data sources, 230
Dearth, 167, 168, 226
Decision-making, 224
Decisions, 1, 14, 22, 92, 96, 97, 166, 167, 169, 170, 172, 175–180, 183, 192, 228, 262, 264, 271, 292
Decreasing, 3, 34, 35, 114, 132, 224, 244
Definitions, 57, 167, 184, 240, 245
Degree programmes, 193, 227
Democratic society, 148, 224, 225
Demographic information, 231
Demotivating, 243
Department, 9, 59, 60, 83, 88, 93, 96, 100, 145, 147–150, 167, 168, 179, 228–231, 234, 248, 262, 265, 269, 270, 288
Department Curriculum Committee, 228
Descriptive language, 225
Descriptive statistics, 27, 28, 31, 34, 37, 124, 125, 127, 271–273
Descriptors, 95, 228, 229, 262, 263
Design, 26, 60, 83, 85, 88, 90, 93, 95–98, 100, 101, 106, 120–122, 151, 153, 169, 175–178, 184, 228, 231, 266, 288, 291, 292, 294
Developments, 1–3, 6, 9–13, 54, 55, 57–59, 62, 63, 65, 67, 69, 70, 74–76, 99, 101, 102, 104, 106, 112–114, 116, 117, 121, 124, 128–131, 139, 143, 148, 149, 153, 155, 160, 166, 167, 175, 177, 192, 201, 221, 222, 226, 234, 254, 266, 267, 287–290

Difficulties, 3, 8, 9, 131, 132, 140, 193, 240, 242
Digital, 148, 225
Digital age, 225
Direct assessment, 222
Disadvantages, 101, 263
Disagreed, 231, 239
Discomfort, 244
Discourse, secondary, 195, 207, 208
Discourses, primary, 195, 208
Discussions, 12, 22, 44, 45, 65, 83, 112, 121, 128–133, 133n1, 141, 147, 153, 156, 159, 183, 184, 204, 212, 225, 230, 233, 246, 269, 273, 274
Dissatisfactions, 242, 294
Doing, 139, 179, 243, 293
Drawbacks, 97, 246, 254

E

Each criterion, 228, 229
Ease, 88, 89, 235, 244, 245
Ease of access, 237, 254, 255
Economic return, 244
Educational, 1–5, 11, 12, 14, 81, 83–85, 92, 96–99, 112, 138, 143, 159, 163–167, 170, 194, 196, 203, 223, 227, 229, 244, 261, 275, 285, 286, 288, 292, 294, 295
Educational integrity, 244
Educational technology, 135
Education for a new era, 138
Education in qatar, 138–144
Educators, 2, 4, 192, 194, 195, 211, 212, 222, 225, 246, 247, 275, 293

Effectively, 76, 103, 106, 116, 117, 149, 153, 243
Effectiveness, 25–27, 42, 44, 45, 58, 112, 119, 164, 222, 231, 286
Effective teaching, 151, 247, 293
Efficiency, 225
EFL assessment, 79, 81, 102, 191, 192, 194, 261–277, 285, 286, 288, 291–295
EFL writing, 1, 22, 34, 45, 46, 81, 101, 169, 172, 183, 198, 261, 285–288, 291–295
Egypt, 2–4, 12, 47, 139, 140, 142, 286
Egyptian ESL students, 57, 62
Egyptian university students (EUS), 4, 59, 60, 65, 66, 71–76, 287
Electronic rubrics, 222, 225, 226
ELT writing, 115, 118, 128, 130
E-mail, 231, 233
Embedded, 124, 147, 158, 201, 212, 230
Emphasis, 7, 71, 104, 106, 113, 115, 131, 151, 193, 226, 240, 241, 245–247, 288, 292
Emphasize, 71, 104, 151, 196
Endeavour, 85, 157, 159, 210, 243, 255
Energy, 236, 247, 293
Energy saved, 234, 236, 244, 254, 255
Engagement, 118, 130
English, 6, 26, 53, 81, 137, 191, 286
English as a second language (ESL), 5, 53–55, 58, 76, 119, 146, 224, 266
English language, 1, 6, 9, 59, 75, 94, 98, 138, 139, 146, 158, 226, 262, 290

English language teaching (ELT) professors, 221–255
English Language Testing System (ELTS), 221
English placement test (EPT), 228
English writing, 1, 4, 6–12, 59, 137–160, 222, 226, 231, 244, 290
Enhancing, 58, 75, 111, 225, 239, 240, 245, 268, 273, 293
Environmentalist, 235
EPT, *see* English Placement Test
Equality, 125, 226
Errors, 7, 9–11, 13, 27, 84, 99, 123, 144, 150, 156, 181, 245, 276
E-rubrics, 83, 221, 293
ESL, *see* English as a second language
Essay progression structure, 287
Essay writing, 10, 59, 61, 150, 222, 276, 286
Ethical imperative, 245
Evaluation, 3–5, 9, 12–14, 22, 24, 25, 82, 91, 155, 156, 244, 245, 261, 294
Examine, 3, 7, 9, 23, 25–27, 29, 32–35, 37–39, 41, 43, 46, 56, 60, 80, 88, 90, 112, 118, 119, 125, 127, 132, 183, 193, 199–201, 222, 225, 231, 246, 265, 271, 275, 289
Expectations, 8, 85, 92, 193–195, 197, 198, 211, 223, 238, 293
Experiences, 54, 81, 91, 94, 97, 98, 104, 115, 116, 138, 140, 141, 149, 155, 156, 171–174, 184, 194–197, 201–203, 207–210, 232–234, 240, 242–244, 252, 253, 269, 288

Explains, 44, 55, 56, 61, 71, 74, 128, 140, 153, 158, 159, 163–165, 167, 168, 171, 177–182, 196, 198, 212, 222, 224, 230, 234–238, 240–242, 255
Exploratory, 60, 172, 201, 203, 229, 246
Expository writing, 104, 153, 286
Extended parallel progressions, 55, 56, 58, 59, 61–64, 66, 67, 69, 71, 72, 74, 75

F

Facial expressions, 232
Factors, 4, 10, 12, 14, 25, 46, 73, 80, 88, 93, 227, 244, 262, 266, 286, 291
Faculty, 83, 84, 93, 95, 97, 101, 102, 120, 146, 149, 158, 193, 222, 228–230, 232–234, 239, 240, 243, 244, 254
Faculty collaboration, 292
Faculty members, 59, 75, 231, 232, 246
Failing, 66, 99, 171, 175, 176, 180, 182, 246, 262, 264
Fair assessment, 245
Familiar, 7, 74, 75, 133, 165, 178, 195, 199, 244
Familiarity, 178, 229, 243, 244
Federal National Council's (FNC), 227
Feedback, 3, 7, 8, 22, 112, 113, 115–117, 121, 123, 126–128, 130–133, 148, 151, 156, 157, 171, 172, 178, 181–184, 200, 207, 212, 222, 228, 229, 231, 234–241, 244, 245, 247–250, 252–255, 265, 267, 275, 289, 290, 293
Feedback functions, 242, 244
Feedback (on) writing, 159, 200, 210, 233, 252–254
Figures, 63, 71, 86, 127, 179, 206, 230
Final tests, 36
Findings, 2–5, 7–12, 25, 27, 31, 32, 34, 36, 37, 39, 41, 43–46, 54, 57, 65–72, 87–90, 95, 97–101, 129–131, 133, 172, 184, 192, 204–211, 233, 238, 243, 245–247, 267, 268, 272–274, 285–292, 294, 295
First-Year Writing Seminars (FYWS), Cornell university, 145, 147, 150, 151
Flexibility, 202, 235, 246
Flexible data collection, 231
Follow-up interviews, 232, 233, 236, 238, 241
Formalized, 147, 150, 246
Formative assessment, 4, 111, 176, 226, 245
Foundation Program, WCM-Q, 138, 146
Framework, 54–59, 75, 91, 95, 100, 102, 115, 145, 146, 164, 194, 201, 229, 266, 276, 289, 292
Freedom, 84, 96, 97, 143, 171, 226, 242, 254, 294
Freshmen, 26, 293
Full time faculty, 231
Funding, 14, 149

G

Gap, 11, 74, 90, 95, 192, 270, 288, 295
Gender, 118–120, 171, 173, 232, 234
Generating, 21, 60, 144, 177, 241
Genres, 44, 46, 61, 63, 80, 88, 115, 151–153, 156, 158, 177, 225, 290
Globalization, 226
Good writing, 240, 245, 261
Gottschalk, Katherine, 148, 149
Governance, 225
Graders, 157, 247
Grading, 86, 98, 155, 157–159, 212, 223, 225, 229, 234–238, 241, 244, 247, 253–255, 290
Grading procedures, 96, 170, 180, 183
Graduate, 138, 145, 147, 149, 153, 193, 223
Guide, 5, 22, 46, 82, 106, 157, 171, 210, 230, 246, 286, 287
Guidelines, 88, 91, 93, 96, 102, 104, 106, 116, 158, 170, 176, 177, 223, 238, 264, 288
Gulf region, 192, 199, 226
Gulf States, 226

H

Handwriting, 144, 236, 239, 255
Hard copies, 235
Hassle free, 242, 254
Head of the department, 228
Hesitance, 240
Hesitant, 245
High, 2, 3, 6, 7, 13, 55, 56, 59, 73, 74, 90, 99, 130, 139–141, 145, 153, 155, 157, 168, 173, 198, 207, 209, 210, 231, 242, 261, 272, 274, 290, 294
Higher education, 5, 6, 11, 81–85, 99, 101, 102, 111, 143, 159, 168, 172, 173, 184, 192, 199, 227, 244, 286, 288, 293, 294
Highlight, 1, 3, 4, 9, 11, 12, 42, 59, 60, 83, 92, 116, 191, 193, 198, 200–202, 230, 236, 243, 287, 294
High-rated essays, 56
High return rate, 232
High-stakes decisions, 92, 262
Holistic, 6, 12, 14, 96, 97, 112, 146, 155, 157, 158, 234, 243, 246, 254, 264, 265, 267, 268, 270–275, 288, 293
Holistic grading, 155, 157, 159, 290
Holistic grading rubrics, 223
Holistic rubrics, 6, 14, 264, 265, 267, 268, 270–272, 274–276
Homogenization, 224

I

IBT, 221
I-learn, 235, 243, 244, 255
Illinois, 224
Immigrants, 1, 164, 226
Impact, 4, 81, 83, 85, 93, 142, 191, 192, 194, 201, 204, 209, 210, 225, 229, 231, 237, 244–246, 254, 255, 261, 262, 264, 266, 287, 290, 292, 294

Implementation, 45, 91, 95, 123, 241, 242, 287, 289, 291
Implications, 60, 75, 76, 80, 99, 100, 132, 133, 159, 211–213, 243, 287, 289, 290, 293
Imposition, 242, 243
Inclusion, 118, 225, 266
Incomplete, 197, 232
In-depth qualitative investigation, 230, 232
Indispensable Reference for Teachers of First-Year Writing Seminars, 145
Individual, 3, 41, 55, 92, 103, 114, 130, 145, 146, 150, 151, 153, 156–159, 167, 170, 199, 212, 229, 241, 246, 255, 267
Inefficient, 226
Influx, 226
Information, 55, 76, 85, 96, 98, 101, 105, 133n1, 139, 151, 169, 171, 172, 174, 179, 185, 192, 231–233, 265, 285, 288
Informed consent, 233
Institution Review Board (IRB), 233
Instructions (test), 95, 96
Instructors, 5, 7, 8, 12, 14, 59, 75, 76, 80, 81, 85–89, 93–96, 98, 100, 116, 133, 141, 145–148, 150–153, 155–159, 194, 199, 202, 206, 211–213, 223–225, 231, 233, 235, 236, 239, 244, 247, 289, 290, 293
Integrating, 138, 150, 164, 222, 243, 264
Interact, 113–115, 144, 200, 202, 224, 227, 229
Internal coherence, 53–76, 287

International English Language Testing System (IELTS), 198, 221, 227, 228
Interpretive, 158, 191, 201–203, 229
Inter-rater agreement, 62, 64, 264, 268, 274
Inter-rater reliability, 157, 264, 265, 271, 274
Intra-class correlation coefficient, 271–274
Intra-rater reliability, 267, 272, 274
Investigating, 3, 5, 6, 24, 40, 41, 46, 55, 57, 58, 61, 85, 101, 116, 118, 128, 156, 194, 202, 229, 271–274, 288
Iran, 226
Issues, 25, 71, 81, 83, 84, 90, 91, 96, 98–100, 116, 117, 121, 123, 127, 130–132, 144, 145, 150, 151, 153, 172, 193–195, 203, 208, 211, 225, 229, 233, 241–243, 245, 246, 265, 286, 287, 291–294

J

John S. Knight institute for writing in the disciplines, 137, 145, 148–150

K

Khaliji, 144
Knowledge, 2, 7, 10, 59, 81, 82, 89–91, 93, 94, 98, 101, 111, 114, 115, 119, 130, 138–140, 142, 143, 147, 150–153,

156–160, 165–169, 172, 174, 176, 178, 180, 182, 184, 192, 202, 206, 211, 223, 226, 242, 266, 267, 270, 271, 276, 288, 291–293
Knowledge schemata, 267
Kuttabs, 141–143
Kuwait, 10, 226

L

Labelling, 207
Lack of resources, 69, 75
Lack of teachers' professional development, 101
Language learning, 10, 115, 197, 229
Language policy, 227
Language structure, 81
Language testing, 163, 164, 168, 172, 262, 266
Laptop, 235
Large classes, 3, 13
Large-scale assessment, 264, 265
Learning environments, 46, 247, 293
Learning outcomes, 84, 91, 92, 99, 100, 103, 151–158, 289, 290
Learning tool, 25, 237, 245, 254
Legitimacy, 225
Level of assessment, 92, 169, 174, 183
Levels of attainment, 228
Liberalism, 226
Likert-scale, 231
Limitations, 45, 46, 81, 115, 167, 171, 243, 244, 276
Limited, 46, 58, 82, 97, 147, 166, 167, 176–178, 184, 225, 242–244, 276, 291

Limiting, 240, 241
Lingua franca, 139, 192, 197, 227
Linguistics, 102, 115, 129, 140, 144, 146, 158, 194–200, 207, 226, 232, 289, 290
Lists, 2, 7, 22, 177–179, 181, 183, 184, 230, 263
Literature review, 25, 26, 31, 34, 194–201, 222–226, 231, 263–268
Low-rated essays, 55, 56, 67, 74

M

Major-related, 224
Majors, 7, 8, 11, 12, 21, 25, 36, 45, 53, 81, 99, 101, 111, 112, 123, 130, 131, 138, 148, 153, 167, 192, 193, 198, 204, 225, 227, 236, 240, 245, 263, 293
Management system, 112, 228
Many-Facets Rasch Model (MFRM), 276
Master, 153, 157, 199, 207, 227, 233, 234, 246, 247
Meaning, 82, 116, 140, 159, 208, 229, 292
Meaning-level comments, 123, 127, 128, 131, 132
Measurement, 84, 99, 111, 113, 118, 124, 165, 167, 176, 262
Measures, 3, 27, 37, 55, 76, 83, 84, 88, 97, 100, 112, 123–126, 128–130, 132, 155, 164, 168, 175, 178, 244, 263, 266, 271, 272, 274, 276, 294
Measuring coherence, 55
Medium of instruction, 227

Mentors, 246, 247
Messages, 76, 240, 255
Methodology, 26, 27, 86, 201, 202, 225, 229–231
Methods, 3, 6, 13, 54, 59, 60, 81, 103, 119–122, 141, 146, 148, 155, 157–159, 166, 169–172, 176–178, 198, 201, 203, 204, 211, 222, 228–231, 235, 239, 240, 242, 246, 247, 252, 254, 255, 262, 265, 268–272, 275, 290, 291
Minister of Higher Education, 227
Ministry of Education, 10
Minors, 26, 227
Mission statement, 227
Mixed method, 81, 229, 230
Mixed research method, 246
Modelling, 116, 212, 226, 292
Modernism, 226
Moodle, 113, 121–123, 133, 289
Moodle workshop, 111–133
Morocco, 2, 4, 5, 12, 81–84, 98, 286
Multiple methods, 229

N

Name, 172, 182, 202, 205, 230
Nationalities, 227, 232, 233
Nationality/ethnicity, 234
National Writing Project, 225
Nations, 1, 227
Neglecting, 246
Negotiated, 242
Notes, 152, 156, 198, 231, 233, 246, 292

O

Objectives, 26, 80–82, 84, 97, 99, 100, 102, 106, 112, 113, 122, 123, 128, 147, 153, 157, 159, 175, 177, 203, 223, 225, 228, 231, 234, 236–239, 244–247, 254, 255, 262, 263, 292
Objective testing, 222
Oil boom, 226
Old-fashioned, 226
Oman, 2, 5, 6, 12, 144, 286
Online, 90, 91, 112, 113, 120, 121, 124, 126, 128, 130–132, 229, 235, 238, 241, 243, 255
Online e-rubrics, 245
Online writing assessment, 244
Open-ended, 7, 10, 171, 231, 236, 238, 242
Open University, 224
Oppenheimer, D., 80, 83, 84, 87, 99
Organizational patterns, 55
Organizing, 53, 149, 230

P

Palestine, 2, 6, 7, 12, 286
Paper-based medium, 234
Parallel progression, 55–59, 62–67, 69–75
Participant, 12, 26, 46, 60, 61, 93, 113, 117, 119–121, 124, 125, 132, 133, 169, 172, 174, 175, 177–184, 191, 192, 194, 197, 201–204, 206, 211, 231–236, 239, 241–247, 252–254, 268–270, 289
Pedagogic demand, 261

Pedagogy, 21, 24, 47, 91, 98, 138, 145, 148, 149, 158, 193, 197, 229
Peer assessment, 6, 225, 290
Peer-feedback, 3, 111, 112, 116, 117, 122, 130, 159, 289
Perceived, 7, 74, 82, 123, 167, 176, 193, 204, 206, 211, 235–237, 255, 293
Perceived academic control (PAC), 204, 205
Perceptions, 5, 7, 80, 142, 193, 229
Performance, 6–8, 22, 24, 25, 27, 37, 38, 40, 45, 47, 80, 82, 85–87, 89, 92, 95, 96, 101, 112, 114, 116, 118, 119, 122, 124, 130, 148, 156, 165, 166, 171, 179, 181, 183, 223, 224, 228, 263–268, 270–275, 287, 288, 291
Permissions, 233
Perspective, 26, 64, 112, 115, 130, 155, 191, 197, 201–203, 221, 285, 295
Philosophies, 10, 148, 158, 159, 226
Placement test, 60, 120, 221
Platform, 121, 131, 133, 229, 247
Political, 139, 143, 148, 227
Portfolio assessment, 222
Portfolios, 3, 5, 6, 12, 118, 150, 156, 157, 222, 223
Position/positioning, 65, 143, 173, 191, 192, 194, 196, 200, 201, 204, 207, 208, 210, 213
Positive, 3, 12, 35–37, 40, 42, 44, 45, 75, 84, 85, 118, 119, 195, 204, 224, 225, 235, 239, 255, 275, 293
Power, 199, 207, 208, 211, 226, 264, 266
Practices, 4, 5, 7, 9, 14, 79, 80, 82–87, 90, 92, 93, 95, 96, 98, 99, 101–103, 105, 106, 111, 115, 138, 141, 145–149, 151, 157–160, 163–165, 167, 168, 178, 179, 182–184, 196–199, 202, 208, 210–213, 222, 226, 240, 245, 246, 288, 291–293
Predictions, 229
Pre-fabricated tests, 292
Preferences, 42, 139, 231, 233, 252–254
Preparing, 137, 230
Pressure, 54, 149, 244
Primary language, 227
Problem solving, 114–116, 224
Process, 2, 5, 21–23, 25, 26, 47, 55, 58, 62, 88, 91, 93–95, 105, 107, 111, 112, 117, 121, 130, 131, 133, 140, 145–147, 150–153, 155–159, 166, 172, 174, 177, 193, 196, 205, 209, 210, 223, 225, 230–233, 235, 236, 242, 244, 246, 247, 254, 287, 289
Process writing, 25, 26, 46, 103, 104, 106, 107
Professors, 145, 147, 152, 157, 172, 173, 221
Progress, 21, 79, 81, 97, 101, 113, 115, 123, 124, 126, 132, 156, 159, 169, 170, 175, 176, 179–183, 222, 223, 226, 238
Proponents, 71, 99, 244
Pseudonyms, 202, 203, 232
Psychometric statistics, 268, 275
Public concern, 244

310 Index

Purposes, 1, 3, 13, 25, 59, 60, 62, 79, 81, 83, 88, 90, 91, 93, 95, 96, 99–102, 106, 123, 142, 146, 149, 156, 158, 165, 169, 170, 172, 175, 176, 182–184, 188n1, 191, 197, 202, 224, 225, 229, 261, 267, 268, 273, 275, 290, 291

Q

Qatar foundation for education, science, and community development, 139
Qualifications, 232–234, 269
Qualitative analysis, 231
Qualitative methods, 229
Quality, 2, 5, 11, 14, 56, 58–60, 73, 74, 76, 85, 94, 98, 101, 112, 116, 117, 119, 122, 131, 132, 148, 163, 164, 171, 181, 184, 212, 223, 262–264, 266, 267, 275, 289, 292, 294
Quantifiable assessment, 238
Quantitative, 25, 60, 65, 146, 155–157, 159, 171, 229, 230, 290
Questionnaire, 5–7, 10, 12, 27, 40–45, 156, 167, 169–172, 174, 175, 184, 185, 197, 231
Questions, 22, 24, 27, 31, 34, 37–40, 59, 72, 80, 81, 83, 89–92, 94, 113, 117, 119, 121, 124, 126, 131, 132, 141, 157, 168, 169, 171, 172, 174–176, 179, 180, 182, 185, 192, 203, 204, 212, 227, 229–234, 236–239, 242, 246, 254, 268, 269, 291, 292, 294
Quick, 231, 238

R

Rand corporation, 138
Record keeping, 234, 235, 244, 245, 254, 255
Reducing, 224, 230, 233
Relationship, 11, 46, 54, 55, 61, 96, 115, 118, 119, 123, 139, 144, 199, 202, 203, 206, 231
Relevant, 121, 123, 126, 128, 167, 233, 234, 237, 240, 255, 262, 264
Reliability, 2, 25, 26, 80, 84, 90, 99, 157, 172, 203, 263, 264, 268, 271–274, 285, 286, 290, 292–294
Remedial language, 227
Representing, 149, 230
Requirements, 26, 83, 91, 99–101, 103, 165, 223, 228, 237, 241, 244, 289
Research, 1–7, 9–11, 14, 21, 25, 27, 36, 44, 46, 59, 72, 74, 80–84, 87, 90–93, 97, 99, 101, 102, 111–113, 118, 119, 123, 124, 137, 145, 165, 167, 168, 171, 172, 193, 196, 201–204, 211, 222, 224–226, 229, 230, 233, 234, 264, 276, 287, 290–294
Research questions, 24, 27, 38–40, 59, 72–75, 126, 131, 192, 203, 204, 229, 231, 234, 237, 240, 271
Research team, 230
Reservations, 237, 239–241
Respondents, 171, 174–181, 197, 202, 236–238, 241, 242
Responses, 40–43, 94, 111, 117, 118, 150, 157, 171, 172, 174–182, 184, 191, 200–202, 204, 206, 211, 227, 228, 230–232, 236, 238–242, 246, 247, 263, 264, 269, 276

Responsibility, 96, 148, 210, 231
Restrictions, 10, 240–243, 254, 255
Restrictive tool, 240
Results, 3, 6–9, 14, 25–29, 31–38, 40–45, 56–59, 62, 63, 65–67, 69, 72–75, 79, 82, 84, 85, 87, 89, 92, 96, 99, 101, 102, 116, 118, 119, 124, 125, 129, 130, 164–167, 169–171, 174–184, 191, 192, 197, 199, 200, 204, 210, 211, 230, 231, 244, 247, 262, 271–275, 288, 289, 291, 293
Revised, 25, 121, 150, 242
Revision, 149, 150, 157, 206, 286, 287
Rhetorical discourse, 53
Rhetorical foundations, 228
Rhetorical knowledge, 267
Rhetoric and composition, 232, 234
Rigidity, 241
Rubric, 6, 25, 80, 145, 222, 263, 288
Running record, 235

S

SAT, 223
Saudi Arabia, 2, 7, 8, 12, 138, 142, 143, 286
Scholars, 81, 83, 140, 145, 196, 223
Scholars, 142
Scientific Research, 227
Scoring, 5, 7, 9, 12, 14, 96–98, 100, 146, 155, 157, 158, 165, 166, 170, 171, 178–181, 184, 227, 262–265, 267–269, 271–276, 288, 294
Scoring method, 262, 272–275

Scoring procedures, 87, 91, 96, 97, 288
Scoring rubrics, 12, 82, 83, 91, 123, 263–268, 271–275, 293, 294
Screen computer, 243, 255
Second language learners, 53, 57, 73
Seconds phase, 230
Self-assessment, 3, 6, 9, 112–119, 121, 122, 124, 127, 129–133, 224, 226, 286, 289, 290
Self-expression, 225
Semi-structured interviews, 7, 118, 191, 202, 230, 233
Sentence, 2, 36, 54–57, 61–67, 70, 72–74, 76, 92, 95, 102–104, 123, 150, 153, 157, 159, 223, 287
Sequential progression, 55–58, 62–67, 69–75, 287
Series, 63, 67, 111, 150, 152, 210, 227, 228, 292
Shape, 246
Sheikha Moza Bint Nasser, 144
Significance, 27, 29, 30, 32, 33, 35, 37, 38, 59, 60, 118, 124, 245
Simplification, 224
Social reality, 229
Socio-cultural theory, 114
Socioeconomic benefits, 226
Solutions, 8, 157, 244, 294
Sources, 84, 90, 139, 152, 155, 203, 209, 231, 236, 241, 273
Space, 46, 140, 211, 213, 235, 245, 247
Specifications, 94, 177, 178, 183, 184
Sponsors, 247

Standard, 4, 5, 9, 13, 14, 27, 31, 34, 37, 81, 84, 95, 96, 124, 127, 128, 144, 157, 163, 164, 166–171, 193, 195, 197–199, 207, 209, 227, 228, 233, 243, 263, 270, 271, 288, 291, 292
Standardization, 14, 195, 224, 225
Standardized, 137, 145, 198
Standardized tests, 90, 99, 100, 292
Standard rubrics, 225
Standards international, 4, 9, 14, 137, 163, 164, 168, 197
Standards of teaching competence, 166, 169, 175, 183
State of Qatar, 138
State universities, 79, 101, 227
Strategic competence, 267
Strategy, 2, 8, 13, 47, 54, 57, 75, 76, 80, 88, 98, 103, 112, 118, 152, 168, 204, 210, 227, 228, 230, 231, 266, 267, 287, 292
Strengths, 114, 146, 238, 239, 264, 275, 294
Strict ethical standards, 233
Strongly, 40–43, 141, 231, 236, 237, 239
Students, 1, 22, 54, 57–59, 63, 65, 67, 73, 75, 76, 79, 138, 164, 262, 287
Student-teacher relationship, 224
Study, 2, 22, 56–60, 62, 65, 73–76, 79, 113, 138, 167, 191, 222, 265, 286
Styles, 7, 55, 57, 115–117, 140, 152, 156, 181, 207, 210, 225
Subheadings, 230
Subjective and, 26, 82, 99, 201, 203, 237

Subsamples, 230
Successful written texts, 54
Sudan, 2, 8, 9, 12, 139, 286
Surface-level comments, 123, 127, 128
Survey, 225, 230–238, 240–242
Syllabi, 147, 148, 228, 286

T

Targets, 53, 81, 91, 92, 95, 100, 148, 223
Teacher-centred, 141, 226, 227
Teachers, 21, 54, 55, 59, 61, 75, 79, 141, 191, 224, 265, 287
Teachers' beliefs, 3, 4, 14
Teachers' conceptions, 80, 85, 93, 95, 288, 292
Teachers' roles, 226, 289
Teaching and learning, 4, 12, 59, 99, 151, 224, 240, 245–247, 286, 293
Teaching experience, 171–173, 232–234, 269
Teaching methods, 103, 141, 211
Teaching writing, 11, 21, 145
Technical, 2, 4, 5, 142, 143, 153, 176, 240, 242–244
Technical difficulties, 242–244, 254, 255
Technical issues, 229, 243, 247
Tertiary education, 5, 81, 124, 199, 226, 292
TESL, 232
Test administration, 262
Test construction, 167, 168, 176, 177, 184
Test design, 88, 178

Testing, 2, 4, 6, 9, 14, 81–83, 85, 87, 92, 95, 97–99, 163–169, 174, 176, 178, 221, 223, 224, 261, 265–268, 291, 292
Testing specialists, 222
Test interpretation, 39
Test items, 166, 178, 179
Test of English as a Foreign Language (TOEFL), 90, 99, 198, 221, 227, 228, 265
Test progress, 169, 170, 175, 176, 179–183
Test purpose, 95
Test results, 7, 34, 166, 181, 182, 184
Texas A&M University, 224
Textbooks, 98, 144, 228
Thematic development, 54, 57–59, 65, 75, 288
Themes, 55, 57, 69, 90, 192, 203–205, 230, 234, 236, 237, 240, 242, 245, 255, 256, 287, 293
Thorny issue, 83
Time, 22, 76, 81, 83, 94, 96, 97, 99, 114, 117–119, 121, 128, 131, 145, 149, 155, 172, 173, 198, 200, 202, 206, 210–212, 221, 222, 225, 230, 233–236, 244–247, 254, 255, 264, 267–269, 290, 293
Time-to-degree, 244
Top-down management, 11, 14
Topical development, 55, 58, 59, 62, 63, 65, 67, 69, 70, 74, 75
Topical structure analysis, 53–76
Topical subjects, 61–67, 70, 72, 73
Topic formulation, 88

Topics, 7, 54–56, 58, 61–67, 69–75, 80, 84, 88–90, 137, 140, 150, 151, 153, 168, 170, 177, 178, 230, 254, 255
Top priorities, 244
Track changes, 243
Training, 1, 2, 4, 6, 9, 14, 25, 80, 93, 95, 98, 102, 112, 116, 119, 133, 143, 144, 147, 149, 151, 168, 171, 174, 184, 242, 244, 265, 269, 275, 289, 292
Transcribed, 202
Transcripts, 230, 232
Transitional signals, 54
Transparency, 234, 244
Transparent evaluation, 245
Triangulating, 156, 203, 229
T-test, 28–33, 35, 36, 38, 39, 43, 124, 125, 129, 271
Tunisia, 2, 9, 12, 286
Turkey, 232–234
Types of progressions, 57–61, 64, 65, 71, 72, 75, 76, 288
Typing, 63, 228, 236, 239, 249

U

UAE, *see* United Arab Emirates
Undecided, 239
Undergraduate, 11, 53, 60, 95, 120, 145, 146, 148, 168, 174, 223, 227, 228, 261, 262, 268
Undergraduate education, 53
Under investigations, 80, 81, 85, 88, 93, 101, 117, 122, 229, 230, 286, 288
Unethical and illegal practices, 167, 171, 182, 183

Unified, 14, 120, 247, 293
United Arab Emirates (UAE), 2, 10–12, 84, 191, 192, 194, 195, 198, 221, 286, 293
United States Of America (USA), 165, 232, 233
University, 2–4, 6–14, 26, 30, 39, 57–59, 63, 83, 119, 120, 143, 147, 164, 167–169, 172, 184, 191–213, 221, 265, 291, 293
University contexts, 9, 294
University environment, 228
University policy, 233
University professors, 147, 221
US colleges, 244
Use of results, 56, 82, 87, 92
User-friendly, 243

V

Vague, 24, 88, 232, 241
Valid discrimination, 263
Validity, 2, 26, 80, 88, 90–92, 99, 169, 172, 203, 204, 263, 265, 266, 285, 286, 292–294
Value-added, 83, 244
Version, 111, 121, 140, 242, 270
Views, 10, 12, 80, 82, 84, 147, 197, 199, 201, 202, 212, 213, 227, 236, 239, 245, 246
Virtual course, 228, 244
Virtual course management systems, 244
Voiced, 4, 237, 241–243
Voices, 211, 225
Volunteers, 230, 232, 233, 236

W

WAC, *see* Writing Across the Curriculum
Washback, 101
Waves, 164, 221–223, 294
Weaknesses, 60, 75, 117, 210, 238, 239, 275, 294
Weight, 122, 229, 266
Weill Cornell Medicine–Qatar (WCM-Q), 138, 145, 158, 159, 290
Women's writing, 144
Writer identity, 192, 194, 195, 199–201, 209
Writing, 12, 144, 224
Writing ability, 12, 100, 113, 115, 118, 119, 132, 155, 261, 262, 267, 270, 275, 289
Writing Across the Curriculum (WAC), 145, 146, 149, 152, 159, 223, 224, 290
Writing as discovery, 149, 159, 160
Writing as learning, 140, 149, 159
Writing assessment, 3, 5, 7, 9, 10, 12, 14, 81, 137, 159, 285, 286, 288, 291–295
Writing assessment at WCM-Q, 145–148, 150, 158, 290
Writing challenges, 159, 240
Writing classroom, 192, 234, 290
Writing components, 36, 92, 224, 265
Writing conventions, 54
Writing courses, 75, 76, 112, 137, 193, 202, 207, 228, 269
Writing goals, WCM-Q, 145, 148, 150, 151

Writing in Islam, 12, 139, 141
Writing instruction, 3, 21, 58, 117, 138, 143, 148–151, 158, 265
Writing in the disciplines (WID), 137, 145, 146, 149, 152, 159, 290
Writing problems, 7, 8, 13, 180, 183, 275
Writing process, 22, 25, 111, 112, 150–152, 155, 157, 210, 287
Writing proficiency, 2, 13, 27, 39, 40, 46, 88, 118, 123, 262, 263, 271
Writing skills, 1, 4, 8, 9, 11–13, 27, 40, 41, 80, 102, 114, 118, 119, 144, 150, 175, 176, 180, 182, 185, 193, 200, 206, 210, 212, 222, 239, 240, 254, 261, 268, 269, 276, 287, 293
Writing topics, 4, 10, 13, 121
Written discourse, 54, 55, 287
Written feedback, 159, 181–183, 199, 200, 210

Y

Yemen, 2, 11, 12, 139, 261

CPSIA information can be obtained
at www.ICGtesting.com
Printed in the USA
BVHW010345180619
551200BV00006BA/906/P

9 783319 877242